THE RIGHT TO DIGNITY

THE RIGHT TO DIGNITY

*Housing Struggles, City Making,
and Citizenship in Urban Chile*

Miguel Pérez

Stanford University Press
Stanford, California

Stanford University Press
Stanford, California

Printed in the United States of America on acid-free, archival-quality paper

Library of Congress Cataloging-in-Publication Data

Names: Pérez, Miguel (Pérez Ahumada), author.
Title: The right to dignity : housing struggles, city making, and citizenship in urban Chile / Miguel Pérez.
Description: Stanford, California : Stanford University Press, 2022. | Includes bibliographical references and index.
Identifiers: LCCN 2021048844 (print) | LCCN 2021048845 (ebook) | ISBN 9781503614963 (cloth) | ISBN 9781503631526 (paperback) | ISBN 9781503631533 (ebook)
Subjects: LCSH: Low-income housing—Chile—Santiago. | Right to housing—Chile—Santiago. | Housing policy—Chile—Santiago. | Poor—Political activity—Chile—Santiago. | Social movements—Chile—Santiago. | Citizenship—Chile—Santiago.
Classification: LCC HD7287.96.C52 S25 2022 (print) | LCC HD7287.96.C52 (ebook) | DDC 363.5/96240983315—dc23/eng/20211027
LC record available at https://lccn.loc.gov/2021048844
LC ebook record available at https://lccn.loc.gov/2021048845

Cover photo: Villa Padre Rodrigo Carranza, La Florida, Santiago. Photo by Eugenia Paz.
Cover design: Rob Ehle

To Leila, Emiliano, and Camilo

Contents

Maps, Illustrations, and Tables

Maps

Figures

Tables

Acknowledgments

This book would not have been possible without the generous collaboration of many people. First of all, I am deeply grateful to all the *pobladores* and *pobladoras* who generously helped me conduct ethnographic fieldwork in Santiago, Chile. In particular, I thank the members of the Comité de Allegados Don Bosco of La Florida for allowing me to participate in their organization over fifteen months. I especially thank Fresia, Rafael, Ana, Juan, María José, Nona, Irma, and Claudia for kindly sharing with me moments, memories, and life experiences. Likewise, I thank the other *pobladores* and *pobladoras* who also contributed to this work, especially Mauricio, Lorena, Keila, and Nicolás from the Agrupación Techo Ahora, Luis from the Movimiento Pueblo Sin Techo, and Lautaro and Daniela from the Movimiento de Pobladores en Lucha.

While developing this project, I had the opportunity to discuss my findings with several scholars. Their comments, recommendations, and guidance were crucial to shaping the ideas in this book. Alexis Cortés, Edward Murphy, Mónica Iglesias, Catherine Valenzuela, and Paulo Álvarez provided me with insightful reflections on housing movements of the past. The historian Boris Jofré generously shared with me the map showing the location of squatter settlements in 1971 that appears in chapter 2. I must also express my gratitude to Nicolás Angelcos, a scholar with whom I carried out collaborative fieldwork, published a paper, organized a number of panels, and spent many hours discussing the character and orientation of urban social movements. Many of the arguments in this book are the result of these constructive conversations. Nicolás Somma kindly shared his data set on social protests in contemporary Chile, and my brother Pablo Pérez, a sociologist well versed in statistics, helped me to analyze it. Nancy Postero and Madelyn Boots, from University of California, San Diego, helped me to situate my theoretical perspectives on citizenship practices in Chile within a broader context. Luis Martín-Cabrera, a UCSD associate professor of Spanish and Latin American cultural studies who happened to be in Santiago between 2013 and 2017, accompanied me as an intellectual partner and political *compañero* during my fieldwork. At the Universidad Alberto Hurtado, my colleagues in the Department of Anthropology and my students often encouraged me to assess my academic work in terms of its contribution to Latin American anthropology. I would also like to thank to my former students Constanza Martínez and Gabriel Mallea for their assistance in analyzing interviews. My colleagues in the Anillos Project "Ethnographies of Neoliberalism and Aspiration" provided me with a stimulating intellectual environment and helped me place my arguments within a broader critical perspective. In particular, many thanks to Marcelo González, Diana Espirito Santo, and Piergiorgio Di Giminiani for their constructive comments on several chapters. I am also grateful to Jeremy Geraldo, Cristóbal Palma, and Constanza Tillería, my research assistants in the Anillos Project.

I owe many thanks to Juan Correa, from the Centro de Producción Espacio at the Universidad de Las Américas, who assisted me in the design and edition of maps. The photographer Eugenia Paz kindly shared with me some photos the housing struggles that she took while I was doing the main fieldwork for this book. Nyna Polumbaum, Judy Polumbaum, and the Newseum in Washington, DC, permitted me to reprint a photo by Ted Polumbaum taken in the Campamento Nueva La Habana in Santiago, in the midst of Salvador Allende's government. I thank the public servants who helped me while I was conducting archival research at the Biblioteca del Congreso Nacional de Chile and at the Biblioteca de Santiago. I also thank the Centro de Documentación at the Ministerio de Vivienda y Urbanismo for approving the use of map 3, which appears in chapter 2. Raúl Troncoso and Valentina Acuña helped me with the transcription of interviews. I thank Jordan Harris for proofreading early versions of this book.

Michelle Lipinski and Margo Irvin, the two editors with whom I worked at Stanford University Press, believed in this project from the very beginning and gave me guidance to refine my writing and make this book stronger. I thank them for their commitment to this book. I am also grateful to Stanford

University Press's senior production editor Susan Karani and to manuscript editor Katherine Faydash for their prompt and careful assistance during the production process. Likewise, I thank the two anonymous reviewers for their thorough and detailed reviews.

Many of the reflections expressed throughout the book were presented at the American Anthropological Association annual meetings, the Latin American Studies Association congresses, the Asociación Latinoamericana de Antropología conferences, and the Congreso Chileno de Sociología. I also presented my findings at seminars, colloquiums, and roundtables held at the University of California at Berkeley, and at the Universidad de Chile, the Universidad Alberto Hurtado, and the Pontificia Universidad Católica in Chile. I am sincerely grateful to all of those who shared their thoughts and opinions, compelling me to polish my arguments.

I began studying housing struggles in Chile as an anthropology PhD student at the University of California, Berkeley. The intellectual vigor I encountered there encouraged me to question my assumptions and biases, go beyond my own analytical boundaries, and be open to reformulating my ideas. A number of people ended up guiding me through this process. James Holston advised me from the very beginning of my graduate studies at Berkeley. I thank him not only for introducing me to an anthropological approach to urban politics but also for his selfless commitment to this project and his academic rigor when it came to reviewing my work. This book is the result of a five-year process following my PhD experience, and it could hardly have been completed without his guidance and support. Teresa Caldeira always inspired me to conceive of anthropology as a discipline that can contribute significantly to the study of cities and urban life. Likewise, her in-depth knowledge of Latin American cities stimulated me to situate my research on Chilean *pobladores* in a regional context. Alexei Yurchak introduced me to the anthropological exploration of language, rituals, and performances while inviting me to transcend restrictive geographical dualities such as Global North–Global South, East-West, and so on. I thank him for urging me to look at my own case-study analysis as one that is framed by globally structured processes. Charles Briggs motivated me to revisit Latin American anthropologists as a necessary step for producing innovative anthropological research. Other people I met in Berkeley, with whom I shared countless experiences, were equally important. I thank Samuele Collu, Cole Hansen, Olesya Shayduk-Immerman, Nicole Rosner, Chris Herring, and Carter Koppelman, for their willingness to read, comment, and edit early versions of the text. Among the PhD students I met at Berkeley, my special gratitude goes out to my dear friend Sam Dubal for encouraging me to undertake this project and, quoting his words, for "so many years of friendship and comradery." I miss our conversations about critical anthropology, politics, and soccer, and I wish you had read this book. Although not related to the academic life, Matt Freeman, a musician and a lifelong Berkeley resident, was always eager to spend time with me, allowing me to gain a deeper knowledge of the East Bay. Thank you all for your camaraderie, your kindness, and for making my life in California more enjoyable.

Other people whom I don't know personally also accompanied me in this project during the fieldwork and the writing process. Evaristo Páramos, Fermín Muguruza, Julián Hernández, Javier Soto, BJ Armstrong, Tim Armstrong, Adrian Smith, Steve Harris, Ricardo Mollo, Diego Arnedo, Gustavo Napoli, Indio Solari, and Skay Beilinson helped me get inspired and find peace of mind when I needed.

Last but not least, it is important to mention that this work was made possible by a number of scholarships, fellowships, and research grants. My PhD program was funded by the Government of Chile, through the National Agency for Research and Technology (ANID), as well as by the UC Berkeley Graduate Division. In order to carry out ethnographic fieldwork, I received economic support from the Tinker Foundation and several UC Berkeley institutions. These include the Center for Latin American Studies, the Institute of International Studies, the Center for Global Metropolitan Studies, the Department of Anthropology, and the Graduate Division. The UC Berkeley Institute for the Study of Societal Issues provided me with office space at the Center for Ethnographic Research during most of my time as a PhD student. A significant portion of the ideas presented in this book were developed there, specifically in a small room on the third floor of the old, wooden building located at the corner of Bowditch Street and Channing Way, right in front of the legendary People's Park. While writing this book in Chile, I had economic support from the Department of Anthropology at the Alberto Hurtado University, the Anillos Project "Ethnographies of Neoliberalism and Aspiration" (ANID/PIA/SOC180033), and the Center for Social Conflict and Cohesion Studies–COES (ANID/FONDAP/15130009).

Parts of chapter 3 and chapter 5 originally appeared in "Reframing Housing Struggles: Right to the City and Urban Citizenship in Santiago, Chile," in the journal *City* 21, no. 5 (2017): 530–49. Some ideas in chapter 2 and chapter 4 were published as "De la 'desaparición' a la reemergencia: Continuidades y rupturas del movimiento de pobladores en Chile," in the *Latin American Research Review* 52, no. 1 (2017): 94–109 (cowritten with Nicolás Angelcos). Elements of chapter 3 and chapter 6 appeared in "Toward a Life with Dignity: Housing Struggles and New Political Horizons in Urban Chile," in the journal *American Ethnologist* 45, no. 4 (2018): 508–20.

In 2010, Leila selflessly accompanied me throughout the difficult process of pursuing a PhD program far from our home in Chile. She has been a constant, caring presence in my life. I have no words to express my gratitude for her advice, support, and, more importantly, her love. Emiliano, our first son, came into our lives just months before I finished my PhD program in 2016. Camilo, in turn, arrived when I was revising this book in 2020. I dedicate this book to the three of them, for giving me a reason to live, laugh, and love.

Abbreviations

CAS   Comités de Asistencia Social (Social Assistance Committees)

CASEN   Encuesta de Caracterización Socioeconómica (National Socioeconomic Characterization Survey)

CEPAL   Comisión Económica para América Latina y el Caribe (Economic Commission for Latin America and the Caribbean)

CIDU   Centro Interdisciplinario de Desarrollo Urbano (Center Interdisciplinary for Urban Development)

CNT   Comando Nacional de Trabajadores (National Workers' Command)

COAPO   Coordinadora de Organizaciones Poblacionales (Coordinator of Neighborhood Organizations)

CORMU   Corporación de Mejoramiento Urbano (Urban Improvement Corporation)

CORVI   Corporación de la Vivienda (Housing Corporation)

CTC   Confederación de Trabajadores del Cobre (Copper Workers' Confederation)

CUP   Comando Unitario de Pobladores (Unitary Pobladores' Command)

DESAL   Centro para el Desarrollo Económico y Social de América Latina (Center for Social and Economic Development of Latin America)

EGIS   Entidades de Gestión Inmobiliaria y Social (Entities of Social
                and Real Estate Management)
FENAPO   Federación Nacional de Pobladores (National Federation of
                Pobladores)
FOCH   Federación Obrera de Chile (Chilean Workers' Federation)
IC   Izquierda Cristiana (Christian Left)
MINVU   Ministerio de Vivienda y Urbanismo (Ministry of Housing and
                Urbanism)
MIR   Movimiento de Izquierda Revolucionaria (Movement of the
                Revolutionary Left)
METRO   Coordinadora Metropolitana de Pobladores (Metropolitan
                Coordinator of Pobladores)
MPL   Movimiento de Pobladores en Lucha (Movement of Pobladores
                in Struggle)
MPST   Movimiento Pueblo Sin Techo (Movement of People Without
                a Roof)
PC   Partido Comunista (Communist Party)
PDC   Partido Democracia Cristiana (Christian Democratic Party)
PI   Partido Igualdad (Equality Party)
PN   Partido Nacional (National Party)
PNUD   Programa de las Naciones Unidas para el Desarrollo (United
                Nations Development Program)
POS   Partido Obrero Socialista (Workers' Socialist Party)
PPD   Partido por la Democracia (Party for Democracy)
PRSD   Partido Radical Social Demócrata (Social Democratic Radical
                Party)
PS   Partido Socialista (Socialist Party)
PSAT   Prestador de Servicios de Asistencia Técnica (Provider of Tech-
                nical Assistance)
SERVIU   Servicio Metropolitano de Vivienda y Urbanismo (Metropoli-
                tan Service of Housing and Urbanism)
UF   Unidad de Fomento (Inflation-Indexed Currency Unit)

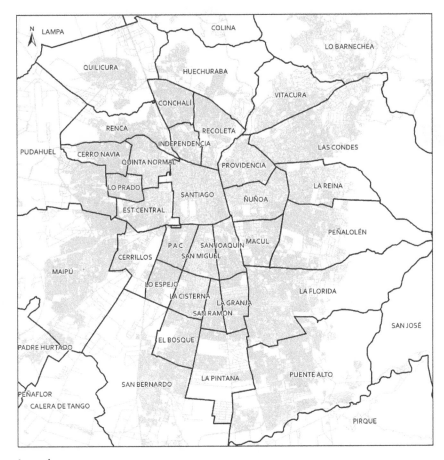

Legend

District limits

―――――

Main road networks

MAP 1. Santiago metropolitan area. Source: National Institute of Statistics, 2017. Credit: Juan Correa.

THE RIGHT TO DIGNITY

I   COLLECTIVE ACTION

1   Housing the Poor in a Neoliberal City

Tuesday, June 17, 2014. Early in the morning, around 7:00 a.m., I got together with over two hundred members of the Comité de Allegados Don Bosco—the housing assembly with which I had been conducting ethnographic research—in downtown Santiago. It was a typical winter morning: cold and a bit foggy, but I knew that the sun would break through the clouds later. We gathered on the corner of Pío Nono and Andrés Bello. The area is known as Plaza Italia, named after the square located directly across from our meeting spot. Plaza Italia is an urban "node," meaning that it is a strategic, as well as a symbolic, point in the city (Lynch 1960). Plaza Italia is not only situated at the convergence of four major avenues—Alameda Bernardo O'Higgins, Providencia, Vicuña Mackenna, and Andrés Bello—it also is the cornerstone for popular protests and demonstrations in Santiago. Whether the site of a "spontaneous" celebration of a victory by the national soccer team or the starting point of a planned political march, demonstrators usually gather and organize together at Plaza Italia, which makes it a site of constant clashes between the police and the people. This explains the permanent presence of law enforcement at the site, a presence that increased considerably since October 18, 2019. That day marked the onset of the most significant rebellion against social inequality in the past thirty years in Chile. During the *estallido social*, or social uprising, in 2019, protesters rechristened Plaza Italia as "Plaza de la Dignidad" (Dignity Square), making it clear that the question of dignity was at the core of the protests against neoliberalism.

But Chileans' claims for dignity and social justice did not start in 2019. The activists I met between 2011 and 2015 were part of an emerging movement through which they sought to achieve the right to housing and the right to *la vida digna* (a life with dignity). And that is why the Don Bosco members had congregated at that particular place on that winter morning in June 2014. On that occasion, they had gathered together to complain about what Ernesto, one of the organization's leaders, called the "paradox" of Chile's neoliberal housing programs. While handing out pamphlets to passersby, he explained: "We are here to fight against subsidy-based housing policies, because we can't endure another winter without a home of our own. Although most of us [the members of the Don Bosco committee] have been granted state subsidies, we're still waiting for private construction companies to build our houses. They are not interested in building housing units for the poor. Real estate developers don't want to build social housing projects for us because it is not profitable for them. This is what the poor endure in a neoliberal country."

This "paradox," as Ernesto explained to me when I first met him in 2013, was even more flagrant in peripheral districts like La Florida, where the Don Bosco housing assembly was formed. There, the sustained increase in land prices over recent decades had led to a context in which, despite the availability of vacant plots, "there is no money to pay for all the expenses related to homebuilding." The idea to meet early in the morning in downtown Santiago, which is about an hour away from La Florida by public transportation, was a strategic decision. On the one hand, it is the time when most *santiaguinos* are on their way to work. This means that if protesters were to barricade any of the major avenues, they could easily draw media attention because of the impact that such an action would have on urban traffic flows. On the other hand, for those Don Bosco members who were not able to take the day off, they would still be able to get to work on time or, if things were to escalate, be just a little late.

On June 17, 2014, things got out of hand. After dozens of housing activists attempted to block Andrés Bello Avenue at 7:30 a.m., the police intervened and detained six or seven of them. The rest of us, who had not been arrested, gathered again at Pío Nono Bridge and remained there for another hour and a half. At around 9:00 a.m., someone who I could not identify shouted: "Let's go to the MINVU [Ministry of Housing and Urbanism]!" In a completely improvised move, we took over two lanes of Bernardo O'Higgins Avenue, known as La Alameda and the main artery of downtown Santiago, and began marching toward the ministry. The crowd, made up mostly of women, flew Chilean flags and sang the national anthem two or three times during our march. However, people's passions soared even more when chanting "La vivienda es un derecho, no un privilegio" ("Housing is a right, not a privilege") and "Somos caleta, más que la chucha, somos pobladores unidos en la lucha" ("We're a lot, a hell of a lot, we're *pobladores* united in the struggle").

· · ·

This book talks about what Chileans commonly refer to as *pobladores*, that is, poor urban residents. It is an ethnographic account of *pobladores*' participation in social movements for the right to housing and the right to the city in Santiago; their constitution and recognition as ethical-political subjects engaged in both squatter settlement movements in the mid-twentieth century and in subsidy-based housing programs in neoliberal Chile; their modes of collective action arising from the struggle to obtain subsidized housing; their power to articulate political agency in different historical contexts based on their involvement in the making of the city; their capacity to formulate novel understandings of citizenship and rights by demanding the right to remain in their neighborhoods of origin; and their capacity to generate new political horizons grounded in demands for dignity. By scrutinizing how Chilean *pobladores* constitute themselves as political subjects, this book reveals the mechanisms through which housing activists develop new imaginaries of citizenship in a country in which the market was the dominant force organizing social life for almost forty years. It does so by interrogating the limits and potentialities of urban movements, which are framed by both poor people's involvement in neoliberal programs and the capacity of those same individuals to struggle against the commodification of social rights by claiming the right to live with dignity—a demand based on a moral category that helped give shape to the 2019 *estallido social*.

An Ethnographic Exploration of Subjects and Political Movements

In Chile, the word *poblador* is a class- and territory-based category commonly used to refer to poor urban residents. The notion of *poblador* is closely bound up with the term *población*, a concept that has been utilized since the late nineteenth century to allude to working-class neighborhoods located in the urban peripheries.[1] A commonsense definition of *poblador* would thus be anyone who lives in a *población*. *Pobladores* have historically been considered a heterogeneous mass of people who have been able to "micro-colonize" the spatial and social outskirts of society (Salazar and Pinto 2002, 240). As residents of the peripheries, public opinion has generally depicted *pobladores* as a "marginal population" located at the bottom of the social ladder. In turn, *poblaciones* have frequently been conceptualized as the spatial expression of such a marginal condition. Edward Murphy (2015, 11) argues that the words *pobladores* and *poblaciones* have had "specific, varied, and at times contested meanings" throughout the twentieth century. The nuances in their meanings are a result of the tense relationship between housing activism and state policies, a relationship that has played a key role in the formation of the state and the public sphere. In this book, I expand upon Murphy's assertion by arguing that the category *poblador*, in addition to being exposed to resignifications, has also operated as a political category for subject formation. I hold that the Chilean urban poor, by recognizing themselves as *pobladores*, become political subjects capable of addressing the state by using a rights-based language. To do so, I examine past and present housing movements through which working-class families have been able to form their subjectivities as subject-citizens endowed with rights and dignity.

Looking at *pobladores* as a specific type of political subjectivity anchored in poor people's participation in housing movements does not imply that they have a cohesive identity or identical worldviews. Although working-class residents have long drawn on the term *poblador* to give shape to their struggles, the term itself has had different connotations, depending on who has used the word and why (see Murphy 2015). The category of *poblador* has been indistinctively utilized to allude to marginal groups, political clients, or revolutionary subjects. Thus, there is no a single definition of what it means to be a *poblador*, nor has the usage of the term been the same throughout the twentieth and early twenty-first centuries. This openness in the meaning of the word is crucial to understanding the processes of subject formation and the specific forms of social distinction that such a term has made possible among the urban poor. In the following chapters, I show that, both in the past and at present, the social category of *pobladores* has been composed of individuals with diverse political affiliations, opposing ideological discourses, and different moral comprehensions of themselves as housing activists. However, regardless of *pobladores'* internal differences, it is striking to note that contemporary housing activists—such as those I encountered during the fieldwork for this book—think of the word *poblador* as endowed with a generative power, as if the very the usage of the term enables them to become collective actors. In this book, I do not seek to propose a normative definition of the word *poblador*, nor do I argue that the term has a singular meaning. Rather, I reflect on a historical process in which, while poor urban residents have long been subject to social exclusion, their discourses and political practices around housing have helped transform the meaning of the term *poblador*. In particular, I explore how new generations of housing activists make sense of this category in their everyday interactions and how their subjective understanding of it has allowed them to both construct collective memories of the past and carry out social protest movements for rights and social justice.

In English, the word *housing* has two connotations, depending on how speakers use it in their linguistic interactions (Turner 1972). When used as a noun, *housing* alludes to a material product, a commodity through which people seek to satisfy their need for shelter. In contrast, the verb "'to house' describes the process or *activity* of housing" (Turner 1972, 151). As a political anthropologist, understanding *housing* as a verb leads me to examine the role of housing in people's everyday life and, more specifically, how their aspirations for homeownership inform their involvement in urban politics. Focusing on the case of Chile, this book seeks to accomplish this through an ethnographic study on what scholars have called the *movimiento de pobladores* (*pobladores* movement) in order to describe poor residents' protest movements for housing rights.[2] My focus, then, is on the political interventions through which people struggling for housing seek to transform their precarious living conditions as urban residents and on how such practices help develop new types of subjectivities.

The phrase *movimiento de pobladores* evokes various meanings, all of which allude to different, historically situated urban struggles for rights to the city. When reflecting on the *pobladores* movement, social scientists have generally elaborated on two theoretical fields, both of which relate to the capacity of the urban poor to participate in politics as collective actors. On the one hand, they have analyzed the extent to which large-scale housing-related mobilizations— like the mid-twentieth-century squatter movement—give rise to transformative urban social movements. On the other hand, they have long examined the relationship between *pobladores* and the political system as a means to discuss the capacity of such movements to propose an agenda for social change as autonomous political agents. But what happens when, as I show in the opening field note, low-income urban dwellers seek to achieve their right to housing by participating in neoliberal housing programs? I address this question by delving into how poor residents struggling for subsidized housing configure their political agencies in an era of neoliberal governmentality.

The Claim to Housing Rights from the Urban Peripheries

In Latin America, poor urban dwellers have long understood housing as a social right, that is to say, as a right that must be guaranteed by the state to all citizens so that they can attain an adequate standard of living. This conceptualization of housing has led to widespread demands for homeownership, which contrasts with the circumstances in countries like the United States where homeownership is primarily seen as one's own personal responsibility (Murphy 2015). In Chile, *los sin casa* (those who do not have a home of their own) have historically conceived of the lack of legal residence in the city as an "affront to the dignity and the sociopolitical status of the urban poor" (Murphy 2015, 267). The category of *los sin casa* can include people with a variety of different residential situations, some of which I explore in this book. For example, it can refer to poor families living as squatters in informal settlements, as room renters, or as *allegados*, the latter alluding to individuals who reside in relatives' homes, generally in overcrowded conditions. In any case, *los sin casa* have long mobilized for housing rights and homeownership through different forms of activism. This largely explains why, since the beginning of twentieth century, the Chilean state has developed homeownership-oriented housing policies, even during governments inspired by progressive and socialist ideals.

In Santiago, as in many other cities in the so-called Global South, poor city dwellers engaged in mass urban movements for housing in the mid-twentieth century as a way to access homeownership. Between the early 1950s and 1973, *los sin casa* conducted large-scale land seizures in the urban peripheries, developed self-built *campamentos* (squatter settlements), and organized for improving the conditions of their residential spaces. In a context of increasing urban struggles, the term *poblador* took on a uniquely political character as it began to refer to poor residents who had organized powerful social justice movements. *Pobladores* constituted themselves as transformative, collective actors, which allowed them to become one of the more recognizable social forces backing the socialist project of Salvador Allende (1970–1973).

However, the *pobladores'* actions were severely constrained once General Augusto Pinochet overthrew Salvador Allende's government. The subsequent military dictatorship (1973–1990) steadily quashed land occupations, carried out massive evictions of squatter settlements located in the wealthiest areas of Santiago, and killed hundreds of poor residents. *Los sin casa* could no longer occupy urban lands as part of their movement, and the state persecuted those who engaged in housing struggles. Incapable of obtaining housing solutions through land takeovers, lower-income families without a home of their home came to be characterized predominantly as *allegados*. The category of *allegados*, as a term referring to people sharing a house with relatives, was already in use in the mid-twentieth century. However, it was in the 1980s that the word began to circulate more widely in public policy discourse, as residing in other people's houses became the most common strategy used by the poor to deal with the lack of social housing.[3] To become homeowners, *allegados* were forced to enroll in new, subsidy-based housing programs created in the late 1970s as part of the military regime's "modernization" process. Consistent with the neoliberal orientation of the dictatorship's reforms, these programs conceived of poor families as rational actors who would be able to obtain housing as a commodity in the private market. Homeownership, in that sense, came to be understood as the result of an individual effort rather than a collective one. But *pobladores* assumed a renewed political role by shifting the focus of their protests from housing to democracy. Being one the most active segments of the working classes in the struggle for democracy, poor urban residents played a decisive role in the Jornadas de Protesta Nacional (Days of National Protest) by drawing on the social networks and organizing skills they had attained through their neighborhood associations. This led to certain *poblaciones*—especially those that received the support of the Communist Party—becoming an important setting for political resistance against the military regime.[4]

The remarkable political significance of *pobladores* vanished once Pinochet's regime ended. To maintain the neoliberal economic, political, and institutional arrangement created by the military regime, the center-left governments that followed the dictatorship attempted to prevent the proliferation of grassroots movements. The return to democracy in 1990 thus marked the beginning of a state-led demobilization in which the ruling classes dismissed the popular sectors as valid interlocutors when it came to discussing the type of social compact that would regulate the new democratic period.[5] To avoid the resurgence of large-scale land seizures, these governments started to allocate considerable public expenditures for subsidized housing projects on the basis of the neoliberal urban policies implemented in the late 1970s. At the same time, poor families were increasingly compelled to enroll in *comités de allegados* (state-regulated housing assemblies) to be able to apply for housing subsidies and become homeowners.

The utilization of subsidy-based housing policies allowed postdictatorial governments to expand access to social housing among the lowest-income groups. During the 1990s, when Chile had a population of over thirteen million people, the state endeavored to construct at least ninety thousand subsidized housing units per year (Arriagada and Moreno 2006). This eventually helped reduce the quantitative housing shortage—that is, the number of housing units needed for everybody to have adequate housing—from 918,756 units in 1990 to 743,450 in 2000, which represents a decrease from a 53 percent housing deficit to a 37 percent deficit (Ministerio de Planificación 2001). The reduction of the housing deficit persisted in the following decades, dropping to 497,560 units in 2017 (Fundación Vivienda 2019). Nonetheless, the housing shortage increased again because of the joint effect of the economic crisis provoked by the COVID-19 pandemic starting in 2020 and the inefficiency of subsidy-based housing policies. Official MINVU data showed that the housing deficit increased to 600,000 units in 2021 (*Diario Financiero* 2021), meaning that around 11 percent of households in Chile did not have a home of their own in 2020 and 2021.

Despite the increase in the housing shortage in recent years, since 1990 Chile's subsidized model has stood out for helping the governments lower the number of families in need of housing. But the significant progress in building subsidized housing turned out to be paradoxical for the poor. Since the early 1980s, low-income families have been forced to move to the distant outskirts of the city in order to obtain subsidized housing (map 2). Homeownership has become a means of segregating and socially excluding low-income families. This is what Rodríguez and Sugranyes (2005) understand as the dilemma of *los con techo* ("those who have housing"): the quandary of those who, to fulfill the dream of their own home (*el sueño de la casa propia*), have had to abandon their original neighborhoods and live in subsidized housing projects in the urban peripheries.

This paradox largely explains the reemergence of housing movements since the mid-2000s. As I show in this book, the resurgence of social protests around housing is closely related to both novel claims for the right to a life with dignity and the transformation of the ways in which poor residents conceive of themselves as urban citizens with dignity. Although *pobladores* had been actively involved in housing assemblies since the early 1990s, it was only in the mid-2000s that such involvement transformed into public forms of activism. The

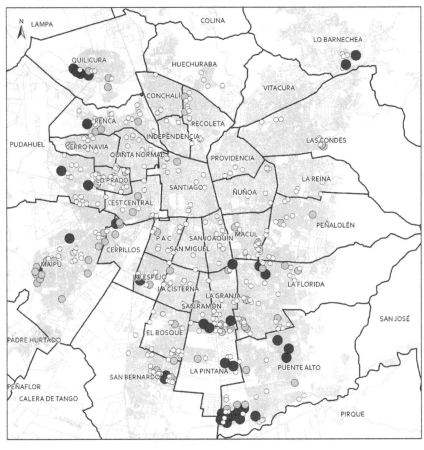

Legend

Social housing projects
units by project

District limits

○ 10 - 500
◎ 501 - 1000
● 1001 - 3200

Main road networks

MAP 2. Social housing units built by housing project, 1980–2003. Source: Ministry of Housing and Urbanism, 2015. Credit: Juan Correa.

tactics used in these new protests consist not of land occupations but of participation in subsidy-based housing programs, similar to those that were used in the 1990s to demobilize the urban poor. What occurs, then, when low-income residents demanding the right to housing and dignity are no longer squatters but recipients of state subsidies? This book addresses the question of how to account for the formation of transformative political agencies when neoliberal housing programs frame poor people's claims for housing and dignity.

The Right to Housing in Neoliberal Chile

Chile's recent political history is framed by massive state repression, broad-reaching neoliberalization, and intense protest movements for social rights. The case of this country, however, contrasts with other "post-neoliberal" states in Latin America like Bolivia, Argentina, or Venezuela, as neoliberalism remained firmly and solidly embedded in Chile for over forty years. Implemented in the in the mid-1970s during Pinochet's regime and entrenched in the country's 1980 constitution, the neoliberal reforms enacted in Chile founded a political, economic, and cultural project that remained practically unaltered until the late 2010s. The 2011 student movement, a mass reaction to the commodification of the right to education, questioned the ideological principles of Chile's neoliberalism. But the movement lost momentum between 2012 and 2013, and some of its demands were addressed by President Michelle Bachelet's second administration (2014–2018). Around the same time, other social movements came into play and, in different ways, denounced the privatization of social life by demanding gender, environmental, labor, and indigenous rights.[6] These mobilizations, along with those related to housing demands that I describe in this book, helped to configure the 2019 social uprising. In October of that year, what started out as students engaging in mass fare dodging to protest against a 4 percent hike in Santiago metro fares, quickly transformed into a widespread movement against social inequality. Millions of people flooded the country's major cities calling for an end to the 1980 constitution, which they saw as the embodiment of Chile's market-driven economy. The 2019 social uprising resulted in a plebiscite to rewrite the constitution, which eventually took place on October 25, 2020.

Chile's initial turn to neoliberalism in the mid-1970s emerged as a violent response to President Salvador Allende's socialist project and sought to reestablish the conditions for capital accumulation and restore power to economic elites (Harvey 2005). Allende's presidency had attempted to expand the welfare system for the poor by, among other measures, redistributing land through a significant agrarian reform program and nationalizing both the foreign-owned copper industry and the banking system. Advised by economists trained at the University of Chicago—the so-called Chicago Boys—Pinochet executed a radical macroeconomic restructuring to revert Allende's "Chilean road to socialism." Based on the idea that the free market is the best way to achieve development and wealth, the military dictatorship "reversed the nationalizations and privatized public assets, opened up natural resources (fisheries, timber, etc.) to private and unregulated exploitation . . . , privatized social security, and facilitated foreign direct investment and freer trade" (Harvey 2005, 8).

In terms of urban planning, the dictatorship's market-oriented reforms entailed an early and extreme liberalization of urban land markets.[7] The 1979 National Policy of Urban Development followed three main principles. First, urban land is not a scarce good. Its "apparent scarcity," the policy said, resulted from the lack of consistency between state regulations and the real estate market's balance between supply and demand (Ministerio de Vivienda y Urbanismo 2012, 16). Second, use of urban land is to be defined by its profitability. This meant that the free market would be able to balance the *rentabilidad social* (social profitability) of real estate developments and the private interests of developers. Third, the use of urban land must be regulated by flexible norms in accordance with market requirements. This meant that state regulations, rather than acting to regulate the market, should "follow" it as a way to secure capital accumulation. These and other measures—for example, the displacement of squatter settlements and the creation of socially homogeneous *comunas* (municipalities) in Santiago—were supposed to control speculation and land prices. Quite the opposite occurred, as urban land prices in Santiago increased by almost 1,000 percent between 1982 and 2012 (*El Mercurio* 2012). In chapter 3, I show that the sustained increase in land prices in the city is at the core of *pobladores'* struggles for housing, as it makes it more difficult for the poor to obtain housing.

Current subsidy-based housing policies are grounded in the neoliberal urban reforms developed during the dictatorship. Developed in the late 1970s, subsidy-based policies brought about a radical change in the way Chilean *pobladores* access and conceive of social housing. In the mid-twentieth century, housing activists expected to obtain social housing through collective action. With technical supervision by the state, they usually became homeowners by either creating housing cooperatives or building their residential spaces themselves. Nonetheless, since the late 1970s, state policies have come to conceptualize housing as a consumer good that the poor can access individually through the market using both state subsidies and private savings. In essence a voucher-based system, these policies provide housing subsidies to low-income individuals who, understood as rational economic agents, purchase homes built by real estate developers.

This subsidy-based system of housing provision has been the model for housing policies implemented elsewhere in the Global South. The World Bank and other international agencies supported Chile's neoliberal housing programs and even persuaded other countries to adopt them. Since the early 1990s, Colombia, Costa Rica, South Africa, Mexico, and Brazil, among others, introduced their own subsidy-based policies inspired by the Chilean experience. In all these cases, international agencies suggested that governments withdraw from the construction market to make way for the privatization of housing. Governments, in fact, were "advised to limit their involvement in productive activities and to cut much of their regulative intervention. . . . Along with education, health, infrastructure provision, and transport, housing became an eminently suitable candidate for private sector initiative" (Gilbert 2004a, 14).

This market-led modality of social housing production has resulted in three main outcomes. First, housing has turned into a commodity that is attained as means-tested assistance, that is, as a finished product distributed individually among the poorest families. Second, housing is often located in peripheral areas that lack infrastructure and services, which has consolidated class separation and spatial inequality.[8] Third, prospective homeowners are expected to enroll in subsidy-based housing programs to fulfill their aspirations for homeownership. As technologies of government, these programs seek to form the urban poor as responsible citizens capable of governing themselves by instilling values of self-sufficiency and individual autonomy.[9] Chile's housing programs have long aimed to inculcate ideas of civility and responsibility among the poor. In the 1960s, for instance, prospective homeowners had to demonstrate that they were "responsible workers and family members" (Murphy 2015, 87) by depositing monthly quotas into saving accounts that the Ministry of Housing and Urbanism had opened for them. There is certainly a continuity in the moralizing language used by the state when imagining the poor as civilized citizens. However, what is new in the neoliberal period is that, since the late 1970s, the poor began to be conceptualized as individualized, rational economic agents rather than as rights-bearing subjects. As technologies for infusing individuals with this new economic ethos, subsidy-based housing policies can thus be understood as underlying the cultural project of Chile's neoliberalism; one in which the poor become citizen-consumers able to make rational choices in every domain of their lives.

Neoliberalized Pobladores?

Through the Foucauldian notion of governmentality, scholarly debates have elaborated extensively on the cultural dimension of neoliberalism. For Foucault (2003), advanced liberal societies rely on a kind of power that depends less on surveillance and discipline than on calculative operations and regulation. Foucault calls this form of power *government*. Rather than subduing the capacity of action of the governed, this type of power recognizes the subject's faculty for agency in order to act instrumentally upon it. Thus, to manage the conduct of individuals and populations, neoliberal technologies of government presuppose the freedom of the governed. This is what Foucault and others have referred to as "government through freedom," a mode of exerting power grounded in the rationalization of procedures in every domain of social life and the promotion of autonomous and self-responsible citizens.[10] What is at stake in neoliberal societies is thus to diffuse "market logics throughout society" (Goodale and Postero 2013, 8). Building on this perspective on governmentality, Ong (2006, 13) defines neoliberalism as "an art of governing whose logic is the condition of individual active freedom." It is precisely in neoliberalism where a new "game of powers" emerges that Rose (1999) calls *ethico-politics*. If disciplinary power focuses on maximizing the utility and docility of individuals, and biopower deals with maximizing the health of populations, ethico-politics "concerns itself with the *self-techniques necessary for responsible self-government* and the *relations between one's obligation to oneself and one's obligations to others*" (Rose 1999, 188, original emphasis).

The successful process for the mass provision of subsidized housing to the urban poor since 1990 has led social scientists to stop thinking of *pobladores* as transformative political agents. Their involvement in neoliberal housing programs seemed to relegate them to a cast of responsible citizens who were forced to wait, whether to receive subsidies, to become homeowners, or something else. This has been interpreted as a tangible expression of their pacification. Over the past three decades, scholars have analyzed the category of *poblador* as primarily a social identity signifier, alluding to a heterogeneous aggregation of low-income urban dwellers, now exposed to new forms of power. Three fields of scholarship on the Chilean urban poor have emerged in this context. The first one has focused on the examination of how the implementation of neoliberalism altered the characteristics of poverty and how the poor have subjectively made sense of these changes.[11] The second has focused on the demobilization of popular social sectors. With respect to urban movements, scholars have also scrutinized the pacifying role of subsidy-based housing programs in the vanishing of land seizure movements.[12] The third field of research has delved into how former squatters signify the process of becoming homeowners by both acquiring middle-class values and re-creating nostalgic views of their past life experiences in the self-built settlements.[13]

The issue of how new generations of poor residents configure their political agencies as welfare recipients who are "in waiting,"[14] and how their participation in subsidy-based programs frame their demands for housing and dignity, has barely been explored. When speaking on the political character of *pobladores*, scholars tend to look to the past and the events surrounding the emergence of the old *pobladores* movement. In doing so, they construe the agency contained in the category *poblador* as depending exclusively on the collective practices that working-class urban dwellers engaged in during the mid-twentieth century. Such a perspective conceives of *pobladores'* agency as fixed and static in time, which hinders our ability to understand how their political capacities reemerge in a period of neoliberal governmentality. To approach this reemergence, I argue that the word *poblador* operates both as a social identity category and as a political signifier, which urban activists draw on in certain conditions to formulate political subjectivities. I do so by first examining the constitution of *pobladores* genealogically as political subjects and, second, by ethnographically describing how such a subject-formation process takes place in the context of current housing struggles.

The housing activists I met considered their political actions directly rooted in the old housing mobilizations. They conceived of the movements that they were engaged in as a contemporary expression of the movements that their parents and grandparents had carried out in the mid-twentieth century. In situating their struggles within a broader historical framework, the people I encountered looked at the past as a source of symbolic and political power, allowing them to take part of a particular form of subjectivity. In doing so, they conceptualized the category of *pobladores* as containing a consistent type of identity, as if the *pobladores* of the past were "the same" as those of the present. However, confronted with the need to bring this subjectivity into the present to determine what it means to be a *poblador* in this day and age, and which rights one is entitled to, they established strict mechanisms of distinction based on moral evaluations of themselves and others. By inquiring into prospective homeowners' ethical and political practices, this book seeks to account for how urban activists re-create their subjectivity as *pobladores* while enrolled in neoliberal programs.

In this book, I'm not interested in determining whether housing protests in neoliberal Chile lead to subversive urban social movements, nor do I seek to affirm or deny the existence of *pobladores* as revolutionary collective actors per se. Such approaches, I argue in the following chapters, have prevented the social sciences from scrutinizing how the poor become political agents by claiming the right to housing through their participation in state policies and programs. Some crucial questions thus arise: What kind of subject is formed when working-class social movements are carried out through the subject's involvement in market-based housing programs? What kind of values do these welfare programs seek to instill in people waiting to obtain subsidized housing, and how do those values inform their everyday practices? What type of citizenship comes about in circumstances in which state policies conceptualize housing as a commodity rather than as a social right?

Anthropologists have persuasively argued for the need to transcend Eurocentric approaches to neoliberalism, to situate neoliberal cultural and political projects—which are always fragmented, incomplete and contested rather than fully realized—within the particular settings in which they develop.[15] I take this challenge as an invitation to reflect ethnographically on the specific directions that neoliberalism has taken in a country of the Global South, such as Chile. The main argument in the book is that, in advanced neoliberal societies, the process of citizen-subject formation that results from social movements framed by poor residents' engagement in welfare programs is paradoxical: although low-income inhabitants' participation in these programs fosters the development of a neoliberal ethics through which they become entrepreneurial and self-reliant rights bearers, it also makes the emergence of new political agencies aimed at contesting the commodification of social rights possible. I understand the idea of agency as a process of political and ethical formation in which meanings are open to unexpected delimitations rather than fixed in advance.[16] This book questions the limits and potentialities of political resistance to neoliberalism when working-class residents draw on neoliberal programs to articulate their demand for rights. In this regard, I argue that poor people's engagement in welfare programs not only sets the condition for the production of "responsibilized and entrepreneurialized" subject-citizens (Rose 1999, 139). It also makes social protests appear to resist the dominance of the market over the allocation of social rights. At the core of this paradox, poor urban dwellers formulate their political narratives through moral categories such as "dignity," to ethically signify their everyday experiences with vulnerability and to shape the strategic orientations of their movement against neoliberal policies.

Words and Actions

I hold that the social identity category *poblador* enables the formation of political subjects capable of directing a rights-based discourse at the state, as it is endowed with a "performative" power. Following Austin (1962), by "performative" I mean the capacity of words to do or constitute what they say.[17] This implies that, when uttered, the word *poblador* makes the formation of subjects possible, a process that has taken place at different historical conjunctures since the 1950s. But where does the performative power of words come from? Austin and others have paid attention to the role of repetition, citationality, and social conventions.[18] If words produce what they name, it is because they unfold in ritualized acts—as in a baptism ceremony—in which speech acts are constantly repeated. This is why Austin (1962, 14), when explaining the conditions for a performative utterance to be effective, says that "there must exist an accepted conventional procedure having a certain conventional effect." This has two implications for my argument, which I account for in detail in chapter 4. First, the performative power of the category *poblador* materialized only when such a word began to circulate widely in public discourses, which ultimately led to the transformation of the poor into political subjectivities. Second, because performative utterances operate through repetition, the political agency anchored in the signifier *poblador* can reemerge every time that such a category is brought into the present through citation. I do not, however, reduce *pobladores'* subject-formation process to mere linguistic operations of naming. Ritualized bodily encounters can also act in a performative way. This means that, like speech acts, rituals also have the capacity to create meaning on the basis of their repetition.[19] Accordingly, this book examines how the urban poor have become *pobladores* by looking at both the social discourses that have spoken about them and the everyday actions that, since the early 1950s, low-income residents have developed to obtain housing.

As words and actions can assume a formative character, the effect of these performatives in terms of meanings and significations must be understood as open ended, unpredictable, and potentially subversive. For Derrida, every single repetition of a linguistic sign is, at the same time, its transformation. He calls this property "iterability" (Derrida 1977, 180). Derrida's iterability entails a force of rupture, as the linguistic sign has the power to break from the context of its own production. Repetition, thus, implies a form of alterity as, when quoted, the linguistic sign changes. Adapting Derrida's approach to the performative, I think of *pobladores* not as a fixed or static type of political subjectivity, but as one whose character, agency, and identity cannot be fully determined in advance. This book explores ethnographically the types of political agencies that, by reinvoking the word *poblador*, contemporary poor urban dwellers develop in their housing struggles.

Performances of City Making: Land Occupations and Autoconstruction
It is the acknowledgment of the poor as city makers that enabled the formation of *pobladores* as a particular type of working-class agency. *Pobladores* became visible to the Chilean public as political agents, and subject to Chilean public opinion, once they engaged in mass housing protests. The irruption of the *pobladores* movement in the mid-twentieth century came hand in hand with the spread of public discourses accounting for the poor as unprivileged urban dwellers who had organized for the right to housing. Whether through the news media, politicians' speeches, the Catholic Church's journals, or the political propaganda produced by grassroots organizations, these narratives generally depicted *pobladores* as recognizable political subjects whose agency stemmed from two interrelated performances of city making: *tomas de terrenos* (land seizures) and *autoconstrucción* (self-building) of houses and neighborhoods.

By "land seizures" I mean the illegal occupation of plots, located most often in the urban peripheries, by organized families struggling for housing rights. As national governments were incapable of managing the housing crisis derived from growing rates of urbanization, land seizures proliferated in Latin American metropolises in the 1940s and 1950s. The so-called marginality theory looked at squatters as anomic and dysfunctional urban dwellers who, as part of what Lewis (1961) defined as the "culture of poverty," were unable to contribute to society on their own.[20] Other approaches, to the contrary, saw squatters as active, productive city dwellers, endowed with organizing skills and able to provide housing for themselves by self-building their neighborhoods.[21] The anthropologist William Mangin (1967, 74), who studied the rise of *barriadas* (squatter settlements) in Lima, argued that "one major contribution [of squatter settlements] is that millions of people have solved their own housing problem in situations where the national government was practically unable to move." Mangin and others highlighted the capacity for collective action of squatters who, by taking over vacant plots, sought to access urban land and acquire title deeds in order to eventually achieve the right to housing.

In Santiago, *pobladores* drew on the illegal seizure of urban land to develop a mass housing movement. Especially between the late 1960s and 1973, they carried out over three hundred *tomas de terrenos* in the city, which is explained by the generalized radicalization of working-class protest movements. The events surrounding the invasion of urban lands were composed of performative actions, which helped create social imaginaries of land occupations as a distinguishable strategy used by the poor. Upon arrival at the occupied plot, squatters would plant the Chilean flag as a sign of victory, as if they were colonizing an unknown land that they could then claim as their own. Likewise, they would give the emerging *campamento* a name, which generally evoked Marxist figures like Lenin, Pablo Neruda, Ho Chi Minh, or Che Guevara. For both the right and the left, it was the conjunction of illicit actions and revolutionary symbols that revealed the disruptive, or even revolutionary, capacities of those socially recognized as *pobladores*.

But *pobladores'* performances of city making were not restricted to land seizures. In the same period, the urban poor engaged en masse in practices of self-building homes and neighborhoods. In Chile and elsewhere in Latin America, this modality of city making has been known as *autoconstrucción*, a concept that the anthropologists James Holston and Teresa Caldeira literally translate as "autoconstruction." Autoconstruction, Holston (1991, 451) contends, involves a variety of activities that share two main attributes: first, that of a particular social production of space in which "the need to build a house represents the builder's relation to a set of conditions that we might call peripheral urbanization; and second, that of home building as the figure or measure of an imagined future quite different from those conditions." As a defining feature of mass urbanization in the Global South since the mid-twentieth century, Caldeira (2017) says, autoconstruction entails specific forms of agencies and temporalities. First off, residents, rather than being merely consumers of spaces, are themselves the main agents involved in the urbanization of the peripheries. Second, they build houses and neighborhoods that grow "little-by-little, in long-term processes of incompletion and continuous improvement" (Caldeira 2017, 5). Third, by autoconstructing their residential spaces, the poor become citizens, acquire the capacity to deal with the state as subjects of rights, and develop novel forms of civic participation.[22] The autoconstruction of the peripheries thus results in the emergence of a kind of subjectivity fundamentally anchored in the acknowledgment of the poor as city makers. As autoconstructors, residents at the periphery are thus able to become citizens, transform their patterns of consumption, and legitimize their rights to the city.

Holston and Caldeira argue that autoconstruction in Brazil became essentially a private enterprise because of, among other aspects, the scarce control and assistance from the state.[23] As expected, this gave rise to fraudulent land transactions. As in São Paulo, poor families were also exposed to illegal land dealings in Santiago. The so-called *loteos brujos*—illegally subdivided plots sold by fake real estate agents—were the most common expression of this. However, the kind of autoconstruction that emerged in Santiago was different from that of Brazil. First, *pobladores* participated in the building of their homes and neighborhoods not so much as private entrepreneurs than as collective actors. Since the early 1950s, members of housing organizations like the Agrupación Provincial de Pobladores (Pobladores' Provincial Association) claimed that the state supplied them with construction materials to autoconstruct their residential spaces. There was, in that sense, an explicit political demand for autoconstruction that housing activists used to claim urban rights. This demand, I show in chapter 4, increased as housing protest movements escalated.

This leads to the second element, which relates to the role of the state in autoconstruction processes. Unlike the Brazilian case, in Chile the state strongly promoted autoconstruction through housing programs such as Jorge Alessandri's (1958–1964) Housing Plan and Eduardo Frei Montalva's (1964–1970) Operation Site. To become homeowners, *pobladores* were expected to do the work themselves, building their own houses under the technical supervision of public agencies like the Urban Improvement Corporation (CORMU) and the Housing Corporation (CORVI). As a collective and state-led phenomenon, the Chilean variety of autoconstruction sought to moralize the poor by acknowledging them as civilized, citizen city makers. This act of "interpellation"—using Althusser's (2001) terminology (for more on this, see chapter 4)—led *pobladores* to, in some cases, establish clientelistic relationships with populist governments like that of Eduardo Frei Montalva. But the kind of subjectivity that derived from the recognition of *pobladores* as city makers did not involve their total subordination to the state's interests. Quite the opposite, the consolidation of *pobladores* as transformative agents helped them to radicalize their struggles for the right to housing. By creating self-defense militias, self-managed grade schools, and popular courts, among other community-based institutions, *pobladores* could even develop innovative experiences of *poder popular* (popular power) in squatter settlements.

In today's neoliberal Chile, the poor no longer become homeowners through autoconstruction. This is not to say that autoconstruction does not still occur. Contemporary *pobladores* who have already obtained subsidized housing become invested in their homes through small-scale forms of self-building. Although they receive housing as a finished commodity ready to be consumed, they usually autoconstruct when, for instance, making home additions to accommodate family needs or renovating their homes on their own. Likewise, as of this writing, the economic crisis caused by the COVID-19 pandemic has fostered the reappearance of mass land occupations in Chile's major cities. The number of families living in autoconstructed *campamentos* increased dramatically from 47,050 in 2019 to 81,643 in 2021, which suggests that the poor still draw on autoconstruction to achieve the right to housing.[24] There is thus a continuum, rather than a clear distinction, in terms of how the poor have produced their residential spaces both materially and symbolically over the past seven decades. Nonetheless, autoconstruction as it was extensively practiced in the mid-twentieth century is no longer the dominant force intervening in the urbanization of the peripheries, nor do families in need of homes consider it their first and foremost strategy to become homeowners. Neoliberal urban policies, as I had previously explained, force prospective homeowners to apply for subsidies to obtain housing through the market. This fact compels us to reflect on how poor residents reconfigure their agency as *pobladores*, when their historical modalities of subject formation—land seizures and autoconstruction—do not play a central role in the emergence of the housing movements anymore. Here, then, emerges the problem of citizenship and political membership, expressed through the question of how contemporary *pobladores* constitute themselves as citizen city makers when they deal with the state not as autoconstructors but as recipients of welfare programs. This book examines the types of citizenship that result from contemporary *pobladores*' struggles for housing and the ways they negotiate their membership in the political community as beneficiaries of state subsidies.

Struggling for Citizenship Rights

Drawing on debates in political anthropology, I understand citizenship as a regulatory system through which societies manage their social conflicts and power relations in order to consolidate their identity projects.[25] Citizenship regimes operate on the basis of a logic of inclusion-exclusion materialized through criteria for political membership, which delimits the rights that those considered full members can exert (Kipnis 2004). Citizenship alludes thus to the relation "between the person and the political community" (Lazar 2013, 111), a relation that, while framed by how societies answer the question of belonging, results in specific subject-making processes.[26] In the following chapters, I show that, since the early mid-1950s, poor residents without a home of their own have addressed the question of belonging by claiming the social right to housing, which has entailed the emergence of *pobladores* as a distinctive political subjectivity.

While housing activism in Chile has historically allowed the working classes to achieve homeownership, it has also contributed to reinforcing liberal notions of citizenship linked to specific forms of property and expectations of propriety (Murphy 2015). Nevertheless, this has not prevented *pobladores* from conceiving of housing as a social right. For the activists I spent time with, housing is a universal right that—drawing on Marshall's (1977) classic definition of social rights—provides the poor with a minimum level of economic welfare and security. The definition of what constitutes a "minimum level" of well-being, of course, varies according to the standards prevailing in any given society. What was considered acceptable living conditions for the poor in the 1950s may not be suitable now. This explains why *pobladores'* claims for dignity have changed significantly over time.[27] Their ideas of dignity, as I show in detail in chapter 6, no longer constitute a reaction to their residential situation as squatters. Rather, they arise as a political response to welfare programs that, while constructing the poor as individual beneficiaries of subsidies, segregate them by forcing them to live in the urban peripheries. What remains unchanged for the *pobladores* is their view of housing as a social right. Such an understanding has been crucial to the emergence of urban, residency-based types of citizenship. By developing new forms of participation in urban politics, *pobladores* have helped expand social rights while questioning dominant criteria regarding how rights are distributed in society.

National Citizenship, Equality, and Difference

In the modern formulation of citizenship, nationality has been understood as the principal criterion for the definition of who belongs to society. The regime of citizenship that appeared along with the development of the modern state was thus grounded in the delimitation of a national community, which was thought of as the group of people over which political sovereignty resides, that is to say, as a defined political community entitled to a set of rights (Anderson 1991).[28] Citizenship has since come to be understood as a "status" that makes those who possess it equal with respect to rights and duties, meaning that full members are endowed with the same corpus of rights as well as protected by common law.[29] Modern citizenship thus conceived of equality as the capacity of those who participate in politics to exercise the same set of rights.[30]

Critical approaches to citizenship have, however, argued that the promotion of formal equality among citizens has resulted in the subordination of social difference—be it in terms of class, gender, race—to dominant cultural structures.[31] Iris Marion Young (1989) notes that modern citizenship has understood universality from a twofold perspective: as a synonym of that which is "general" and as a set of norms that are the same for all. These two conceptualizations of universality—that is, as generality and as equal treatment—have contributed to an understanding of equality as sameness, which has homogenized citizenry by relegating citizens' identity claims to the private domain.[32] To subvert this "unreal universality"—paraphrasing Marx (1978, 34)—Young advocates the concept of a differentiated citizenship. This is a kind of special treatment regime, one that would ensure the full inclusion and participation of all by granting more rights to deprived groups.[33]

Advocacy for differentiated citizenship and special treatment for certain groups has triggered a number of debates about the unintended outcomes that could result from giving special rights to minorities, women, immigrants, or any kind of underprivileged group. Okin (1999), for instance, maintains that granting more rights to patriarchal cultures could be used to imprison women in an oppressive and inegalitarian gender status. For Holston (2011), the problem of differentiated citizenship is that such a model, by legalizing existing social differences, consolidates and perpetuates them.[34] Both Okin's and Holston's reflections invite us to think critically about forms of citizenship and the politics of recognition. In spite of being inspired by liberal or progressive ideals, such perspectives may give rise to new types of oppression and social inequality. As Holston suggests, Young's analysis fails to notice that citizenship regimes have in fact implemented special treatment models, which have been far from promoting substantive social justice. In this sense, rather than to ahistorically categorize citizenships as "difference blind" or "difference specific," it is instead more important to historically and ethnographically scrutinize how "a citizenship problematizes the legalization and equalization of differences and struggles with the problems of justice that result" (Holston 2008, 32).[35] By examining *pobladores'* long-term housing protest movements, this book seeks to account for how low-income residents have handled the problem of equality as an excluded population. This issue is particularly relevant in the context of planetary urbanization, in which the city has become a "strategic arena" (Holston and Appadurai 1996, 188) for reconstructing the notion of citizenship and expanding it on a new social basis.

Urban Contestations: Rights to the City, Rights to Dignity

Explosive urban growth in the Global South since the mid-twentieth century has led to the emergence of mass protest movements, by means of which underprivileged collectivities have struggled for social inclusion by claiming rights to the city. The city has thus turned into a renewed political community capable of undermining the foundations of national models of citizenship.[36] Greatly influenced by Henri Lefebvre's (1996) politics of inhabitance, scholars have begun to think of novel types of citizenship grounded in people's everyday contribution to urban life. In this context, the concept of urban citizenship has emerged forcefully over recent decades to account for how marginalized groups legitimize their claim to rights as residents of the city. Drawing on Holston's (2008) work on Brazil's insurgent citizenship, by "urban citizenship" I mean a form citizenship that presents three main characteristics: (a) it deems the city, rather than the nation, as the foremost political community; (b) political membership is defined by residency rather than nationality; and (c) the rights to be distributed are understood as rights to the city. As I discuss in detail in chapter 5, *pobladores'* urban citizenship reveals itself through what I call a "politics of effort"—a system of rights distribution based on the evaluation of people's behavior in terms of their political and moral commitment to the struggle for housing. *Pobladores*, in that sense, look at citizenship as a "claim rather than a status" (Das 2011, 320; see Lazar and Nuijten 2013). This suggests that, for them, claims to citizenship are determined not by formal legal procedures but by the very act of demanding rights, through which they seek to justify state provision of housing. Rights, in their view, are not a prerogative that the state "gives" to the people but, rather, are gained through *la lucha* (the struggle).

Understanding citizenship as a claim enables us to question some theoretical efforts proposing normative, or even utopian, models of urban citizenship that do not allow for an ethnographic scrutiny of how people's demands for rights generate historically situated conceptualizations of citizenship.[37] Likewise, in the case of advanced liberal societies like Chile, it compels us to analyze how the poor conceive of citizenship and rights when participating in subsidy-based programs. Current debates on citizenship and right-to-the-city movements in metropolises of the Global South are overwhelmingly focused on examining the subversive effects of those who have directly engaged in auto-construction processes.[38] The vast literature on this matter contrasts, however, with the scant attention that has been paid to housing protests framed by poor residents' enrollment in neoliberal policies. Those who have accounted for this phenomenon in Chile argue that there is little room for insurgencies when the poor make use of such programs to claim housing rights.[39] For them, participating in state-regulated housing assemblies entails both the internalization of neoliberal values and, accordingly, the political demobilization of the poor. In the following chapters, I question these assumptions by demonstrating that *pobladores* who are enrolled in state-regulated housing assemblies, despite articulating their citizenship claims through a neoliberal moral grammar grounded on the ideas of effort and individual responsibility, are capable of mobilizing against exclusionary housing policies. They do so by incorporating two kinds of rights into their struggles: the right to stay put and the right to live with dignity. While the former is used to avoid being displaced from their neighborhoods of origin, the latter helps *pobladores* signify their engagement with welfare programs in ethical and political terms.

I conceive of the right to stay put as a type of right to the city that arises from *pobladores'* understanding of themselves as city makers. The right to stay put is not entirely new in the political language used by housing activists. In the mid-twentieth century, residents of *campamentos* usually claimed this right when confronted with imminent eviction. In neoliberal Chile, however, the right to stay put took on a new meaning. Rather than being claimed by squatters, in the current context it is claimed by individuals living in legally sanctioned houses who formulate their demands by attaching their subjectivity to the place in which they were born and raised. Most of the people whose stories I share throughout this book have lived most, if not all, of their lives in the municipality of La Florida, specifically in the Población Nuevo Amanecer. Initially known as Campamento Nueva La Habana, this neighborhood was created in 1970 by poor residents who were members of the Movement of the Revolutionary Left (MIR). These residents autoconstructed their houses under the technical supervision of Allende's government.[40] The people I met were actually the children and grandchildren of the original autoconstructors. Organized through the Comité de Allegados Don Bosco, they claimed to have rights over the neighborhood spaces that their parents and grandparents had built through autoconstruction; rights that, according to them, were being denied by market-based housing policies. This explains why the motto of their Don Bosco housing committee was "porque aquí nacimos y aquí crecimos, aquí nos vamos a quedar" ("because we were born and raised here, here we're going to stay"). It is critical to comprehend how contemporary *pobladores*—who have not engaged in mass autoconstruction processes—express their citizenship claims as "heirs" of the rights acquired by their parents and grandparents in the old *movimiento de pobladores*. Likewise, it is necessary to understand how such symbolic identification with the past, based on operations of collective memory, informs their present agencies as citizen city makers.

The activists I encountered also drew on the right to live with dignity, in reaction to subsidy-based programs. In this book, I do not suggest that excluded populations' claims for dignity are by definition oppose to hegemonic cultural norms, or that their actions necessarily entail resistance to power. Hashemi (2020, 6) suggestively points out that, as a culturally situated social practice, "the search for dignity takes multiple forms." She shows that disadvantaged Iranian youth maintain dignity by assuming an "accentuated conformism," which involves the configuration of a moral compass through which they seek to integrate into, rather than confront, dominant social structures. That is certainly not the case of Chilean *pobladores*, who claim dignity in order to question how the state deals with poverty. As I show specifically in chapter 6, their claim for the right to *la vida digna* (a life with dignity) emerges as a response to both the lack of social housing and the neoliberal programs through which the state allocates social welfare among the poor. *Pobladores'* demands for dignity, I argue, makes the constitution of a new political language possible, one that is grounded in everyday experiences as individuals in need of housing. As a right based on a moral category, the right to live with dignity allows *pobladores* to reframe the strategic demands of housing movements while endowing their political actions with specific ethical connotations.

This book accounts for how *pobladores'* mobilizations for housing and dignity have contributed to the development of a kind of citizenship in which residency emerges as a key type of political membership. Although national membership continues to be the main form of political allegiance among *pobladores*, the act of living in the city—and contributing to its everyday reproduction—becomes a source of legitimacy for their demands. By participating in state-regulated housing committees, they engage in citizenship practices as subsidy recipients who are forced to wait—in some cases for more than ten years—to become homeowners. Through this process of subject-citizen formation, they are situated as responsible, dignified city makers, for whom it takes blood, sweat and tears to *llegar a fin de mes* (make ends meet). In doing so, they generate a political imaginary in which the capacity to claim rights—even those widely recognized as universal, such as housing, education, or health care—becomes inseparable from the act of fighting for them. This book reflects on how housing activists in neoliberal societies make sense of the universal character of social rights and how their ideas of universality help configure their criticism of subsidy-based welfare programs.

A Note on Methods

This book is based on seventeen months of fieldwork carried out in Santiago de Chile in three stages: the first stage between May and July 2011, the second between July 2013 and August 2014, and the third and final stage between June and August 2015. My analysis of *pobladores'* protest movements draws on two types of data: historical and ethnographic. The historical materials used include press articles, newspaper editorials, statements by political parties, *pobladores'* publicity campaigns, and artistic works (songs and films) produced between the late 1940s and the early 1990s. These materials allowed me to unpack the discursive interpretations of *pobladores* and housing protests in different historical contexts. The ethnographic data stems from around eighty interviews with past and present housing activists, politicians, and government representatives. I also conducted participant observation in a *comité de allegados*, focusing on the various activities that members carried out as prospective homeowners (e.g., attending general assemblies, meetings with local and national authorities, participating in marches and protests). I use pseudonyms for the housing activists and state officials quoted. The names of public figures, politicians, grassroots organizations, and neighborhoods are unchanged.

When I began fieldwork as a PhD student in 2011, I first contacted the Movimiento de Pobladores en Lucha. I conducted a dozen interviews to explore the discourses and practices of poor residents resisting gentrification processes in the municipality of Peñalolén. In doing so, I was able to capture a broad picture of the contemporary *pobladores* movement, familiarize myself with the language the activists used to articulate their political claims, and identify the strategies they drew on to achieve the right to housing. In July 2013, I returned to Santiago for thirteen months of continuous fieldwork. During this time, I began participating in the Comité de Allegados Don Bosco, a housing assembly formed in 2002. As a way to acquaint myself with people's routines, codes, and everyday practices, I initially assumed a role of "pure" observer, trying not to interfere in their interactions (I use quotation marks because having no effect whatsoever on the people with whom we work in the field is impossible). After two months of observation, I began to assist the Don Bosco social leaders in tasks related to the daily management of a *comité de allegados*, such as photocopying documents, designing propaganda, or writing reports on housing issues to be disseminated through social media. Working as an assistant contributed significantly to gaining the *pobladores'* trust. This later allowed me access to more reserved meetings such as those held at the Ministry of Housing and Urbanism (MINVU), the Metropolitan Service of Housing and Urbanism (SERVIU), and the La Florida City Hall. At almost the same time, I was able to contact members of the National Federation of Pobladores, FENAPO. FENAPO is a political organization that was founded in 2010. By 2015, it had organized around thirty housing assemblies nationwide, including the Don Bosco *allegados* committee. The reflections contained in this book, although grounded primarily on my ethnographic immersion in the Don Bosco assembly, also derive from findings I obtained through work with other FENAPO organizations, such as the Movimiento Pueblo sin Techo, Agrupación Techo Ahora, and the Movimiento de Pobladores en Lucha.

During the fieldwork, I had to adapt my own expectations of what it means to do ethnography. As I was a young, middle-class Chilean who had studied at the Universidad de Chile—one of the most prestigious higher educational institutions in the country—and, at that time, was pursuing a PhD in the United States, some *pobladores* understandably distrusted me. I often thought that they saw me as a *cuico*—a slang word commonly used in Chile to allude disdainfully to upper-class men—although I was never referred to as such in our interactions. In fact, I was never treated in a way that I might consider disrespectful or rude. Quite the opposite, the people I encountered made me feel welcome every time we saw each other. And they still do so whenever I meet with them. However, my anthropological anxiety about entering the field, gaining admittance to a housing assembly, and living with some of its members at times clashed during daily experiences. After introducing myself to Don Bosco members—most of whom lived as *allegados*—I was allowed to attend the organization's public activities with no problem. Things were different, though, when it came to accessing their private lives. At first, I insisted on spending as much time as possible with them in order to build what anthropologists call rapport. But I stopped doing that once a young guy commented: "Do you want to find a place to live here? Why don't you get into the committee?" Later on, I realized that even though some members would have been willing to have me as a guest in their homes, most of them had a hard time making their own decisions on how to organize their time within the houses where they lived. To avoid being considered intrusive, I stopped asking for a place to stay and attempted to conduct conversations in public spaces. After four or five months, the *allegados* themselves worked out strategies to be able to host me in their homes, often seeking out a time or a day in which they were sure that the homeowner—generally a parent or a parent-in-law—would be away so that we could talk without being disturbed. As visits to my interlocutors' homes became more regular, some homeowners began to treat me as a family friend, which eventually allowed me to stay overnight at their homes. This book is the result of an anthropological experience in which, to secure an ethnographic immersion in the *allegados'* domestic sphere, I had to negotiate my role as an anthropologist with both my informants and the owners of the houses in which they live.

Chapter Outline

Chapter 2 positions the argument of the book in a historical and regional context. Emphasizing the similarities and differences between right-to-housing protests in Chile and elsewhere in the Latin America, I analyze the role played by poor individuals' aspirations for homeownership in the appearance of social movements within urban peripheries. I show that these protests have been crucial for the constitution of low-income city dwellers as urban citizens, which enables them to address the state using a rights-based language. This chapter focuses on how the long-lasting housing crisis in Santiago throughout the twentieth century has given rise to different mass protest movements fighting for social rights. While explaining the appearance and development of housing protests starting in the early twentieth century, I concentrate on what scholars describing the squatters' movements of the mid-twentieth century have called the *movimiento de pobladores*. The chapter scrutinizes the institutional and political context in which this movement emerged, as well as the role of social sciences in the production of such an urban social movement. Drawing on both archival research and oral history from poor residents who participated in these movements, I reflect on how these protests help us to frame the contemporary housing movement in a historical context.

Chapter 3 offers an ethnographic account of contemporary housing protests in Santiago by discussing the case of the Comité de Allegados Don Bosco. This state-regulated housing assembly at the time consisted of around seven hundred families, many of which became homeowners after participating in subsidy-based housing programs for almost ten years. Through this case study, I show that *pobladores'* enrollment in housing programs is structured around different modalities of waiting—to be recognized as eligible for welfare, to receive subsidies from the state, to have the housing projects built—that frame their activism. Several scholars have understood welfare programs—and the act of waiting they entail—as technologies of government that regulate, civilize, and pacify the poor. To challenge these approaches, I argue that the *pobladores'* experience with waiting emerges as a specific modality of social action through which they articulate their right-to-the-city claims.

Chapter 4 reflects on the process of subject formation of Chilean poor residents, drawing on what scholars have referred to as performative theory. If chapters 2 and 3 concentrate on the political and intuitional arrangements contributing to the rise of social housing movements, then chapter 4 inquires into the types of subjectivities that have emerged from these movements. I first analyze genealogically how the processes of city making and autoconstruction of the 1960s and early 1970s—which I conceive of as performative practices—provided the urban poor with the capacity to claim rights. Then, by looking ethnographically at the Don Bosco *allegados* committee, I explore how such a capacity develops when contemporary *pobladores* obtain housing through neoliberal housing programs. This chapter concludes that poor residents in neoliberal Chile re-create their political agencies as city makers by both reclaiming the legacy of the old housing movements, and evoking land seizures and autoconstruction through collective memories. Likewise, I show that contemporary housing activists draw on effort-based narratives to morally differentiate themselves from other poor residents who are not considered *pobladores*.

Chapter 5 discusses how the process of subject formation described in chapter 4 informs *pobladores'* views and practices of citizenship. I first contend that contemporary housing mobilizations have given rise to a formulation of citizenship that is grounded on *pobladores'* subjective recognition as producers of space entitled to rights to the city. Collective memory plays a key role in this process, as it enables *pobladores* to bring individual experiences into a collective history of struggle for housing rights. Then, I show that urban activists think of their housing assemblies as political communities formed by members who bear political and moral obligations to the collectivity, to their families, and to themselves. It is this sense of obligation that helps them establish a particular criterion for allocating rights: the right to have rights is reserved for those who struggle (*luchan*). Accordingly, I argue that when it comes to distributing rights among the members of housing committees, *pobladores* consider the acquisition of rights to be essentially a matter of effort, responsibility, and self-sufficiency. This politics of effort shows the transversal rationalities of housing movements in contemporary Chile: although *pobladores'* concept of residency-based citizenship rests on a moral ground specific to a neoliberal regime, their struggles are structured by demands that challenge market-based urban policies.

Chapter 6 focuses particularly on the right to a life with dignity, which *pobladores* understand as the new political horizon of housing movements. In this focus, I critically engage with contemporary anthropological debates on ethics and morality, which have been concerned with ethnographic analysis of the ways that practices of self-fashioning and self-subjection turn individuals into ethical subjects. Although these approaches examine how vulnerable populations' search for dignity results in ethical practices performed mainly in the private or domestic sphere, I hold that the quest for dignity also gives rise to political demands that are expressed in public. In this way, I maintain that moral concepts such as dignity, while allowing for the formation of ethical subjects, enable vulnerable people to signify their everyday experiences in political terms. This chapter concludes that moral concepts can take the form of political signifiers, by means of which poor urban residents frame their claims to rights, equality, and social recognition in a context of neoliberal governmentality.

In the conclusion, I reflect on the shifting nature of housing protests in Santiago de Chile. I do so by highlighting the paradoxical nature of social movements organized around vulnerable populations' engagement in neoliberal welfare programs. The conclusion focuses on three points in particular: how new generations of *pobladores* constitute themselves as citizen-subjects by both looking to the past as a source of symbolic power and producing ethical narratives of themselves as dignified individuals; the extent to which *pobladores'* understanding of rights and citizenship contributes to questioning the commodification of social rights beyond housing; and the extent to which the use of moral categories such as dignity enable excluded populations to articulate broader claims for social transformation, such as those that led to the 2019 social uprising.

2 Peripheral Struggles for Housing

The Pobladores *Movement*

My first ethnographic encounter with housing activists occurred right at the outset of a period of social unrest. It was May 2011, the month that marked the beginning of what the international media later called the Chilean Winter. The term referred to the mass social movement led by high school and university students who struggled against the commodification of the social right to education. Since the restoration to democracy in 1990, Chile had stood out for increasing college enrollment among middle- and working-class families. But it did so by compelling them to get state-backed loans, which "sentenced" hundreds of people to a lifetime of debt (Pavlic 2018). The primacy of the market as the mechanism for allocating social rights had been unchallenged for over twenty years. But everything seemed to break down when millions of students poured into the streets week after week, demanding an end to for-profit academic institutions, the termination of the loans-based funding model, and, more interestingly, structural reform that guaranteed free education for all.

It was precisely in May 2011 when, as part of my pre-dissertation summer fieldwork, I got in touch with members of the Movimiento de Pobladores en Lucha—the Movement of Pobladores in the Struggle, or MPL—a grassroots organization founded in 2006 in the district of Peñalolén. I specifically met with Lautaro, a social leader in his early thirties, whom I contacted through Facebook. At that time, he was serving as a democratically elected councilman for the City of Peñalolén, the municipality in which he had performed his political activity as a housing activist. Lautaro lived in Lo Hermida, an autoconstructed *población* (working-class neighborhood) that was founded in 1970. In the early 2000s, he gained social recognition as a leftist, grassroots community organizer. His dedication to the cause enabled him to be elected as a councilman to the city hall in 2008, after a campaign that promised to represent the voice of *pobladores* within local administration.

Lautaro invited me over his office at city hall. There, he said on a phone conversation, I could explain what type of involvement I would have in the housing struggle and, as a young, middle-class Chilean pursuing his graduate studies abroad, what my "contribution to the movement" would be. Such suspicion, I would come to learn later on, was common among the most radicalized *pobladores* and, in retrospect, I do indeed understand it. Why should they trust a privileged doctoral student if, as housing movements in Chile and elsewhere in Latin America have demonstrated, the urban poor have essentially achieved the right to housing through their own means? Nonetheless, Lautaro's mistrust did not prevent him from allowing me to conduct research on his organization, so I got to his office as agreed, at 10:00 am.

When I arrived, one of his consultants—another member of the MPL whom I will identify as Cristián—opened the door. After presenting myself, he let me in. Lautaro had not yet arrived. While waiting for him, I took a look at the graphics adorning the room, most of which were associated with leftist icons such as Che Guevara, Víctor Jara, and Fidel Castro. Then, I unsuccessfully attempted to initiate a conversation with Cristián. Although I asked him a couple of questions to break the awkward silence, his answers were rather monosyllabic. Seated at a desk and handling his cell phone, he seemed more interested in checking and replying to messages than talking to me. Suddenly, he stopped paying attention to his phone and, without looking at me, said: "You've got to see this. Come with me." Cristián took me to the City Council Chamber where Lautaro, together with the mayor of Peñalolén, Claudio Orrego—a prominent Christian Democratic politician[1]—and the rest of the council, was having a council meeting. "This is a public act, so we have the right to enter," Cristián told me at the entrance to the venue while holding the door for me. We walked in and spotted Lautaro, visibly irritated, arguing with the mayor about the modification to the Plan Regulador Comunal (municipal master plan), an initiative proposed by the mayor. Lautaro was the youngest member of the council, but his determination and conviction made him look like an experienced politician: "There is a housing crisis in Peñalolén, and thousands of families still live as *allegados*, but the mayor wants to sell the municipality to real estate agents and make a profit [*lucrar*] out of it. Mr. Orrego says that there is no land available for social housing in Peñalolén, but we know that's not true. He, with the complicity of other member of the council, wants to gentrify Peñalolén, to displace the poorest citizens. But we, the *pobladores*, won't allow that to happen, and will organize against and protest the mayor's master plan. While students defend the right to education, the *pobladores* movement will defend our right to obtain housing in Peñalolén."

Once the meeting ended, I approached Lautaro and introduced myself. We walked back to his office and chatted briefly about his argument with the mayor and what, in his view, the proposed changes to the master plan would imply. He said, "This is what's going on: the rich don't want the poor around and use the state and its tools, like master plans, to *echarnos* (expel us)." He went on: "But we're ready to fight because *pobladores* are organizing *again*; the *pobladores* movement is reemerging. That's why I'm here, because *el pueblo* (the people) put me here as its representative."

The fact that Lautaro understood his office as subordinate to a collective struggle, one that he conceived of as a social movement, was not trivial. His words, uttered at the beginning of the Chilean Winter, can be understood as a contingent expression of a larger political conjuncture, which provided housing activists with concepts, categories, and ideological frames through which they signified their political action. But Lautaro's opinion also revealed the role of broader historical processes in the contemporary articulation of political narratives. If Lautaro and other activists were expressing a rights-based language to demand housing, it is because they looked to the *pobladores* movement of the past as a source of symbolic and political power, a power that—using Lautaro's terms—can "reemerge" in the present. Analyzing contemporary housing movements from a historical perspective is, thus, key to fully comprehending how, in neoliberal Chile, low-income individuals' aspirations for homeownership appeared as forms of collective action.

Drawing on archival research and oral history, in this chapter I discuss the role played by poor city dwellers' claims to housing rights in the rise of social movements based in the urban peripheries. I particularly analyze how, at specific historical conjectures, *pobladores* have been able to develop forms of what Tilly and Tarrow (2015) call "contentious politics."[2] I do so by examining the institutional and political setting in which mass housing movements developed, as well as the role of scientific discourse in the construction of such urban social movements. The chapter begins by offering a brief description of how the urbanization of Latin American societies, while construed by national states as a precondition for modernity, entailed the manifestation of new regimes of inequality. This helps to frame the emergence of the Chilean housing crisis in a regional context. Then, I set forth the main characteristics of the so-called *movimiento de pobladores* (*pobladores* movement) by dividing it into three historical "cycles of protest" (Tarrow 2011). In emphasizing the cyclical character of social movements, this approach allows me to account for the notion of re-emergence that Lautaro and others usually drew on when making sense of *pobladores'* contemporary struggles. This historical description of the *movimiento de pobladores* is complemented by a review of the scholarly debates that, especially between the 1960s and 1980s, elaborated on how transformative a social movement organized around the demand for urban rights could be. In doing so, I am able to examine current housing mobilizations in a larger historical context and, as suggested by my interlocutors, reflect on them as if there existed a genealogical link between past and present urban movements in Chile.

Latin American Urbanization and Modernizing Agendas

Over the past two centuries, Latin American states have constantly strived to take part in Western modernity through the implementation of "modernizing" projects and processes. In this endeavor, urban settlements have long been conceptualized as spatial arrangements in which societies can embrace modern values and ideologies.[3] The sociological significance of urbanization, in this regard, was defined early on by Louis Wirth (1938). With a clear ethnocentric bias, Wirth's notion of urbanization alluded to both the geographical expansion of the city and the incorporation of traditional societies into a new, modern "mode of life"—what he called "urbanism"—which occurred exclusively in industrial capitalist cities.

Similarly, a significant portion of Latin American narratives on development understood urbanization and industrialization as a necessary and unavoidable step on the path to modernization. Latin American nation-states saw the formation of large metropolises as a material expression of social, economic, and cultural progress, an ideology that, as Holston (1989) argues, manifested most paradigmatically in the building of Brasília in the late 1950s. But equating urbanization and modernity is profoundly problematic in the region, as well as elsewhere in the Global South. Latin America's explosive urban growth led to never-before-seen forms of social exclusion, placing the promises of Western modernity out of reach for many.

In the first three decades of the twentieth century, Latin American economies depended primarily on agricultural or mining production. By 1930, even in the most developed Latin American countries, industry represented only a minor portion of total gross national product: 23 percent in Argentina, 14 percent in Mexico, and 12 in Brazil (Almandoz 2008). To follow the path initiated by the so-called developed countries, nation-states implemented an import-substitution industrialization model based on the economic theory of developmentalism.[4] Assuming that Latin America's underdevelopment was the effect of its condition as a provider of raw materials for industrialized countries, developmentalist thought compelled these countries to implement reforms aimed at promoting national industry through state intervention. However, developmentalist agendas were confronted with rapid urbanization that resulted from an influx of rural migrants into cities, a process that experienced its fastest rates of expansion between 1950 and 1990. The number of people living in urban areas increased from 40 percent in 1950 to 70 percent in 1990. Since then, urbanization rates continued to rise but at a slower pace (UN-Habitat 2012).

Anthropologists examined this shifting scenario closely. In paying attention to the cultural effects of urban growth, a number of ethnographers began to conduct research with the various problems surrounding urbanization as a backdrop. By making use of either structural-functionalist perspectives (Redfield 1947) or culturalist approaches (Lewis 1951), they sought to shed light on the influence of the urban on small, *mestizo* villages as a means to account for the collapse of, using Redfield's conceptualization, folk societies.[5] This new perspective encouraged anthropologists to scrutinize cultural conflicts in urban settlements, with marginalized communities being the main focus of inquiry.[6] In doing so, they critically examined the unintended consequences of Latin American modernization, the most dramatic expression of which was the spread of squatter settlements at the margins of large cities.[7] As a phenomenon specific to large metropolises, the proliferation of informal neighborhoods came to be understood as an adaptive phenomenon. Through this process, the poor could deal successfully with housing shortages by generating new cultural arrangements based on, for example, the "culture of poverty" (Lewis 1961), or the development of an economic system sustained on networks of reciprocity (Adler Lomnitz 1977). The spread of self-built neighborhoods would also have unexpected political consequences related to the formation of novel social movements through which low-income city dwellers would become constituted as urban citizens. Chile is an exemplary case in this regard, as the *pobladores* movement demonstrated "the potential and the limits of squatters' participation in a revolution" (Castells 1983, 179).

Housing Crisis in Urban Chile, 1900–1950

In the early twentieth century, Chile's economy depended overwhelmingly on the export of saltpeter, which was used primarily as a natural fertilizer. However, the creation of synthetic nitrate in the context of the First World War and the subsequent boom in other types of artificial fertilizers brought about a profound economic crisis, which compelled thousands of workers to leave the *salitreras* (saltpeter mining towns) and to settle in cities. The migration of these miners from the north of the country, along with that of impoverished *campesinos* (peasant farmers) from the central provinces, contributed to accelerating the urban growth of Santiago. The city's population was 330,000 in 1907, but by 1930 more than 700,000 people lived there.[8] A similar trend was observed in other Latin American metropolises. For instance, Buenos Aires went from 663,000 inhabitants in 1895 to 2,178,000 in 1932; Mexico City from 328,000 in 1908 to 1,049,000 in 1933; and São Paulo from 240,000 in 1900 to 1,075,000 in 1930 (Almandoz 2008).

In these changing circumstances, the so-called social question became a topic of public discussion in Chile. On the one hand, working-class movements gradually began to demand social and political rights through emerging leftist organizations such as the Chilean Workers' Federation (FOCH, founded in 1909) and the Workers' Socialist Party (POS, created in 1912).[9] On the other hand, new forms of poverty appeared in the largest cities, due to an unprecedented housing crisis that led to an astonishing portion of the urban poor having to live in overcrowded houses lacking basic services like drinking water, electricity, and adequate sanitary facilities. Low-income residents began demanding that the state ensure affordable living conditions, asserting their rights for various needs to be met, from "the consumption of meat to housing conditions" (Murphy 2015, 51). According to Garcés (2002) and Hidalgo (2002), poor urban dwellers inhabited three types of housing: First were inner-city slum tenements, called *conventillos*, formed through the subdivision of a one- or two-floor house with a single entrance from the street. The rooms resulting from this subdivision were usually located around a central patio, which served as a common space. *Conventillos* were the most representative kind of housing for the urban poor during this period.[10] Second were *cuartos redondos*—literally "round rooms"—subleased rooms that, unlike *conventillos*, had neither windows for ventilation nor access to any open area. And third were *ranchos*, precarious adobe houses with straw roofs that represent a housing typology with origins in rural areas. By 1910, one hundred thousand people—approximately 25 percent of Santiago's population—resided in twenty-five thousand rooms distributed among *conventillos*, *cuartos redondos*, and *ranchos* (Garcés 2002, 30–31). Some estimates indicate that more than 97 percent of working-class dwellers were room renters living predominantly in *conventillos* (Salazar and Pinto 2002, 245).

As the social problems derived from urbanization became apparent, the Chilean state attempted early on to confront the lack of affordable housing for the poor by passing a number of laws. President Germán Riesco's government (1901–1906), for instance, passed the Ley de Habitaciones Obreras (Law of Worker Housing) in 1906, which is considered the first housing law in Chile.[11] Through this legislation, the state sought to *sanear* (sanitize) slum tenements by establishing a set of regulations to improve their sanitary conditions. As a homeownership-oriented policy, this law also promoted the construction of housing projects by creating local housing councils, through which lower-middle-class and working-class families could access loans from credit institutions and banks.[12]

But the Law of Worker Housing "quickly demonstrated its total inefficiency" (Garcés 2002, 31). Though deemed a pioneering legal initiative in Latin America, the law was incapable of providing the poorest sectors with affordable housing, and it prevented landlords from raising rent.[13] This issue led to the foundation of the Liga de Arrendatarios (Renters' League) in 1914, a grass-roots organization strongly influenced by anarchist ideals (Grez 2007). Along with demanding that landlords sanitize *conventillos*, this organization claimed a 40 percent reduction in rent prices (V. Espinoza 1988). The actions of the Renters' League and other unions of poor inhabitants, like the Sociedad de Arrendatarios de la Defensa Mutua (Renters' Association for Mutual Defense) carried out a nationwide strike in 1925, in which *conventillo* residents stopped paying rent for six months.[14]

These protests triggered the passing of two housing laws in 1925, the Ley de Arrendatarios (Renters' Law) and the Ley de Habitaciones Baratas (Law of

Affordable Housing), both of which "improved regulatory oversight and helped to establish the state's responsibility in ensuring affordable housing of a minimal quality" (Murphy 2015, 55). While the former tried to regulate rent prices and endow the poor with rights to help avoid evictions, the latter sought to stimulate the creation of housing cooperatives. This last aspect turned out to be one of the most innovative elements of the Law of Affordable Housing, as these cooperatives facilitated the building of neighborhoods for workers and employees. These neighborhoods came to be known as *poblaciones* (Hidalgo 2002, 101). All these measures together, however, did not result in the building of a significant number of housing projects, and not nearly as many as was needed to mitigate the lack of two hundred thousand *viviendas salubres* (sanitary housing units) that the country required.[15]

The ineffectiveness of housing policies was not, by any means, the only reason for the widespread emergence of shantytowns in the following decades.[16] Another crucial factor was the implementation, in the 1920s and 1930s, of important urban renewal projects aimed at "modernizing" Santiago (Cáceres 1995), an undertaking that even entailed the hiring of renowned city planners such as the Austrian Karl Brunner. The implementation of large-scale urban regeneration plans in Santiago's downtown, which in some cases involved the demolition of entire blocks, triggered land speculation and a general rise in land prices. As a result, landlords seeking to increase their profit margin sold their properties, forcing thousands of families living as tenants to move out of their neighborhoods. The press called these events *lanzamientos* (evictions), which in the eyes of leftist newspapers like *El Siglo*, were orchestrated by *enemigos del pueblo* (enemies of the people) who wanted to make a profit by expelling the poor out of the city center.[17] In the late 1940s, it was common to read stories of injustice, desperation, and abuse of poor families who, even when up to date with rent payments, were dispossessed by unscrupulous landlords carrying out "inhumane evictions."[18]

The combined action of ineffective housing policies, the increase in land prices in central areas, and mass evictions all produced the conditions for the spread of squatter settlements in the peripheries of Santiago. As these settlements tended to emerge quite suddenly, at times literally overnight, and because of their proximity to water sources, public opinion referred to them as *poblaciones callampas* (mushroom neighborhoods) or simply *callampas* (mushrooms). Pedro Lemebel (2003, 14), a Chilean writer who during his childhood lived in the Zanjón de la Aguada—one of the largest squatter settlements in the

1950s—describes the rise of *poblaciones callampas* as a quick, unexpected event, the result of "clandestine" action by poor city dwellers who took over empty plots in "the dull quagmire of the fatherland." By 1952, approximately 75,000 people lived in *callampas* in Santiago, which amounted to about 6 percent of the total population (De Ramón 1990). Two decades later, 456,000 people were living as squatters in Santiago's peripheries, which represented 16 percent of the population (Santa María 1973).

The significant increase in informal settlements accounted not only for the aggravation of the housing crisis in Chile but also for the consolidation of urban protest movements. From the 1950s until 1973, the urban poor used land seizures as a preferred strategy for making claims to the right to housing. In what follows, I describe how the extensive occurrence of land occupations enabled the configuration of a radical, social mobilization that would come to be known as the *movimiento de pobladores*.

The *Movimiento de Pobladores*

Between 1930 and 1960, Santiago continued to undergo important demographic changes. A quick look at census data shows this sharp transformation: whereas Santiago's population numbered only 712,533 in 1930, the population had reached almost 2 million by 1960. In the midst of an accelerating housing crisis, some governments attempted to implement reformist agendas. This implied that the poorest sectors acquired never-before-seen political significance, especially for center-left and leftist parties. By developing strong grassroots organizations, the urban poor assumed a leading role in a process of democratization that culminated with the election of the socialist Salvador Allende as the president of Chile in 1970.

In this political scenario, residents in need of housing engaged in social movements for social recognition and dignity by demanding citizenship rights from the state. To achieve their goals, they shifted their forms of protests. Instead of advocating for the right to housing from inner-city *conventillos* through rent strikes—such as the one that had occurred in the 1920s—starting in the mid-1940s *pobladores* made use of a specific, geographically situated political action: mass land seizures (*tomas de terreno*, or simply *tomas*) in the peripheries of Santiago. As sociospatial practices carried out through, in paraphrasing Turner (1968, 354), the "autonomous action of low-income squatters and clandestine developers," land occupations represented a determining factor in the formation of *pobladores* as a specific type of political agency. As my reflections on the performative role of *tomas de terreno* in the emergence of political subjectivities is covered extensively in chapter 4, here I concentrate on how these practices helped configure what scholars have called the *movimiento de pobladores*.[19]

The activists I met considered their struggles to be directly rooted in the old housing protests. In chapter 4, I show that by identifying themselves as part of a long-term social movement, they were able to endow their subjectivities as *pobladores* with a sense of shared beliefs, values, and experiences. This did not make their political organizations impervious to tensions and conflicts over who qualifies as a *poblador*. In fact, chapter 5 discusses how contemporary housing activists use strict evaluation systems based on a moral understanding of effort, to determine who should enjoy the right to housing. In any case, among the interlocutors involved in my research, the idea that past and present housing movements are genealogically related was widely shared. The MPL, for example, stated that its success in the struggle for housing in the gentrifying district of Peñalolén derived from the capacity to "show themselves as a continuity of the historical struggle of people in need of housing" (Movimiento de Pobladores en Lucha 2011, 26). Based on my interlocutors' perspective on the *movimiento de pobladores*, my description of the historical progression of this movement assumes thus that there is a genealogical link between its past and present manifestations. This means that current urban movements, expressed through the poor's involvement in neoliberal housing programs, can be thought of as belonging to the "same" social movement that gave rise to squatter settlements in the mid-twentieth century. Sydney Tarrow's (2011) work on the cyclical character of social movements helps us understand the "historical continuity" that the MPL's members and many other housing activists speak of.

For Tarrow (2011, 199), a cycle of contention is a "phase of heightened conflict across the social system, with rapid diffusion of collective action from more mobilized to less mobilized sectors." In each of them, social movements draw generally on groundbreaking means of protest—what Tarrow calls repertories of contention—and new or transformed frames of collective action. The cycles of contention can trigger different outcomes. They can lead to reforms, drastic repression, or a revolution, permitting social movements to redefine their relationship with the state. Tarrow's framework helps me reflect on what my interlocutors thought of as cyclical nature of the housing movement. It also allows us to conceive of its multiple expressions as the consequence of historically established sociopolitical circumstances. Thus, the different cycles of protest by the *pobladores* movement must be understood not as the ahistorical configuration of spontaneous uprisings, but as critical conjunctures at which organized low-income dwellers have reacted to a long-term housing crisis. In what follows, I present the old *pobladores* movement by dividing it into three cycles of mobilization. In the next chapter, I ethnographically analyze how activists' engagement in subsidy-based housing programs allowed for the reappearance of the *movimiento de pobladores* in neoliberal Chile.

First Cycle of Protests (1950s–1970): Callampas as an Expression of Urban Marginality

The first cycle of protests was characterized by the irruption of large-scale land seizures—mostly on state-owned plots—which resulted in squatter settlements located predominantly among the urban peripheries. Once settled on the occupied land, *pobladores* sought to become homeowners by demanding two primary elements: construction materials that allowed them to initiate processes of autoconstruction and title deeds as a means of avoiding further evictions (see more in chapter 4). To accomplish these goals, *pobladores* organized into local housing assemblies and larger organizations such as the Pobladores' Provincial Association, created in 1952.[20] In addition, they received support from civil-society associations such as political parties, the Catholic Church, and student unions. Those relationships were key for the future development of the right-to-housing movement during this cycle of protests.

During this first cycle of contention, the *pobladores* movement employed a strategy that was oriented more toward demands for housing-related rights than toward seeking out radical transformation of social structures. People in need of housing aspired to become homeowners, not to incite a revolution. The rationale of *pobladores* was structured by their interest in finding a quick solution to the lack of affordable housing. The very act of occupying lands, V. Espinoza (1998) argues, was thus construed as an act of citizenship through which they sought to be recognized as rights-bearing citizens by the state.

The date October 30, 1957, was decisive for the housing movement in Chile. In the early morning of that day, over one thousand families living as squatters on the riverbank of the Zanjón de la Aguada took over empty plots in the district of San Miguel. This event would be the genesis of the Población La Victoria, one of the most iconic working-class neighborhoods in Santiago. Rather than describing the incidents surrounding the emergence of this *población*—something that several authors have already done in depth[21]—I want to point out two elements that allow for an assessment of the relevance of this *toma de terrenos* in terms of the further development of the right-to-housing protest movements. First, both the occupation and the subsequent events that made possible the building of the Población La Victoria were not the result of a spontaneous action of poor families with no political affiliations. Quite the contrary: *pobladores* received constant support and assistance from left-wing parties—particularly the Communist Party (PC), which was outlawed between 1948 and 1958[22]—student associations, and the Catholic Church. Second, it is necessary to question the idea, as it is widely understood among the public opinion in Chile, that La Victoria was the "first" organized land seizure in the country and that the autoconstruction processes that defined it were exceptional.[23] Both land seizures and the demand for construction supplies to carry out autoconstruction processes had already emerged within *pobladores'* political discourse at least ten years prior to the emergence of the Población La Victoria.[24] Thus, the appearance of La Victoria was not totally unexpected. Rather, it seems to be an expression of a set of transformative sociospatial practices that had been long performed by the urban poor. La Victoria's contribution to housing protest movements, therefore, has less to do with being the founding event of the *movimiento de pobladores* than with its ability to provide future land seizures with a sort of technical, political, and even "symbolic inspiration" when it comes to collectively autoconstructing a *población* (Cortés 2014, 242).

In the late 1950s and early 1960s, there were important attempts to tackle the shortage of affordable housing. Then president Jorge Alessandri's (1958–1964) Plan Habitacional (Housing Plan), for instance, attempted to address the issue by centralizing the building of large-scale housing units through the Housing Corporation (CORVI, created in 1953). In practice, Alessandri's plan led to massive displacement of *callamperos* (squatters) to Santiago's southern areas between 1959 and 1962, giving rise to densely populated *poblaciones* like San Gregorio, José María Caro, Clara Estrella, and Santa Adriana. Altogether, these neighborhoods included over one hundred thousand *pobladores* (Garcés 2002, 197). In most cases, *pobladores* themselves were in charge of the construction of their houses under the technical supervision of CORVI. As discussed in depth in chapter 4, this modality of state-led autoconstruction turned out to be a significant determining factor regarding the formation of *pobladores* as political subjectivities.

Regardless of the growing concern over housing issues of both Jorge Alessandri and his successor Eduardo Frei Montalva (1964–1970), *pobladores*
continued to take over empty lands in order to demand the right to housing
throughout the 1960s. Between 1964 and 1969, there were fifty-eight large-scale
tomas in Santiago, thirty-five of which occurred during 1969 (Duque and Pastrana 1972). These occupations led to the formation of well-known *campamentos* that, given the increasing influence of the PC and the Socialist Party (PS),
were identified with leftist ideals. Herminda de la Victoria (1967), Violeta Parra
(1969), and Primero de Mayo (1969) were three of the most prominent *campamentos* of this period.

The emergence of squatter settlements built by highly politicized *pobladores*
resulted in passionate ideological debates in the arena of public opinion. These
were expressed through the appearance of editorial notes in both conservative
and progressive newspapers, which generally elaborated on what the *pobladores
movement* represented and the kind of social transformation it could entail.
The right-wing daily *El Ilustrado* argued that the existence of a severe housing
crisis was an excellent battleground for the action of "agitators interested in
subverting the social order."[25] On the opposite side of the political spectrum,
the communist newspaper *El Siglo* contended that the mobilization of *los sin
casa* (those who do not have a home of their own) embodied the transformative nature of *el pueblo* (the people):[26] "The struggle of *los sin casa* is one the
most exemplary chapters of the country's social history at present. It is about a
movement with a great vitality that grows and reproduces itself on the basis of
the unity and spirit of achievement of our people. It is a movement that, in spite
of repression, threats, and low blows, wins its battles and raises its triumphant
flags all throughout the national territory."[27]

As poor urban residents were acquiring a growing political recognition,
they began to be systematically studied by the social sciences. Chilean *pobladores*, just like the urban poor of other Latin American countries, were mostly
analyzed through the lens of "marginality," a concept that became a catchphrase
when it came to problematizing the increasing impact of squatter settlements
on large cities. But the idea of marginality, rather than being a univocal concept, was understood from different perspectives. Perlman (1976), in fact, accounted for this diversity by showing seven schools of thought that examined
the sociocultural dimensions of the so-called marginal man in different ways.[28]
Regardless of this multiplicity of approaches, the theoretical formulations
were generally predicated on the consideration of marginality as something

"dysfunctional" (Cortés 2013, 4), which led scholars to reflect on the capacity of squatters to turn themselves into collective actors. As a consequence, the "marginal mass"—borrowing José Nun's (2001) terminology[29]—was considered politically disruptive because of its capacity for revolution (Ribeiro 1971) or contribution to forms of chaotic and inorganic violence (Vekemans 1969; Vekemans, Giusti, and Silva 1970; Bonilla 1970).

In Chile, the theory of marginality was formulated by scholars from the Center for Social and Economic Development of Latin America (DESAL), of which the Belgian Jesuit priest Roger Vekemans was the most prominent figure. According to DESAL authors, Latin American marginality was historically rooted in the ethno-cultural and ethno-social superposition inherited from Spanish colonization (Vekemans, Giusti, and Silva 1970). Colonization, they argued, triggered the conformation of a dual society in which traditional, indigenous cultures were subjugated by the modern ones, creating a social system based on the existence of two different social groups: those who participate in society and those who do not. The Latin American urban poor, as heirs of the historically marginalized segments of the population, were thus incapable of fully participating in society given their structural exclusion in sociocultural, economic, ecological, and political terms.[30]

This view of marginality saw the participation of marginal groups in society—or, rather, the lack of it—as made up of two dimensions. The first one was the "passive or receptive" (Vekemans 1969, 58), which was linked to the inability of *los marginales* (the marginals) to take part in the dominant system of values, the means of production, and the social division of labor. This primary form of marginality supposed that the so-called marginal man could not access the resources and services that society distributes among its members. The second dimension of participation was the "active or contributive," associated with the marginal population's incapacity to contribute to either overcoming its own disadvantaged position, or "solving social problems in general" (Vekemans 1969, 59). In having no "functional integration into society" (Vekemans 1969, 62), the marginal groups were thus disarticulated from one another. In addition, the marginal populations were understood as being unable to establish relationships with larger political structures, unless they fell into the politics of clientelism. This is why, for DESAL, the "marginal man is a *hombre disminuido* [disabled man], not in terms of his moral values (which sometimes may be heroic) but in terms of his capacity for acting individually or collectively in a rational way" (Vekemans, Giusti, and Silva 1970, 71).

This understanding of *pobladores* as limited, marginal individuals—a belief that reminds us of Lewis's (1961) culture of poverty—was the framework that Eduardo Frei Montalva's Christian Democratic government used to back his Program of Popular Promotion. As the urban poor needed to be moralized and civilized, Frei Montalva's popular promotion encouraged the creation of state-regulated grassroots organizations in order to facilitate their integration into state policies. This aspiration, fundamental for Frei Montalva's patronizing politics, materialized through the Ley de Juntas de Vecinos y Organizaciones Comunitarias of 1968 (Law of Neighborhood Councils and Community Organizations). This legislation led to the rise of over twenty thousand grassroots associations nationwide (Garcés 2002).

With respect to housing issues, Frei Montalva's populist regime considered *pobladores'* organizations as essential for the development of a new housing policy, known as Operación Sitio (Operation Site). Through this policy, the government expected to provide the poorest families with urbanized plots—generally nine by eighteen meters—and title deeds. *Pobladores*, in turn, were supposed to save money, pay monthly quotas, and engage in the construction of social housing units by either forming housing cooperatives or auto-constructing their houses. Throughout the process of home building, the state gave *pobladores* constant technical and financial support,[31] along with training workshops in community skills oriented toward endowing the emerging *poblaciones* with a "sense of community."[32] Between 1965 and 1970, around seventy thousand housing units were constructed in the context of Operación Sitio (Garcés 2002).

Frei Montalva's housing programs came far, however, from fulfilling expectations and the promises made at the beginning of his term. The government had the ambitious plan of constructing a total of 360,000 housing units between 1964 and 1970 (around 60,000 per year).[33] However, it eventually produced 228,398 units, of which only 121,000 were intended for low-income groups (Murphy 2015, 88). Compared to its predecessors, Frei Montalva's administration certainly stood out for the total number of housing units built, but it was unable to prevent the housing shortage from growing worse. By 1970, the housing deficit had reached 585,000 housing units, around 100,000 units more than in 1960 (CIDU 1972). In this context, left-wing parties strongly criticized Frei Montalva's Operación Sitio, claiming that it was based on the self-exploitation of the working classes. Likewise, in many cases, rather than supplying formal urbanized plots as it was supposed to, it provided poor families with only a piece of land demarcated with white chalk. This led leftist politicians to ironically call the program Operación Tiza (Operation Chalk).[34]

The lack of decent housing contributed significantly to the spread of housing protests, leading to the escalation of land seizures. At the end of Frei Montalva's presidency, the state reacted more violently to squatters' actions, to the point of killing ten *pobladores* who tried to seize an empty plot in the southern city of Puerto Montt on March 9, 1969. The Pampa Irigoin Massacre, as it is known, was the most harrowing sign to date of the disjuncture between Frei Montalva's government and the radicalized *pobladores*. While the former persisted in the idea of offering housing solutions without questioning the foundations of Chilean dependent capitalism, the latter intensified their struggles. All this occurred in a context in which the working classes were decisively committed to an agenda for social transformation that triggered the election of Salvador Allende as president of Chile in 1970.

Second Cycle of Protests (1970–1973): Revolutionary Pobladores
When Allende's Unidad Popular (Popular Unity, or UP) came into power in 1970, an important part of the *pobladores* movement acquired a clearly class-based orientation. Land seizures were no longer performed as a means of making the demands of poor residents visible but as a way to both challenge the right to property and generate innovative experiences of popular power.[35] In fact, the most characteristic elements of this cycle of protests are related to the appearance of highly politicized *campamentos* and the radicalization of the political language utilized by the *pobladores'* organizations, especially in the case of those more inspired by leftist ideals. The radicalization of the housing activists coincided with increasing influence of the Movement of the Revolutionary Left (MIR) on the urban poor. Until then, the working classes had overwhelmingly supported traditional parties such as the PC, the PS, and the Christian Democratic Party (PDC). While these parties would continue to have an unquestionable influence on housing organizations, the growing involvement of the MIR would be crucial to the progression of the housing movement during Allende's government.

Between 1970 and 1973, political parties—from the centrist PDC to the leftist MIR—began to use land occupations as a strategy to deploy their own partisan objectives at the local level.[36] This suggests that the *movimiento de pobladores* was made up of different, even opposing, ideas of society rather than a cohesive, unified ideology. Nonetheless, if we consider the support that

Allende's government received from poor urban residents, it seems clear that the influence of left-wing parties on the poor was far more significant. Allende's policy on illegal occupations was therefore ambivalent. On the one hand, he considered *tomas de terreno* a reasonable and legitimate claim by the working classes in need of housing. This implied that the Allende's administration barely repressed *pobladores* at all in the way that previous administrations had done, especially when pro-government parties were involved in the occupation. On the other hand, Allende also imagined a city in which poor families could live with dignity as homeowners in state-regulated housing projects. Allende's programs sought to achieve this by delivering finished housing to low-income groups through the mass production of housing units, in contrast to the autoconstruction-based policies used in Frei Montalva's Operación Sitio. In fact, the Unidad Popular built around sixty-six thousand housing units in 1971, a record production that would not happen again until the 1990s (Ministerio de Vivienda 2004, 143). The government assumed that this would eventually end illegal land occupations. However, Allende's permissiveness, as well as the interest of political parties in co-opting the *pobladores* movement, resulted in a dramatic explosion of land seizures.

Although historians do not agree on the actual number of *tomas de terreno* that arose between 1970 and 1973 in Santiago, some estimates are indicative. For Murphy (2015), the number of cases went from 23 in 1969 to 103 in 1970 and 350 in 1971.[37] Based on thorough archival research, the historian Cofré (2011) holds that *pobladores* conducted at least 344 successful land seizures in that period, producing a similar quantity of *campamentos*.[38] Altogether, these settlements included over 450,000 people, which was 16 percent of the city's population (Santa María 1973). This increment is graphically depicted in map 3, which shows the 338 *campamentos* that existed in Santiago in 1971. The map illuminates another aspect related to Allende's tolerance of *pobladores'* takeovers: the proliferation of a dozen, leftist squatter settlements in the northeastern part of Santiago at the heart of Las Condes, the richest municipality in the city. Bourgeois families considered the appearance of *campamentos* such as Fidel Ernesto, Ho Chi Minh, and Ñancahuazú as a direct threat to their class privilege, which even led to episodes of violent physical encounters between *pobladores* and their rich neighbors. Right-wing newspapers described these events as the result of an indulgent regime seeking to promote class struggle by allowing the poor to both "invade" Las Condes and violate property rights (fig. 1).[39] On the opposing side, pro-government dailies depicted the violent

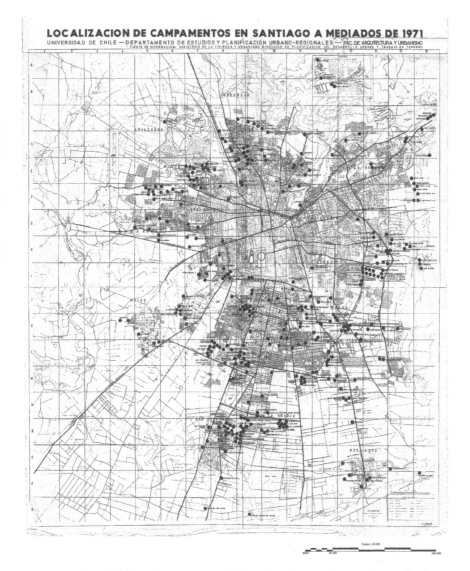

MAP 3. Localization of *campamentos* in Santiago in 1971. Source: Personal collection of René Urbina. Credit: Ministry of Housing and Urbanism, and School of Architecture and Urbanism, University of Chile.

FIGURE 1. "The invasion of Las Condes. *Pobladores* build up *campamentos* either legally with the government or illegally with *miristas* [MIR's militants]." Source: *Mundo 72*, September 21, 1972, 19.

clashes as the resistance of "fascists" unwilling to let go of their class preroga-tives.[40] Regardless of the rich families' reaction, Allende's government carried out some pioneering social housing developments in Las Condes, such as the Villa Compañero Ministro Carlos Cortés—renamed Villa San Luis by the dic-tatorship—as a means of creating a more socially integrated city (Chiara and Pulgar 2008).

As the working classes embraced the Unidad Popular's political project, the social sciences considered *pobladores* as capable of constituting a truly trans-formative social movement. Sociologists and planners began to examine squat-ter settlements, no longer to scrutinize the sociocultural dimensions of the so-called marginal man, but to delve into the processes for the formation of revolutionary subjects. Scholars examined *pobladores'* groundbreaking experi-ences with self-government in *campamentos* as a way to problematize how the formation of squatter settlements could contribute to the appearance of new, transformative social relations.[41]

The Campamento Nueva La Habana is an exemplary case in this regard. Founded in the municipality of La Florida under the political leadership of the MIR, Nueva La Habana was "probably the most well-known *campamento* in Chile" (Pastrana and Threlfall 1974, 71) because of the unprecedented types of popular power developed by its residents. Once formalized, the *campamento* gave rise to the Población Nuevo Amanecer, the field site where I conducted most of my ethnographic research.[42] More than forty years after this settlement was founded, I heard the voices of new generations of *pobladores* for whom their right to housing was grounded in their parents and grandparents' struggle to build Nueva La Habana. The story of Nueva La Habana began in November 1970, when two thousand families, who had previously been living in three different land seizures sponsored by the MIR—Magaly Honorato, Ranquil, and Elmo Catalán—arrived simultaneously to a wheat farm called Los Castaños. The Campamento Nueva La Habana was one of the most consolidated expressions of *pobladores'* growing political radicalization. High levels of internal organization were expressed through the creation of different *frentes de trabajo* (working fronts), including a self-defense militia, self-managed schools, popular courts, a preventive medicine facility, and a *frente de trabajadores* (workers' front) composed of unemployed *pobladores*.

As a way to form revolutionary subjectivities, Nueva La Habana's residents were supposed to behave in accordance with strict rules of conduct aimed at creating a truly transformative daily lifestyle. Drinking, domestic violence, and other felonies against *pobladores* were prosecuted by a self-managed judicial system that, based on a revolutionary ethics opposed to that of bourgeois institutions, sought to carry out *justicia popular* (popular justice). In light of this *campamento's* spectacular level of organization, newspaper articles treated it either as a breeding ground for "extremists" or as role model for other squatter settlements.[43] Nueva La Habana's reputation even led a Cuban delegation to visit the *campamento* in 1971, in the midst of Fidel Castro's diplomatic visit to Chile.

Magdalena and Adriana were two *pobladoras* I encountered through my ethnographic involvement in the Comité de Allegados Don Bosco, a housing assembly created in the Población Nuevo Amanecer. They had both arrived in Nueva La Habana in the early 1970s, during their early childhood. Like most, if not all, of the *pobladores* who lived in Nueva La Habana with whom I met, they had nostalgic memories of their life in the *campamento*. Magdalena and Adriana separately told me that life was much more difficult in the *campamento* because of the precariousness of living as squatters. However, they both missed the existence of a strong community capable of providing the poor with, at least, a safe place to live. This is how they remembered their lives in Nueva La Habana:

> When any man beat up his wife, everybody got him, beat him up, and kicked him out of the *campamento*. The way of engaging with those matters was that everybody had to follow norms and rules. . . . Drinking was not allowed either,

so everybody who wanted to drink had to go out of the *campamento*. . . . This prevented kids from seeing people drinking on the streets, which could have given them a distorted image, you know? (Magdalena)

[Nueva La Habana] was like a separate country. We had a shack that worked as a preventive care facility, and some old buses adapted as classrooms. I actually went to school there. . . . If anyone lost a spoon, the spoon later appeared! If you fought with your partner and you hit her, everybody got into the fight and beat you up, so it was like a separate world. . . . It was a really good experience. I'd love to go back to those times. (Adriana)

With the passing of the years, Magdalena and Adriana have surely idealized their memories of life in the Campamento Nueva La Habana. But even assuming this idealization, their discourse sheds light on a particular political experience in which the working classes attempted to become revolutionary subjectivities by changing the way in which their everyday life was organized. In doing so, *pobladores* embodied the aspirations of millions of Chileans who conceived of their engagement with Allende's Unidad Popular as relying on their constitution as subjects endowed with class consciousness. The idea that the urban poor could acquire class consciousness by living in *campamentos* drew much attention from social scientists, who analyzed this cycle of protests.[44] By focusing mostly on the *campamentos* under the political leadership of the MIR,[45] scholars questioned dominant theoretical perspectives on urban poverty. The new sociological approaches that emerged in the early 1970s would examine specifically the role of the urban poor in broader processes of social change. They first rejected the idea—widely disseminated by DESAL—that poor neighborhoods were composed overwhelmingly of lumpen proletariat. By denying the so-called economic marginality of *pobladores*, authors attempted to undermine the theoretical foundation of DESAL's marginality and, as a result, its understanding of marginal individuals as agents incapable of acting politically by themselves.[46] Jorge Giusti (1973, 74), in this regard, affirmed that the idea of the marginal man was a "myth": *pobladores*, in his view, "are neither apathetic or pessimistic, nor do they present features of internal disintegration as proposed by DESAL. Quite the contrary, they have the capacity to organize themselves for collective action." For Giusti, *pobladores*' expectations and wishes did not differ substantially from those of the rest of urban society, and even more importantly, they were neither "prisoners of a servant-lord relationship" (75) nor agents excluded from the political arena.

The most consolidated criticism of DESAL's theory of marginality, however, came from the work developed by the Interdisciplinary Center for Urban Development (CIDU), of the Pontificia Universidad Católica de Chile. By conducting in-depth research on *campamentos*, CIDU researchers sought to discover how a social movement organized on the basis of demands for urban rights could result in broader processes of social transformation. To do so, researchers examined the type of social consciousness (*conciencia social*) developed by *pobladores* in their political struggle (Vanderschueren 1971), the rise of subversive forms of grassroots organization in *campamentos* (CIDU 1972), and the actual political significance of the *pobladores* movement as a social protest against a "secondary contradiction" of capitalism linked to the housing crisis and lack of public infrastructure (Castells 1973, 9). The CIDU scholars' reflection on the *pobladores* movement attempted to explain the occurrence of housing protests vis-à-vis the extended process of politicization that Chilean society was undergoing. It is important to acknowledge these efforts, as the urban poor, despite receiving support early on by the PC, were historically cast aside as an object of theoretical analysis by the traditional left, which saw blue-collar workers as the revolutionary subject par excellence.[47]

Manuel Castells's reflections on *pobladores* were significant in this regard. His perspectives on the housing movement in Chile, however, varied significantly over the years. In the early 1970s, as a visiting scholar at CIDU, Castells argued that the distinctive characteristic of *pobladores* was not, as affirmed by DESAL, their belonging to a cultural or ideological universe constituted through their so-called marginal condition. Rather, it was their ability to take part in class struggle by articulating urban-oriented demands (Castells 1973). He envisioned *pobladores'* mobilizations as a type of working-class social movement and considered that demands for collective consumption and public infrastructure might have significantly contributed to Salvador Allende's socialist project. But Castells would substantially reformulate his view of the *pobladores* in *The City and de Grassroots*. By 1983, the year in which that book came out, ten years had passed since Salvador Allende's government had been overthrown by a military coup, which had implied the almost total disappearance of housing movements. By analyzing Latin American squatter protests as an example of urban populism walking the thin line between clientelism and the generation of an urban social movement, Castells concluded that *pobladores* were incapable of developing an autonomous political movement. For him, these social agents relied heavily on the political system to carry out their political demands. Moreover, their very existence and identity as collective actors, framed by their vulnerable status as poor urban dwellers, rested on their subordinated relationship with the state in terms of their demands for rights to a physical presence in the city. In Castells's (1983, 211) opinion, the *pobladores'* protests were themselves part of a patronizing relationship as "only their reliance on the state's permissiveness entitles the squatters to the spatial basis of their daily existence." However, Castells's criticism of *pobladores* seemed to clash with their renewed political role. The very same year in which *The City and the Grassroots* was published, Chile's popular sectors entered into a new phase of protest, this time to resist the brutality of Pinochet's dictatorship. In it, *pobladores* played a leading role, being one of the most recognizable forces struggling for freedom and democracy.

Third Cycle of Protests (1983–1990): Pobladores *against the Dictatorship*

The installation of Augusto Pinochet's military regime on September 11, 1973, entailed the complete dismantling of Salvador Allende's socialist project. In political and ideological terms, the dictatorship gave shape to totally new social order anchored in the application of neoliberalism (Garretón 1983). This implied the implementation of several structural transformations aimed at creating a modern, export-oriented national economy (Harvey 2005). Three sets of reforms in policies linked to social housing, poverty, and urban administration and planning played a key role in the redefinition of the urban and political context in which *pobladores* would carry on their struggles in the years to come.

First, the rise of a subsidy-based housing policy—the 1978 Programa de Subvención a la Vivienda (Housing Subsidy Program)—was predicated on the idea that housing, rather than being a social right, was a commodity that the poor, by then understood as rational economic actors, could individually acquire on the market. While the state began to allocate housing subsidies to poor families that had already demonstrated a capacity for saving money, real estate developers would be in charge of building social housing projects (Gilbert 2004b). Second, and directly related to the emergence of subsidy-based programs, the dictatorship restructured the distribution of social welfare on the basis of a paradigm that, while generating social programs exclusively oriented toward the lowest-income groups, constructed "the poor person" as an individual beneficiary. To do so, Pinochet's regime designed a survey of socioeconomic classification—the Ficha CAS[48]—which categorized working-class families as non-poor, poor, or indigent by measuring their income, level of schooling, and the possession of household goods (Schild 2000). Third, regarding urban administration and planning, Pinochet's regime struck down urban land regulations following the ideology that the market, rather than the state, would be the most effective agent for defining land uses and urban limits. This policy was accompanied by a slum eviction program called *erradicaciones* (eradications), which, between 1979 and 1985, involved the displacement of thirty thousand families who were living in *campamentos* located in high-income neighborhoods (Hidalgo 2004a). These *pobladores* were forced to move to the extreme periphery of the city and to engage in the new subsidy-based policy as individual, rational economic actors. In doing so, according to the dictatorship, these squatters could eventually become homeowners. The direct effect of these changes was the emergence of large-scale subsidized housing projects in highly segregated, peripheral municipalities (Hidalgo 2004a; Tapia 2011). This, as I show in the next chapter, was to become a decisive factor for the reemergence of housing movements in the mid-2000s.

The 1973 coup d'état involved the systematic repression of *pobladores*. While they could no longer squat, *campamentos* and *poblaciones* experienced military interventions. Hundreds of *pobladores* were persecuted, and millions of working-class dwellers suffered the everyday repression of the military regime. Adriana, the resident of the Campamento Nueva La Habana whom I quoted earlier, described her memories of the dictatorship in this way: "You were sleeping and the military suddenly arrived at your house. They knocked on the door, came in, took off the mattress, and searched the attic [*entretecho*]. They messed your home up in two minutes. . . . I also remember that after the coup the military dug a trench inside the *campamento* and stayed there for many days with guns. If you wanted to go out of Nueva La Habana, you had to ask them for permission. That really shocked me."

The actions of the dictatorship toward the residents of *poblaciones* also included some attempts to dispute the hegemony of leftist ideals within neighborhood organizations. Bruey (2012) shows that Pinochet's government, at least during the first few months, endeavored to display a genuine interest in solving the problem regarding a lack of affordable housing for the urban poor. To do so, "high-ranking officials made widely publicized visits, promising services and infrastructure," which led *poblaciones* to become a "scenario for political theatre" (Bruey 2012, 531), just as leftist politicians had done in previous years.

But that strategy was soon abandoned, given the lack of a coherent housing plan which was not developed until at least 1978, the year in which Pinochet's government released its first subsidy-based housing program.

During the first ten years of the military regime, land seizures practically disappeared. Although Bruey (2012) reports the occurrence of around twenty *tomas de terrenos* between 1978 and 1983, most of them were quickly repressed. However, *pobladores* were able to undertake two successful mass land occupations in September of 1983, in the municipality of La Granja, currently La Pintana, located on the southern periphery of Santiago. These occupations turned into two squatter settlements, the Campamento Cardenal Raúl Silva Henríquez and the Campamento Monseñor Juan Francisco Fresno, which ended up housing eight thousand families. The occurrence of these land seizures, certainly exceptional in terms of the number of *pobladores* involved and their success in converting the takeovers into actual settlements, must be understood as an effect of the progressive rearticulating of popular sectors in Chile. Two years prior to the emergence of these land seizures, *pobladores* linked mostly to the PC—at that time outlawed by the military regime—had already founded the Coordinadora Metropolitana de Pobladores (Metropolitan Coordinator of Pobladores, METRO), which became the largest housing federation during the 1980s.[49] The METRO promoted and led the takeovers in La Granja in 1983, in order to question the dictatorship's housing policies, which had been totally ineffective in solving the housing crisis. In fact, between 1978 and 1982, the military government was able to provide the poor with 24,493 housing subsidies nationwide, which represented only 30 percent of the total need (Wilson 1988, 100).

Raised in the Población La Victoria within a family actively involved in the PC, Claudina Núñez presided over the METRO in the 1980s and became a well-known housing activist. Two decades later, her political commitment as a communist leader led her to be elected mayor of the municipality of Pedro Aguirre Cerda for two terms (2008–2012 and 2012–2016). When I interviewed her in 2015, she told me that, during the 1980s, the *pobladores* involved in METRO did not look at the subsidy-based programs as a real alternative for solving the housing crisis. Rather, they demanded that the state allow them to autoconstruct their houses and neighborhoods, using the same demands used by the *pobladores* during the first and second cycles of protests. To do so, the METRO advocated the implementation of the Operation Site programs through which *pobladores* expected to receive urbanized lands and construction material and to be able to do the work themselves in the building of their homes. In her words: "We [METRO] demanded Operation Site or any other alternative that allowed for autoconstruction. . . . We were willing to autoconstruct our houses because we were capable of doing that. Our history had demonstrated that we could do it. But they [the military regime] said that it was illegal."

Tolerating land seizures and permitting *pobladores* to collectively build their residential spaces was not part of the military government's policies on housing. Perhaps foreseeing the risk of letting *pobladores* reorganize grassroots associations, the dictatorship favored the implementation of a subsidy-based policy and allocated subsidies individually among low-income dwellers. The residents of the Campamento Cardenal Raúl Silva Henríquez and the Campamento Monseñor Juan Francisco Fresno thus could not turn their squatter settlements into formalized neighborhoods. They "enrolled in eradication programs and dispersed throughout the city" (Bruey 2012, 548). Although these occupations did not result in the successful development of *poblaciones*, they did have an important symbolic function for those resisting Pinochet's regime. They let the public know that, after ten years of dictatorship, the *pobladores* movement was back.

The year 1983 was a critical one in the struggle against the dictatorship. In that year, nationwide demonstrations exploded against the military regime, which would come to be known as Jornadas de Protesta Nacional (Days of National Protest). On May 11, 1983, workers, students, *pobladores*, human rights organizations, and many other civil-society associations joined the nationwide strike initially organized by trade unions like the Comando Nacional de Trabajadores (National Workers' Command, CNT) and the Confederación de Trabajadores del Cobre (Copper Workers' Confederation, CTC). This would be followed by three other days of protests—June 14, July 12, and August 11—which, in total, involved the participation of hundreds of thousands of demonstrators. The power of the Jornadas de Protesta Nacional for mass protest surprised the military regime, leading it to intensify repression against civil-society protesters. Through all these events, *pobladores* would regain their political significance on account of their strong commitment to the struggle for democracy. Some *poblaciones*, particularly those in which the Communist Party continued to have significant influence over the neighborhood associations, became an important setting for resistance to police repression (Schneider 1995).

Predictably, the *pobladores*' dedicated involvement in the protests against the dictatorial regime was seen by the conservative press as troubling and problematic. The specter of mass urban riots by the so-called marginal groups was at the heart of the debate. In an opinion column in the right-wing newspaper *La Segunda*, the lawyer Ángel Flisfisch (1983) criticized the *pobladores'* participation, arguing that "it is in *poblaciones* where the protests take on forms that threaten the nonviolent means required by political leaders." He went on to say that, since the 1960s, there had been a nightmare associated with the realization "of a great urban revolt by *pobladores* who kill, loot, and burn everything down." Once again, the urban poor became visible through their engagement in urban politics, yet this time they seemed to have shifted from the demand for housing to the demand for democratization (Oxhorn 1994).

The renewed political capacity of *pobladores* was followed by a novel interest in scientifically examining their contribution to the formation of radical social movements. Social scientists began studying the social implications of Chile's neoliberal modernization and the dismantling of the welfare system established during the 1960s and early 1970s. The rise of new forms of social exclusion resulted in the creation of around 1,300 grassroots organizations that involved over 220,000 *pobladores* (Campero 1987). Through these associations, the urban poor developed innovative community-based survival strategies such as *ollas comunes* (cooking cooperatives) and *comprando juntos* (buying together). While the former provided food to poor families, the latter consisted of a system of collective savings through which *pobladores*, by buying in bulk, could purchase products at low cost.[50]

Most of the sociological literature reflected critically on the extent to which these neighborhood associations, the networks of which worked to organize the struggle against the military regime, enabled the formation of a truly transformative protest movement. Authors researching this third cycle of protests maintained that the *pobladores'* mobilizations would not lead to a revolutionary social movement as their actions relied more on community-based orientations than on the definition of a new, revolutionary idea of society.[51] Along this line of reasoning, *pobladores* would be incapable of constituting themselves as collective actors, since their associations were fundamentally predicated upon solidarity and emotional ties, making their articulation with larger political agendas impossible. Deeply influenced by Alain Touraine's work, these researchers conceived of the *pobladores'* actions as mostly oriented toward the preservation of their identity as members of a community of excluded urban residents. For them, the *pobladores'* participation in protests for democracy was equivalent to that of an apathetic mass using violence to make inorganic, depoliticized identity claims, which could even result in chaotic and uncontrolled urban riots.[52]

The end of the military regime in 1990 and the arrival of a center-left alliance—the Concertación de Partidos por la Democracia, which ruled the country until 2010[53]—entailed not only the advent of a neoliberal democracy but also the demobilization of Chilean society (Paley 2001). As a state-led process, the demobilization of social movements was carried out mainly through the expansion of welfare programs oriented toward the integration of the poor into the state bureaucracy.[54] The early 1990s marked the beginning of a shifting scenario for popular protest movements in general and for *pobladores* in particular, who were less and less able to have an impact on the political agenda on the basis of their collective action. In these circumstances, *pobladores*—now understood more as beneficiaries of welfare programs rather than as political actors—participated in the new political cycle as a "dispersed social mass" (Salazar and Pinto 2002, 263). However, starting in the mid-2000s, low-income residents would come to engage yet again in public struggles for housing rights by making use of the very same programs that the state had designed to pacify them. I discuss this process in detail in the next chapter.

3 Mobilizing While Waiting

The State-Regulated Comités de Allegados

"I can't believe she's here." That was what Rosa, evidently annoyed, said at the city hall of the municipality of La Florida, located in southeastern Santiago, after noticing that a *vecina* (neighbor) of hers had arrived. She said this as we—myself and the leaders of the Comité de Allegados Don Bosco—were about to enter a meeting with two communist politicians: David Peralta, a La Florida council member, and Camila Vallejo, the former student leader who had just been elected to congress. As spokespersons of a housing assembly, the activists had arranged a meeting with local and national authorities to generate a network of support for their demands.

The meeting was supposed to start at noon, but neither the councilman nor the congresswoman had arrived on time. While waiting, the *pobladores* held an impromptu coordinating assembly in which they agreed that, as representatives of more than seven hundred families, they had to be consistent in their demands. The idea of adopting a common position and having *una sola voz* (a unified voice) stemmed from the fact that some members of the leadership had profound political and personal differences. Leaving these discrepancies aside, Ernesto, the president of the organization, summed it up: "So we all agree that all of Don Bosco's members must obtain a house in our municipality, La Florida, and that we won't accept any other offer, right?"

After Ernesto's intervention, we all began to chat about trivial things for thirty minutes or so. It was mid-December and the temperature had climbed to 30 degrees Celsius (86 degrees Fahrenheit). Around 12:35 p.m., some were

becoming exasperated about not having started a meeting that had been scheduled for noon. As on many other occasions, Rosa complained loudly. "Once
again these *wevones* [idiots] keep us waiting. Come on guys, show up! I have
to be home soon to cook for my kids and am already starving," she yelled to
no one in particular, as she always did, to make light of an uncomfortable situation. It was precisely at that moment when we encountered Rosa's neighbor.
"No way! Here she is again to see the mayor [the right-wing Rodolfo Carter] to
ask for some assistance," she said aloud, as if wanting to be heard by her *vecina*.
Right after that, Rosa stared directly at me and, as a way of reaffirming her statement, went on: "You know, Miguel? That woman comes to the municipality all
the time to beg for a box of goods [*mercadería*], Christmas gifts, and so on. . . .
She is so lazy; she doesn't even work! You've seen that some *postulantes* [subsidy
applicants] have been waiting for years to get housing, and that it's really hard
to get a meeting with the mayor, haven't you? But for her it's just a matter of
coming in and begging for help."

Pobladores' Experience of Waiting

The experience of waiting structured the modes of collective action of the
allegados I met. They were used to waiting. Yet, as Rosa's complaints clearly
expressed, they certainly did not like waiting and complained about it every
chance they got. Waiting for state officials and politicians to meet with them,
like the ethnographic vignette earlier, was common. But their involvement in
the struggle for housing was also framed by other, more prolonged forms of
waiting that oriented their everyday life as prospective homeowners. Most of
my interlocutors spent roughly ten years participating in subsidy-based programs before obtaining a home of their own. Over that time, they first waited
to be recognized as eligible for housing subsidies by the state's instruments of
socioeconomic characterization.[1] They then waited for the state to formalize the
existence of their housing assembly. Once the state officially recognized their
organization as a *comité de allegados* (state-regulated housing committees),
they waited to receive subsidies. And once they obtained subsidies and had
saved up the required amount of money, they had to wait to have their houses
built by private construction companies.

The relationship between time and power—and more broadly, the role of
the state as the main institution producing and distributing the waiting peri-
ods—has long been subject to analysis. Waiting has been generally conceived

of as a mechanism for reproducing social hierarchies, as it results from a power relation in which powerful agents or institutions have the capacity to subject disprivileged individuals to arbitrary delays.[2] In the case of neoliberal societies, market-oriented reforms and the dismantling of welfare programs throughout the world have produced a "chronic" condition of waiting for the poor, who are "forced to wait for food, housing, education or medical care" (Jeffrey 2008, 954). For Auyero (2012), the social programs mediating the relationship between the state and the poor in Argentina create a power relation that forms subordinate subjects who learn to be patient (of the state). By reducing low-income residents' capacity for collective action, the experience of waiting can ultimately prevent them from acting as rights-bearing citizens. Did the *allegados'* perpetual state of waiting embody only a set of governing, disciplinary techniques through which the urban poor are subjected to the power of the state? Not necessarily. In this chapter, I show that the state of waiting is not mutually exclusive to political mobilization, as the poor can respond collectively to some forms in injustice even when they are entangled in such a power relation. Such is the situation of Chilean low-income families who seek to obtain housing by engaging in *comités de allegados*.[3] These state-regulated organizations, which have been key to the reemergence of housing movements, are the focus of this chapter.

The *comités de allegados* I got to know during my fieldwork carried out their struggles mostly while waiting. The time their activists spent in public performances—which included street marches or the occupation of state buildings—was little compared to the time they were, quoting Rosa, *en el aire* (hanging in the air). My interlocutors felt they were "hanging in the air" because, in short, they did not see their housing projects moving forward. Although they had been granted housing subsidies, were devotedly dedicated to saving money, and in Rosa's words, "do everything that the SERVIU [Metropolitan Service of Housing and Urbanism] tells us," they lived with a heavy sense of uncertainty. They did not know when they would eventually get a home of their own, as the housing projects were usually subject to delays. However, rather than discourage or pacify them, the constant state of waiting seemed to stimulate their commitment to the struggle. In their view, the act of waiting was an indicator of the incapacity of the state to fulfill the promises it had made them, which motivated them to react against what they considered to be an injustice. That explains why Rosa complained about her neighbor. Why, Rosa wondered, did her *vecina* not have to wait to have an appointment with the mayor? Why did she get public benefits if she didn't even have to struggle for them? And, to the contrary, why did the Don Bosco members not have a home of their own after several years of being involved in housing programs?

In this chapter, I argue that prospective homeowners' prolonged state of waiting is a modality of social action that, in the context of a housing crisis, accounts for the *pobladores'* insurgent engagement with state programs. I present the case of the Comité de Allegados Don Bosco, a grassroots assembly formed in La Florida in 2002 to demand the construction of social housing in the municipality. Because housing committees are composed predominately of women, I focus on the case of *pobladoras* (female poor residents) enrolled in the organization. In doing so, I reflect on how state-regulated assemblies, though placing housing activists into a power relation with the state, may in fact establish the conditions for their politicization. The implementation of subsidy-based housing policies seemed to be effective in the pacification of *pobladores*, as in the 1990s the number of land occupations decreased significantly. In this chapter, however, I reveal that the very policies meant to avert massive housing movements generated the conditions for their reemergence in the mid-2000s. This new "cycle" of protests is characterized by the inclusion of claims for the right to the city, which I examine in this chapter.[4] One of these claims is what the National Federation of Pobladores (FENAPO) refers to as territorial demand (*demanda territorial*). In simple terms, FENAPO's territorial demand alludes to the right of poor families to become homeowners in the municipalities where they were born and raised, such as expressed by Ernesto in the opening ethnographic vignette.

I do not argue that right-to-the-city struggles in neoliberal Chile are the direct result of *pobladores'* experience of waiting. As I describe below, there are a number of factors explaining the housing affordability problem to which they have reacted (e.g., lack of regulations in urban land markets, increase in land prices, ineffectiveness of housing policies). Rather, I maintain that any effort to fully understand the role of *comités de allegados* in the resurgence of housing struggles in Chile must consider how waiting has become a widespread and shared experience for those who use subsidy-based programs to achieve homeownership. Examining how prospective homeowners are able to develop right-to-the-city movements while engaging in slow-moving, bureaucratic processes is thus crucial to identifying the main characteristics of the contemporary housing movement.

Demobilizing the Poor through Homeownership

The end of Pinochet's dictatorship in 1990 resulted from strategies of negotia-
tion led by political elites. By ruling out any attempt at radical change through
the collective action of broad-based social movements, these strategies accepted
the conditions for a transition as established by Pinochet's constitution.[5] This
explains why, as of this writing, Chile still has essentially the same constitution
that was created by Pinochet in 1980, and why the former dictator continued
to serve as commander-in-chief of the Chilean Armed Forces until 1998.[6] This
also explains why the Concertación—a center-left coalition that governed the
country between 1990 and 2010—rather than proposing reformist agendas,
strived to preserve and even strengthen the neoliberal project. The consolidation of neoliberalism as a solid and stable mode of development required thus
the demobilization of social movements, a process that paradoxically "could
be accomplished more effectively by political democracy" (Paley 2001, 105).
Among other things, this involved center-left parties persuading labor leaders to postpone their demands, in order to avoid the destabilization of a still
fragile postdictatorial system.[7] In these circumstances, Philip Oxhorn's (1994)
question "Where did all the protesters go?" is pertinent not only to the state's
effort to demobilize the poor but also to the key ideological premise of the new
democratic governments: an understanding of the popular sectors as subjects
unable to intervene politically in the public sphere as collective actors.

Chile's neoliberalization led the economy to grow, on average, at an annual
rate of 7 percent in the final years of the 1980s. But this impressive macroeconomic success was not accompanied by a more just distribution of wealth.
The 1990 National Socioeconomic Characterization Survey (CASEN) indicated
that nearly 52 percent of Chileans lived below the poverty line, which urged the
government of Patricio Aylwin (1990–1994) to make poverty one of its primary
concerns. To handle the "social debt" to the poor caused by the liberalization
of the economy, the state developed poverty alleviation programs based on allocating subsidies to the lowest-income groups.[8] But these programs also had a
hidden agenda. They sought to pacify the working classes by constituting them
as market-based citizens, that is, "as empowered clients, who as individuals
are viewed as capable of enhancing their lives through judicious, responsible
choices as consumers of services and other goods" (Schild 2000, 277).

Subsidy-based housing programs are exemplary in this respect. Postdictatorial governments feared that the return to a democratic political system would

result in the reappearance of what had been the main strategy used by *pobladores* to deal with housing affordability problems: land seizures.[9] This concern compelled them to allocate housing subsidies on a large scale, increasing the number of annually paid subsidies from 32,799 in 1989 to 52,835 in 1999 (Arellano 2011). Likewise, the state constructed an unprecedented amount of social housing units on the basis of the dictatorship's market-based housing policies, reducing the housing deficit from 53 percent in 1990 to 37 percent in 2000 (Ministerio de Planificación 2001).[10]

The reduction of the housing shortage required the integration of the poor into state bureaucracy as a means of transforming them, using Auyero's terminology, into patients of the state. This phenomenon was crucial during the 1990s for the demobilization of *pobladores*, who were increasingly compelled to apply for state subsidies through state-regulated assemblies. In Özler's (2012, 68) view, these housing committees promoted the emergence of a neoliberal rationality, as prospective homeowners "must compete against one another individually or in groups for limited subsidies . . . [which] leads them to seek personal solutions to their housing problems." Edward Murphy (2015, 240) also highlights the disciplinary and demobilizing nature of subsidy-based housing programs. He describes the years after the dictatorship as a period "defined largely by a lack of activism among pobladores . . . a time of political withdrawal and social atomization."

But this period of low levels of activism and social atomization was not necessarily a time of social peace. The Concertación governments reduced the housing shortage through the mass construction of low-quality housing projects, which were commonly located in highly segregated areas. Perhaps the most dramatic expression of this process was the so-called *casas Copeva* (Copeva houses). Named after the private construction company that built them, the *casas Copeva* were part of a housing project developed in the municipality of Puente Alto, located on the south side of the city, specifically in Bajos de Mena.[11] In 1996, over two thousand families became homeowners, living in apartments of roughly 42.5 square meters. However, a storm that hit Santiago in the fall of 1997 caused serious damage to the newly built homes. When the poor-quality constructions led to severe leakage of rainwater into many homes, the government gave the families nylon tarps to cover each building and keep out the rain. This, of course, caused a national scandal. In the midst of this controversy, Chileans learned that Copeva's owner, Francisco Pérez Yoma—brother of Edmundo Pérez Yoma, the minister of defense—had gifted Edmundo Hermosilla, the minister of housing and urbanism, a horse. As the conflict of interest became clear, Hermosilla was forced to leave his position.[12]

The evident failure of the state to provide the poor with decent housing stimulated the rise of new forms of collective action in the mid-2000s. *Comités de allegados*, the same ones used to tackle the reemergence of housing mobilizations in the previous decade, assumed a renewed role, opening up the possibility for the reconfiguration of housing struggles. Depicting how housing activists have fought the exclusionary character of neoliberal policies is not only crucial to questioning the common understanding of *allegados* committees as politically constrained but also key to fully comprehending how the urban poor engage in political action in neoliberal Chile. In what follows, I show that *pobladores*' engagement in *comités de allegados*—even while entrenched in a prolonged state of waiting—has actually played a crucial role in the reappearance of housing mobilizations. I do so by providing an ethnographic description of the current housing movement in Santiago. I first report on the means of protest, and the political language utilized by housing activists affiliated with the National Federation of Pobladores, FENAPO. I then provide an account of my ethnographic participation in the Comité de Allegados Don Bosco, so as both to illustrate how state-regulated assemblies operate on a daily basis and to present a sociological portrayal of those who participate in them as a part of their struggle for homeownership.

Territorially Situated Housing Struggles

Continuing the general trend initiated in the 1990s, the reduction of the housing deficit continued into the following decades, falling to 497,560 units—around 9 percent—in 2017 (Fundación Vivienda 2019).[13] The significant progress in terms of the construction of social housing units, however, caused a dilemma for the poor. Since the early 1980s, working-class families seeking to become homeowners had done so with particular locational constraints. Because of the historically high land prices in Santiago, the urban poor could utilize the state subsidy for homeownership only in highly segregated peripheral areas, which lacked infrastructure and services.[14] In the early 2010s, the urban economist Pablo Trivelli (2011, 181–82) argued, "There is practically no supply of plots that cost less than 1.5 UF/square meters [around US$54.40 per square meter], whereas social housing developments cannot pay more than 0.4 UF/square meters [around US$15 per square meter] for them."[15] To become homeowners, the poor have thus been forced to move out of their neighborhoods and live along the outskirts of the city. This market-led displacement was at the core of the reemergence of *pobladores'* struggles for housing; it was a remobilization process closely related to the appearance of new forms of conceptualizing the right to housing, based on the inclusion of right-to-the-city narratives.

The *pobladores'* demands for anti-segregation were patently expressed through the rise of two organized squatter settlements in Santiago during the 1990s, Esperanza Andina in 1992 and Toma de Peñalolén in 1999.[16] These occupations arose from the desire of thousands of poor families to obtain housing in Peñalolén, their municipality of origin. Since then, *pobladores* have been increasingly engaged in collective action. Nonetheless, unlike the squatter movement that emerged in the mid-twentieth century, they have done so by participating in subsidy-based housing programs. The *pobladores'* renewed involvement in urban politics led to a nationwide escalation of their right-to-housing protests. As table 1 shows, the number of housing protests increased significantly from 2002 to 2012, peaking in 2006, the year in which President Michelle Bachelet's first government (2006–2010) enacted a new housing policy. Bachelet's administration put into practice, among other policies, the new Subsidio a la Localización (Location Subsidy). This policy sought to allocate more public funds to housing projects situated in well-located areas, which is to say, near public facilities, private services, infrastructure, and so on. In addition, Bachelet's housing policy introduced two novel legal entities to mediate the relationship between the state and working-class families—the Entities of Social and Real Estate Management (EGIS) and Provider of Technical Assistance Service (PSAT). The purpose of these entities was, supposedly, to revitalize the building of social housing. Both EGIS and PSAT could be either for-profit or non-profit organizations, including a wide variety of entities such as municipalities, foundations, cooperatives, consulting companies, constructions firms, and others. They were in charge of the entire process of home building, which involved searching for the plot where future housing units would be located, coordinating construction companies and state institutions, supervising the design and construction of housing units, and so on.

In the housing activists' opinion, though, Bachelet's urban reform did little to alter the neoliberal orientation of the subsidy-based housing programs. They said that these policies, while continuing to conceive of the poor as rational economic actors, persisted in providing real estate developers with state subsidies. Accordingly, Bachelet's reform was not designed to prevent private developers

TABLE 1. Nationwide protests for housing-related issues, by year

Year of protest event	Frequency	Percentage of total events
2002	1	1.0
2001	1	1.0
2002	0	0
2003	0	0
2004	0	0
2005	6	6.1
2006	28	28.3
2007	8	8.1
2008	5	5.1
2009	14	14.1
2010	9	9.1
2011	14	14.1
2012	13	13.1
Total	99	100

Source: Data from FONDECYT Project No. 11121147, "Diffusion of Collective Protests in Chile, 2000–2011," led by Nicolás Somma.

from "profiting" (*lucrar*) off poor people's aspirations for homeownership. A consultant for the Ministry of Housing and Urbanism (MINVU), whom I will identify as Ignacio, asserted some further insights that confirmed the *pobladores'* distrust of Bachelet's initiative. When I interviewed him in 2014, he told me that the implementation of location subsidies, by putting more money into the building of affordable housing, contributed to increasing land prices. He also pointed out that the direct result of the appearance of EGIS was that many of these organizations actually operated as real estate companies. This meant that, by fostering affordable housing projects in peripheral municipalities, EGIS sought to make money from building subsidized housing. In his words: "Last year we [MINVU professionals] did some research to know where poor families applying for subsidies came from. We found out that, in the last three years, 80 percent of these applications came from municipalities like Til Til, Colina, El Monte, that is, from the extreme periphery. Interestingly, in municipalities like El Monte, there is no such demand for social housing, which means that some EGIS were buying cheap land there and were then enrolling people from other municipalities in Santiago in order to develop social housing projects."

The trend of developing social housing projects in peripheral areas, even in municipalities outside of the Santiago metropolitan area (as in the aforementioned case of El Monte), persists with the publication of this book. The main reason is that, although governments modified the decrees regulating the allocation of subsidies and the construction of social housing, none of the modifications has substantially changed the market-oriented character of urban and housing policies. For some urban planners, the low level of social housing construction within the city limits is explained by the lack of regulations in urban land markets, which has led to a sustained increment in land prices since the early 1980s.[17] In fact, urban planners have demonstrated that average land prices in Santiago increased by almost 1,000 percent between 1982 and 2012 (*El Mercurio* 2012). As expected, this increment has made it almost impossible for the construction of subsidized housing in central and pericentral areas.

This was the scenario that I encountered while conducting my fieldwork. When I first met some members of the Movimiento de Pobladores en Lucha (MPL) in 2011, I noticed that they had decided to organize in order to obtain housing in their municipality. The *pobladores* whom I encountered afterward in other areas of Santiago would give exactly the same reason for organizing their own committees. Even though they knew how long it could take to get housing through subsidy-based programs, they decided to form *comités de allegados* to collectively resist displacement from their neighborhoods. In the case of the MPL, this organization was made up of five *comités de allegados* in 2011, which involved around two hundred families fighting to become homeowners in the gentrifying municipality of Peñalolén.[18]

To deal with the housing affordability problem, the MPL and other housing assemblies founded FENAPO in early 2010. This federation became the most visible expression of *pobladores'* attempts to reorganize housing associations on a national level, being one of the most influential grassroots associations of this new cycle of protest. In Santiago, it joined poor families from a variety of municipalities—La Pintana, La Florida, Lo Barnechea, Peñalolén, San Joaquín, among others. Regardless of the residential context in which they lived, they all desired to become homeowners in the municipalities in which they were born and raised. To politically signify their aspirations for a life with dignity, FENAPO's members formulated a novel type of claim that they called *demanda territorial* (territorial demand). This demand referred to *pobladores'* right to obtain housing in their neighborhoods of origin, similar to what some authors, when discussing community-based strategies to resist displacement processes, have called the "right to stay put."[19]

State agencies were fully aware of the activists' territorial demand. According to data provided by the MINVU, by July 2015 there were 867 *comités de allegados* in Santiago, representing a total of 57,692 families. "Most, if not all, of these *pobladores*, hope to get a home of their own in their own municipalities," a high-ranking public official from the MINVU told me. Other civil servants also recognized the importance of location for the building of subsidized housing. In June 2014, FENAPO's leaders invited me to attend a meeting at the SERVIU. On that occasion, the director of this state agency told them: "We try to give priority to those housing developments that allow pobladores to stay in their municipalities. We don't want to send the poor to live far away from their home neighborhoods. . . . [W]e don't want to make the same mistake twice, but sometimes that is difficult because of the lack of resources."

"Who cares if you don't have money? We want to have our houses built in our municipalities," replied defiantly a FENAPO leader who often framed his interventions as a matter of rights being denied by "the government." In a similar way, the *pobladores* with whom I worked considered the territorial demand to be unquestionable. For them, this was an inalienable right that the state had to guarantee regardless of the "lack of resources." In the following chapters, I detail how this claim is based on housing activists' understanding of themselves as city makers, an argument that also functions to situate *pobladores* as part of a historically grounded political subjectivity. For now, I discuss what construing FENAPO's territorial demand as a type of right-to-the-city implies, which compels me to briefly look at Henri Lefebvre's seminal work.

Territorial Demand as a Right to the City

Henri Lefebvre's reflection on the right to the city stems from his interest in examining the city from a Marxist perspective.[20] To delineate the defining aspects of the right to the city, Lefebvre (1996) draws on the concepts of use and exchange value through which he makes two hypotheses: First, the city and urban reality—that is, the material base and urban life, respectively—have historically been related to use value. The city, he suggests, can be interpreted as use value, namely, as an oeuvre or work of art created and appropriated by its producers. Second, the generalization of commodities, he asserts, led to the breakdown of the city as an oeuvre. The advance of industrialization had one clear outcome: the city dominated by market relationships (exchange value) began to prevail over the city as a product (use value). Lefebvre's political demand has to do with the capacity to fully realize the urban as a totality, that is, as a mode of life and as a morphological, material base. What is at stake, Lefebvre proclaims, is the reestablishment of the city as an oeuvre able to be produced and appropriated by its inhabitants. Lefebvre's right to the city thus involves the right to appropriation—the right to use, to live, and to represent the urban space—and the right to participation, or to exert control over the decision-making process in the social production of space (Lefebvre 1991).

Lefebvre's proposal moved beyond the classical Marxist dogma in which labor is understood as the primary activity through which the working classes acquire political relevance. In his view, in an urbanized society social change results from the very act of inhabiting the city, which informs a number of everyday actions in which the urban problematic reveals itself in all of its complexity. Urban segregation, in this regard, vividly exposes the incapacity of subordinated groups to fully exert hegemonic power over the production of urban spaces. Although Lefebvre did not see industrial workers as a revolutionary subject per se, he did conceive of working-class residents as the main political force of social transformation. For Lefebvre (1996, 154), they are those who can most effectively resist segregation: "The presence and action of the working class, is the only one able to put an end to a segregation directed essentially against it. Only this class, as a class, can decisively contribute to the reconstruction of centrality destroyed by a strategy of segregation."

In recent decades, social scientists and planners have become increasingly interested in using the frame of the right to the city to reflect on sociopolitical protests reacting against emerging urban inequalities.[21] Despite the revolutionary orientation of Lefebvre's work, the right to the city has become a sort of catchphrase among activists and intellectuals (Purcell 2002). The right to the city, David Harvey (2012, xv) argues, is now "an empty signifier," meaning that its definition depends on those who fill it with a specific political content, be they private developers, homeless people, grassroots organizations, or nongovernmental organizations. It is, in fact, this openness in terms of meaning that permitted Santiago's *pobladores* to articulate their claims for housing as right-to-the-city demands. In a public statement released in 2011, the FENAPO asserted: "We seek to obtain dignified housing through struggle and by getting organized. We also seek to construct a new subject which . . . constitutes a community capable of struggling for the right to the city and the building of a new neighborhood."

The *pobladores*' right-to-the-city demand spoke not only about the constitution of social movements against the exclusionary nature of neoliberal urban policies but also about how they reframed their right-to-housing protests on a territorial basis. A major issue for the analysis of housing movements is how territorially situated housing struggles produced new political demands resulting from *pobladores'* longing to continue to reside in their municipalities. A first and necessary step for the analysis of this phenomenon is to describe the means of political participation through which they carry out their protests for new urban rights. I finish this chapter with a portrayal of the Comité de Allegados Don Bosco of La Florida, the state-regulated housing assembly that I took part in for fifteen months. In doing so, I am able to characterize, in a historical context, the new expressions of the Chilean housing movement in terms of both the socioeconomic and gender-based characteristics of those who mobilized for housing, their modalities of collective action, and the role of the social experience of waiting in the articulation of the *pobladores'* territorial demand.

The Comité de Allegados Don Bosco

I attended a general assembly of the Comité de Allegados Don Bosco for the first time on a cold Friday night in August 2013. There I was supposed to meet with Ernesto, the president of this organization and one of three spokespersons of the FENAPO. Once I got there, I attempted to find him among the two or three hundred attendees. Since March 2013, this *allegado* committee's members had been occupying an empty plot located on the corner of Tobalaba Avenue and Departamental Avenue in the municipality of La Florida. They did so in order to demand the construction of a subsidized housing project there and to avoid being displaced from their municipality. Although no more than three families lived there as squatters, the plot served as Don Bosco's headquarters during the seven months that the land seizure lasted. This is why, on that particular Friday night, I headed there to meet Ernesto. Salvador, a friend of mine who had political connections with the FENAPO, had previously spoken with Ernesto about my presence at the general assembly. On my way to the *pobladores'* gathering, I thought that being "recommended" by one of Ernesto's comrades might function as a sort of political clearance for conducting fieldwork. The possibility that I might not be welcome there honestly worried me.

Trying not to think so much about it, I arrived at the occupation around 8:00 p.m. and started to wander around the crowd as way to go unnoticed. A couple of minutes later, I recognized a man in his forties, brown skinned, average height, and notoriously overweight, who was surrounded by dozens of people asking him questions. I approached this group of *pobladores* and heard the man patiently answer questions about how to get into the housing assembly, how to apply for subsidies, the documents needed to do so, and so on. I had found Ernesto. Trying not to interrupt what I supposed were prospective applicants for subsidies, I introduced myself to Ernesto. "Hi. I'm Miguel, Salvador's friend," I said. "I guess Salvador told you about me coming to meet you today, because I'm doing a research about." Before I could say anything else, he replied: "Sure, sure, but let's meet later. I have to start the assembly now." Five minutes later, Ernesto was directing the general assembly of the Comité de Allegados Don Bosco, the main collective body of this organization.

In his role as the president of the committee, Ernesto reported the most important outcomes of the meeting between the Don Bosco's leadership and public authorities from the SERVIU, which had occurred a few days prior. "As usual, they always find excuses not to offer a concrete solution to our demands. Most of us have already obtained housing subsidies, so we can't keep waiting forever," he stated emphatically while many of the Don Bosco *pobladores* nodded in agreement. He went on: "We're not going to give up until we have our houses built in La Florida." Starting at that first occasion, I would come to hear the same complaint at most of the over eighty Don Bosco committee-related events I attended between 2013 and 2015, which included general assemblies, meetings with state officials, leadership gatherings, public demonstrations, meetings with FENAPO representatives, and so on (fig. 2). A few months after this experience, I said to Ernesto: "It must be hard not to give up on the struggle for housing. The state keeps you waiting for so long and there seems to be so little progress in the construction of the housing projects." He replied: "Sure, sure. But what else can we, the poor, do? If we don't mobilize we get nothing. If we're waiting now, it is because we know that, eventually, we'll become homeowners."

The Formation of a State-Regulated Comité de Allegados

In the early 2000s, around twenty residents of La Florida decided to resist against the housing affordability problem in their district by creating a grassroots organization. All of them came from the Población Nuevo Amanecer, an autoconstructed neighborhood that was founded in 1970 in the midst of the old *movimiento de pobladores*. As discussed in detail in chapter 5, these residents articulated their political claims by conceiving of themselves as heirs to the territorial rights that their parents and grandparents achieved through autoconstruction. However, to apply for housing subsidies and fight for their

FIGURE 2. A Don Bosco *allegados* committee's general assembly. Photo by the author, November 2013.

right to stay put, they first had to turn this organization into a state-sanctioned *allegados* committee. And they did so in 2002.

In simple terms, *comités de allegados* are housing assemblies regulated by the state under Law No. 19,418 of 1995 on Juntas de Vecinos y Organizaciones Comunitarias (Law on Neighborhood Councils and Community Organizations). The *comités de allegados* are functional social organizations through which poor families who qualify for subsidies participate in public housing programs. The formalization of a housing assembly entails meeting a number of requirements. First, prospective homeowners must be classified as eligible for subsidies by the state's instruments of socioeconomic characterization (see chapter 6). Second, they must demonstrate that they had not received housing subsidies before. Third, for those who are married or not formally divorced, they must prove that their spouses are not applying for subsidies elsewhere. Then, they have to hold a meeting with a notary public who, through a performative rite of interpellation,[22] declares the grassroots organization a legal entity (*personalidad jurídica*).

As of July 2015, the Don Bosco committee was composed of 880 members formally enrolled in the organization's member registry (*libro de socios*). This number included the actual applicants for subsidies, some members of their families who wanted to be involved in the housing struggle, and the former applicants who had stopped participating in the assembly. The actual number of subsidy applicants who were officially participating in the committee amounted to 671 people, most of whom lived in relatives' houses as *allegados*. A dozen of Don Bosco's members were Peruvians, who could enter the organization after gaining legal residency (*permanencia definitiva*) in the country. Although Chile and Perú have a long history of disputes over land and maritime territories, I never saw anything that might suggest any form of exclusion or racism against Peruvians. I mention this because immigrants in Chile, especially those who come from other Latin American and Caribbean countries, are usually subject to discrimination based on their race and ethnic identity. But that wasn't the case for the Peruvians I got to know. They seemed to be well integrated into the committee and participated actively in the everyday activities of the organization. One of the Don Bosco leaders told me once that "they [Peruvians] are welcome because they need housing and struggle [*luchan*] for it just like us." As I explain in chapter 5, the idea of *lucha* (struggle) is key to understanding *pobladores'* views of citizenship and rights, which I describe through the concept of politics of effort.

The Comité de Allegados Don Bosco was divided into seven groups (*listas*) that differed by the number of people in each group and how long the groups had existed.[23] From the oldest (2007) to the newest (2014), the *listas* and the number of applicants included in each one were: Alto Tobalaba, 84; Florida Ahora, 120; Buin, 44; Juntos por un Sueño, 66; Ilusión, 83; Suyai, 67; La Herradura, 207.[24] By 2015, all groups, except the newest, had been granted state subsidies. These *listas*, in turn, were split into smaller *comunidades* (affinity groups) made up of anywhere from three to twenty people, who wished to live next to each other when the housing projects were built. As I describe fully in chapter 5, *pobladores* construed these affinity groups as communities with which they had political obligations and emotional ties, compelling them to conduct their everyday behavior under a specific moral code.

The relationship between the members of this *allegados* committee was regulated by a general corpus of rules that the *pobladores* autonomously defined once the organization became a legal entity. "Every person, regardless of his/her individual involvement in any *lista* or *comunidad*, must follow these rules," the leadership of the committee said emphatically to those *pobladores* who wanted to get involved. These norms established, among other things, that every applicant for subsidies had to pay for a monthly committee fee—$3,500 Chilean pesos (around US$4.50)—within the first five days of each month. The payment was generally made during the general assemblies held in the first week of every month. With the money collected, the organization covered all the expenses related to its internal functioning such as photocopies, legalization of documents, transportation, cell phone plans, internet connection plans, and so on. In addition, it was used to give the leaders a salary that usually amounted to US$500 each, which was understood by all as an enforcement mechanism. When talking to prospective homeowners, Ernesto let them know that the income the leaders received allowed "us to be totally dedicated to this, and you to oblige us to do our job right. If we don't do it, you have the right to stop paying us."

The name of this *comité de allegados* was inspired by the figure of the Italian Catholic priest John Bosco, widely known as Don Bosco. My interlocutors decided to call the assembly "Don Bosco" since, prior to founding it, they used to meet at a community educational center run by Salesian priests. These priests, the *pobladores* said, helped create the housing assembly by providing them with legal support and allowing them to hold meetings at the facilities of the educational center. Although during my fieldwork I never saw any member of the Salesian community actually involved in the *comité*, the Catholic Church was still a significant presence in the everyday life of the activists. This presence persisted as a religious influence that was not necessarily expressed through a dogmatic approach to Christian principles but, rather, as widespread acknowledgment of the role of *curas obreros* (worker priests) in the struggle for social justice.[25] In fact, the Don Bosco *pobladores* who became homeowners in the first housing project developed by the committee in 2009, paid tribute to *curas obreros* by calling the neighborhood Rodrigo Carranza, the name of a deceased Salesian priest who worked in the Población Nuevo Amanecer. Likewise, these *pobladores* drew on the names of four priests assassinated by the dictatorship—Andre Jarlan, Miguel Woodward, Gerardo Poblete, and Antonio Llidó—to name the neighborhood streets.

By 2002, most of the founding members of the Don Bosco committee resided in overcrowded conditions in the house of a relative, generally that of their parents. These *allegados* lived in the oldest section of the Población Nuevo Amanecer, specifically in what, back in the early 1970s, was the historical location of Campamento Nueva La Habana. This area was home to around four hundred residential properties, where the original residents of Nueva La Habana had autoconstructed their houses (see chapter 5). Born and raised in this part of the *población*, Rosa was in her thirties when she joined the Comité de Allegados Don Bosco in 2002. Until then, she had lived with her two children in her mother's house, which was built on a residential property of a little over 150 square meters. The availability of space in properties like that belonging to Rosa's mother allowed *pobladores* to make home additions over time in accordance with their emerging family needs. When anyone wanted to move into his or her parents' house with a partner, Rosa told me, the incoming family was supposed to autoconstruct an independent room in the backyard to raise their family in. But having a place to stay was not the same as having a home of one's own. When I asked about why she decided to get into the *allegados* committee, Rosa said: "At some point you just get sick of living as an *allegada* because you want something for your own and for your children. I wanted to be able to do whatever I wanted without being asked about what I did or didn't do. . . . I needed more privacy."

As I discuss largely in chapter 6, *pobladores* signified their desires for privacy in political terms through moral categories such as dignity. In doing so, they conceived of their mobilizations as framed by their aspirations to achieve a life with dignity. In that chapter, I also show that, by understanding dignity as a right that can be demanded through a personal and a collective struggle, poor urban residents in neoliberal Chile reformulated the political horizons of the *pobladores* movement. For now, I want to highlight that the activists I met regarded homeownership as the only possible way to achieve the right to stay put and acquire a sense of entitlement to the place they lived in. But the political demand for the right to housing was also intertwined with gender-based ideas and expectations. This explains why the poor, female residents I met based their struggle on a hope to fulfill their role as self-sacrificing mothers. This also makes it clear why, either in the Don Bosco assembly or elsewhere, it was mostly women who were subjected to the experience of waiting in their everyday life, an experience that, at the same time, allowed them to constitute a collective struggle for the right to the city.

Women, Politics, and Promises

When I began to conduct fieldwork in the Comité de Allegados Don Bosco, I was surprised by the overwhelming presence of women, most of whom were in their twenties and thirties.[26] According to the organization's member registry, 762 of the 880 people ever enrolled were women (87 percent), most of whom were unmarried (62 percent). Women have long worked in housing organizations in Chile and elsewhere in Latin America.[27] This is because homeownership has been traditionally seen as central to women's social role as mothers and caregivers (Levy, Latendresse, and Carle-Marsan 2017), especially in countries like Chile, where single-parent, poor households are mostly headed by women (M. Espinoza and Colil, 2015). In Chile, in fact, the number of poor households headed by women increased from 32 percent in 2006 to 49 percent in 2015 (Ministerio de Desarrollo Social 2016). Likewise, the percentage of poor, single-parent families rose from 26 percent in 2006 to 40 percent in 2015. These numbers suggest that low-income women are particularly vulnerable because they have to perform unpaid care work and provide for their families at the same time. This is why *pobladoras* are so visible in the Don Bosco housing assembly. In comparison with men, women not only participated more enthusiastically in public events, such as street marches, demonstrations, and assemblies, but many more of them held leadership positions, even though women generally tend not to assume leadership roles in urban popular movements.[28] Four of the five leaders of the committee were women.

The applicants' occupations were also gender based. The vast majority of those enrolled in the committee—48 percent, according to the registry (table 2) —identified as *dueñas de casa* (housewives). Although this activity was followed by a job traditionally associated with men—unskilled construction workers (7 percent)—the third most common form of employment is one that is also usually associated with women (domestic and cleaning work, 7 percent). The fact that almost half of the Don Bosco members were *dueñas de casa* implied that they did not have the technical or educational credentials to work in the formal labor sector. Being housewives, however, did not prevent them from earning income. Most of the women I met often worked as informal or self-employed laborers to cope with their families' economic instability. For the urban poor in neoliberal Chile, financial precariousness takes the form of "unpredictable cash flow, irregular work patterns and tasks, and erratic shift-work schedules" (Han 2012, 122). As a means to manage such instability, Don Bosco women used to sell French fries, pizzas, empanadas, and *sopaipillas*—a kind of fried dough made of squash—during the committee's events, or worked as informal street vendors (*coleros*) on Saturdays' at the farmers' market on Departamental Avenue.

In an everyday existence defined by labor instability and economic precarity, the Don Bosco *pobladoras* conceptualized homeownership as the most important struggle to *surgir* (get ahead) in life. In their view, involvement in the struggle for housing required making a number of commitments to themselves, to their families, and to the organization, as well as a set of adjustments in their

TABLE 2. Occupations of Don Bosco members

Major group	Other groups	Frequency	Percentage of total
Technicians and associate professionals	Health associate professionals (e.g., paramedics, nursing technicians)	10	1.1
Clerical support workers	General and keyboard clerks (e.g., secretaries, keyboard operators)	55	6.3
	Client services clerks (e.g., telephone switchboard operators, receptionists)	5	0.6
Services and sales workers	Personal services workers (e.g., cooks, bartenders, hairdressers, childcare workers)	47	5.3
	Sales workers (e.g., market salesperson, cashier)	49	5.6
	Security services workers (e.g., guards)	9	1.0
Craft and related trade workers	Building and related trade workers (e.g., carpenters, joiners)	15	1.7
	Handicraft and printing workers (e.g., shoemakers, upholsterers)	4	0.5
	Metal, machinery, and related trade workers (e.g., vehicle repairmen)	5	0.6
Plant and machine operators and assemblers	Stationary plant and machine operators (e.g., textile machine operators, metal processing and finishing plant operators).	22	2.5
	Drivers and mobile plant operators (e.g., car drivers, truck drivers)	10	1.1
Elementary occupations	Cleaners and helpers (e.g., domestic workers, cleaners)	61	6.9
	Laborers in mining, construction, manufacturing, and transport (e.g., unskilled construction workers)	64	7.3
	Agricultural, forestry and fishery laborers (e.g., gardeners, landscapers)	7	0.8
	Food preparation assistants	16	1.8
	Street and related sales and services workers (e.g., street vendors)	32	3.6
Other employment status	Dueñas de casa (homemakers)	418	47.5
	Students	21	2.4
	Unemployed	5	0.6
	People with disability	1	0.1
Without information or unclassified		24	2.7
Total		880	100

Note: Occupational groups derived from the International Standard Classification of Occupations, 2008.
Source: Own elaboration based on the Comité de Allegados Don Bosco's member registry.

everyday life. First, it entailed reorganizing the family budget and saving money exclusively for housing-related purposes. It also required being ready to spend many hours a week attending meetings and assemblies and, accordingly, dealing with domestic issues such as childcare. It also entailed negotiating with their boyfriends or husbands, many of whom did not want their partners to join in the committee because of jealousy. And, maybe more important, it involved accepting that participation in the organization could last much longer than expected. Not everybody was willing to do so. By 2015, 208 of the 880 people registered in the organization's member registry had voluntarily or involuntarily left the committee. The most common reasons for leaving were not having enough money either to pay the committee fees or to save the necessary amount to apply for subsidies; being expelled from the organization due to "lack of commitment" (see chapter 4); and losing interest in continuing to participate given the frustration of applicants who, after years of involvement, could not obtain housing.

To me, this feeling of disappointment was a completely understandable reaction, considering how long they had been engaged in the organization. As table 3 shows, almost 65 percent of members had joined the committee between 2007 and 2008, the years in which the oldest groups (*listas*) were created (Alto Tobalaba and Florida Ahora). This means that, by 2015, hundreds of families had been taking part in the organization for at least seven years and, although they had received subsidies, they were still waiting to obtain housing. For them, the acquisition of subsidies certainly represented an advance in the pursuit of their own home. But as Ernesto regularly said at the general assemblies as a way to mobilize the Don Bosco members, having a subsidy was "like having a voucher to be used on the market. Nothing else."

On one occasion, Ernesto tried to explain to a *poblador* the reasons for the delay in the building of the housing projects by arguing, "Although we do have subsidies, real estate companies don't want to construct housing for the poor." Ernesto was actually right. By June 2015, official MINVU data indicated that, between 2011 and 2014, the state had assigned 188,769 subsidies nationwide as part of its housing programs for the poorest families. However, almost 100,000 of them had not been used to build housing projects (*El Mercurio* 2015). The reason for this was that the amount of money provided by these subsidies—around 700 UF per family (US$25,300 approximately)—was insufficient to fund housing developments.[29] For Javier Romero, the undersecretary of housing and urbanism in 2014, this was because the real estate market was incapable

TABLE 3. Year of entry into the Comité de Allegados Don Bosco

Year	Frequency	Percentage of total
2007	210	23.9
2008	357	40.6
2009	90	10.2
2010	0	0.0
2011	4	0.5
2012	38	4.3
2013–2014	181	20.6
Total	880	100

Source: Comité de Allegados Don Bosco's member registry.

of "taking responsibility for the construction process" of affordable housing (*La Tercera* 2014).

Don Bosco families who had been granted subsidies between 2012 and 2013 were supposed to be split between three housing projects that SERVIU planned to develop in La Florida: Altos de la Cordillera (180 housing units), Portal La Florida (460 housing units), and Alto Tobalaba (180 housing units). But by 2015, the year in which I ended my fieldwork, none of them had been built. While the first two of the projects were under construction, the third one was still under technical evaluation.[30] The *pobladoras'* prolonged waiting to obtain housing thus framed the relationship they established with the state agencies, a relationship that they construed as anchored in the incapacity of the latter to fulfill their promises. "Stop making promises you can't keep!" and "We are sick of waiting!" were common complaints to MINVU professionals or municipal officials at meetings that were supposedly intended to accelerate the construction of the housing projects assigned to them.

Such complaints, however, seemed to be uttered even more vehemently every time that a *político* (politician) showed up at the committee's activities. Deputies, senators, and council members often stopped by the general assemblies to, paraphrasing one of them, get firsthand knowledge of the poor's needs and give them a prompt solution. But most of the women I worked with considered the physical presence of *políticos* as requiring them to put up with a shameless person who was basically "looking for votes," especially during electoral campaigns. It was actually during the 2013 presidential and parliamentary campaign when I met the senator Carlos Montes, a renowned socialist politician who had made his political career in La Florida. When he arrived at the committee's activities, *pobladoras* generally gave him a warm welcome. But when he left, they immediately began to talk about him behind his back, accusing him of being a phony and a hypocrite.

The *pobladoras'* involvement in formal politics was ambivalent. They expressed strong rejection of political parties, as they were perceived as a function of the elites, who were interested only in preserving the status quo. At the same time, given their ideological identification, some of them usually worked for electoral campaigns in support of traditional political parties. In ideological terms, most of the people I met identified with center-left parties like the Christian Democratic Party (PDC), the Party for Democracy (PPD), and the Socialist Party (PS). Others were more inclined to the left, openly backing the Communist Party (PC) or the Equality Party (PI).[31] I never heard of anyone claiming to support either right-wing parties or the Movement of the Revolutionary Left (MIR), the radical left-wing organization that had helped found Población Nuevo Amanecer in 1970. The *pobladoras'* endorsement of political parties did not necessarily entail a formal militancy. Most of them were not militants at all. As for the few who were formally enrolled in political parties, although I never observed them proselytize, conflicts between them were common. They accused one another of working for the interests of this or that politician rather than for the interests of the committee. In any case, it is fair to say that the Comité de Allegados Don Bosco was not an ideological battlefield. I did not see opposing views of society being discussed, nor did I witness any attempt by political parties to co-opt it. This latter aspect reveals an important difference between the contemporary housing movement and the one that emerged during the mid-twentieth century.[32]

What I did see was some *pobladoras*—both party militants and independents—working for the campaigns of Senator Montes and other local politicians. But I soon realized that such support was contingent on the politicians' capacity to help speed up the building of the housing projects. As the construction of the projects was often delayed, the politicians had to then restore their bond and trust with the activists, a process I observed every time that the former came to the housing assembly, basically to provide explanations to the latter. This endowed the women of Don Bosco with a sense of empowerment when dealing with state agents, which revealed itself in everyday encounters between them. For example, when talking to the La Florida mayor, the right-wing Rodolfo Carter, the women addressed him by using the singular second-person pronoun *tú* instead of *usted*. In Spanish, the former is commonly utilized in

informal, familiar contexts. The latter, instead, is verbalized when the sp[e] considers the addressee to be someone who deserves some kind of respec[t] to his or her rank, age, or social position. That the Don Bosco *pobladoras* on the pronoun *tú* when speaking to politicians suggests that they did no[t] ceive themselves as subdued, inferior, or in a lower position. Rather, the[y] themselves as equals with respect to a political authority; that is, they imag[ined] themselves as citizens endowed with the right to get what they had been p[rom]ised. This is why, when I asked a *pobladora* about the presence of Carlos M[ontes] at an assembly, she said: "I like him to come because, if he breaks his prom[ise,] I can tell him to his face that he's a liar."

The Don Bosco members' sense of empowerment speaks to the pol[itical] implications of waiting for the formation of agencies among the Chilean residents. Unlike what Chatterjee (2004) observed in the case of poor u[rban] residents in India, my interlocutors saw themselves as rights-bearing citi[zens] whose political actions were not necessarily defined by patron-client rela[tion]ships. They were not part of patronage politics in which, to act politically, had to subordinate their subjectivity to that of a political patron. In the co[ntext] of a profound housing affordability crisis, their experiences with waiting—[un]derstood as stemming from broken promises—illuminates how the poo[r en]gage subversively with state programs, transforming state-regulated assem[blies] into right-to-the-city organizations. Both the housing crisis and prospe[ctive] homeowners' insurgent participation in subsidy-based programs explain[s the] mobilizing character of the *comités de allegados*, as well as their role in th[e] emergence of urban movements in Santiago. I argue that this reemergence be analyzed through an ethnographic analysis of three phenomena: (a) the of new modalities of subject formation through which the urban poor reart[icu]late the agency imbued in the category *poblador*; (b) the appearance of ur[ban-] based formulations of citizenship, which enabled them to demand rights the city spaces in which they aspire to pursue their life projects; and (c) the figuration of dignity-based narratives through which urban activists reima[gine] the political horizon of the housing movement. I scrutinize these phenom[ena] in depth in the following three chapters.

II DIGNIFIED SUBJECT-CITIZENS

4   Performances of City Making

"Remove It From the Speech"

My ethnographic immersion in the Don Bosco housing assembly entailed not only spending time in working-class neighborhoods but also participating in several meetings held in public offices such as the Ministry of Housing and Urbanism (MINVU) and the Metropolitan Service of Housing and Urbanism (SERVIU). This allowed me to get to know a number of public servants in different positions of power—from undersecretaries to government consultants—most of whom started to work in the government when the right-wing president Sebastián Piñera came into power in 2010. Their profiles were more or less the same. Most of them were upper-class experts graduated from the Pontificia Universidad Católica de Chile, a confessional private university that is one of the most exclusive universities in Chile. Generally, they had little background in politics and public affairs. "We're working here not for political reasons, but because of our experience in housing-related issues," one of them told me, perhaps as a way to distance himself from the ideological orientation of Piñera's government. A man in his forties, this public servant had worked in the private sector prior to joining the government, specifically in the real estate sector. Other younger professionals had become familiar with the housing problem while volunteering in TECHO, a Jesuit nongovernmental organization created within the Pontificia Universidad Católica in 1997 to provide the poor with affordable housing.

Every time I attended meetings at SERVIU or MINVU, I noticed that both the older and the younger government professionals usually showed kindness, sympathy, and respect to the Don Bosco members. "It's a pleasure to have you here, guys. Why haven't you come by? We miss you!" the bureaucrats often said to welcome the *pobladores*. They acted in this way even when the activists seemed to lose their temper after learning that there had been little progress in the construction of their housing projects. On those occasions, the professionals attempted to show genuine concern by saying things like "We're sorry that the construction of your houses is taking longer than expected and we do understand how you feel. But believe us, we're doing our best." The public servants' justifications clearly concealed a patronizing attitude toward the *pobladores*, as if expressing a sort of Christian guilt was enough for them to put themselves in the other's shoes and erase the institutional, social, and cultural frames mediating their relationship with the poor. What struck me the most was the fact that the government agents barely referred to the Don Bosco members as *pobladores*, which contrasted with the widespread use of that term among my interlocutors. When alluding to the housing activists, government officials drew on the language of public policy, referring to them as *allegados*, *grupos vulnerables* (vulnerable groups), or *familias de menores ingresos* (lowest-income families). Intrigued by how the bureaucrats addressed housing activists, I decided to bring this issue up during interviews. A MINVU consultant, who I will identify as Sebastián, said: "I'm going to tell you an anecdote regarding the word *pobladores*. When the new housing decree [No. 49] was about to be published, my boss [a high-ranking government agent] asked me to spread the news about it to the press, the arena of public opinion, et cetera. So, I wrote a speech in which I started by saying, 'Dear *pobladores* . . .' or something like that. But my boss, after reading it, said: 'Who wrote this? Why do you use the word *pobladores*? That's a communist word; that's a leftist word, remove it from the speech!'"

"Why was it so important for the government agent to prevent the word *pobladores* from appearing in the speech? What, in his view, makes the term *poblador* a 'communist' word?" I wondered after my conversation with Sebastián. With that in mind, I began to ask the Don Bosco members about their own understanding of the word *poblador*. I wanted to delve into how they made sense of such a category within the struggle for housing and how everyday use of the concept helped to inform their demand for rights. José, a construction worker who had been involved in the Don Bosco assembly for six years when

I met him in 2013, conceived of *pobladores* in this way: "*Pobladores* are those who struggle for their right to housing, for their right to feel better, to have a better community. It's the people who need to get ahead in life. . . . I think that a *poblador* is a person who struggles for rights."

For José, the social category of *pobladores* refers to the working class, through which poor residents can "struggle" for better living conditions by demanding rights. Many other housing activists understood the word *poblador* in that way as well. For all of them, this signifier alluded to a kind of consistent political identity that was defined by their engagement in urban struggles, such as the issue of housing. As discussed earlier in this book, *pobladores* as a social segment of the urban poor do not necessarily share a unified identity. Although people enrolled in housing assemblies can be largely described as working class, they engage in a variety of different occupations and ideological affiliations.[1] It was thus striking to hear housing activists articulate a conceptualization of *pobladores* as a cohesive subjectivity, one grounded in their active involvement in the struggle for rights. In this chapter, I show that my interlocutors' view of *pobladores* as a univocal category has enabled them both to form their political agency and to morally differentiate themselves from other working-class dwellers who "did not commit enough to the struggle for housing." As I discuss in the next chapter, this process of moral differentiation is key to understanding *pobladores'* ideas of citizenship and rights.

But where does my interlocutors' conceptualization of *pobladores*, as referring to a unified agency, come from? Anthropologists have argued that social movements for housing, as they result from excluded dwellers' demands for rights to physical presence in the city, have been fundamental to the constitution of the poor as political agents.[2] In chapter 2, I explained that the Chilean urban poor gained significant political recognition by conducting mass land occupations in the 1960s and early 1970s, which triggered the rise of the so-called *movimiento de pobladores* (*pobladores* movement). It was in that context that the signifier *poblador* acquired a political connotation. Although Chileans have used the term since the nineteenth century to refer to impoverished residents (Salazar and Pinto 2002), it was only when land seizures spread throughout the urban peripheries that the social category of *pobladores* began to refer to a segment of the working classes involved in urban struggles. The almost total disappearance of mass land occupations after the return to democracy in 1990, as well as the growing enrollment of poor families in subsidy-based housing policies in that decade, called into question the very existence of *pobladores* as political agents. Prospective homeowners' participation in state-regulated *comités de allegados* was understood as a mechanism used by democratic governments to incorporate the urban poor into state bureaucracy and, accordingly, pacify them. This may explain why authors who have carried out ethnographic studies of the urban poor in neoliberal Chile speak of the word *pobladores* as if there were no agency in that signifier, that is, as if the term were merely a social identity category referring to marginal residents of the peripheries, regardless of their involvement in the struggle for rights.[3]

The ethnographic vignettes I presented here raise certain questions: What leads some people to think of the term *poblador* as a "communist" word while others use it to refer to a person who struggles for his or her rights? Why do the urban poor draw on this signifier when engaging the state with their political demands? Furthermore, why is it important for them to be recognized as *pobladores* by the state? Why do they identify themselves as *pobladores* rather than "proletarians," "workers," or simply "poor people" to make political demands? In chapter 2, I use Tilly and Tarrow's contentious politics to analyze what my interlocutors called the "historical continuity" of the housing mobilizations in Chile, that is, the idea that past and present struggles for the right to housing belong to the "same" urban movement.[4] There, I describe the diverse repertories of actions that activists have performed since the mid-twentieth century, as well as the different of housing policies through which the state has attempted to tackle the shortage of social housing. In this chapter, I delve into how the people I encountered thought of such a historical continuity in terms of the subject that produces—and is produced through—these movements. I do so by focusing on the role of the signifier *poblador* in the constitution of political agency among the working classes.

I argue that the word *poblador*, in addition to functioning as a social identity category, also serves as a political category of subject formation, as it is endowed with a "performative" power (Austin 1962). This means that the term can be rearticulated at different conjunctures by those who utilize it in their political narratives, even during a period in which the old constitutive practices—large-scale land occupations and autoconstruction processes—are no longer part of their repertory of action. Examining the category *poblador* from a performative standpoint entails seeing *pobladores* as the result of a process of subject formation through which they have become political agents. It is thus important to determine which kind of agencies poor residents develop by engaging in urban struggles and the role of language in that process. Following

Saba Mahmood (2012, 18), by "agency" I mean a "capacity for action that specific relations of *subordination* create and enable," a capacity that, materialized in historically situated bodily procedures, allows for the shaping of a moral self. Agency, Mahmood argues, does not necessarily suppose the configuration of a progressive project, as it develops through a process of political and ethical formation, in which meanings and senses cannot be fixed in advance. In this chapter, I explore these meanings and senses by discussing how poor dwellers fighting for housing, in constituting themselves as *pobladores*, are able to make ethical sense of their conditions of exclusion and recognize themselves as subjects of rights. To do so, I briefly examine the idea of subject through both performative theory and poststructuralist approaches, which allows me to present the process of subject formation as associated with both the generative role of language and the constituting character of ritualized social practices. Then, I take a look at cultural, media, and political discourses that, since the 1950s, have spoken of *pobladores* as politicized social agents. Here, I focus on two main aspects: first, the ways these discourses interpreted *pobladores'* performances of city making, and second, how the doing of these social practices of city making contributed to the formation of *pobladores'* subjectivity. Finally, I show ethnographically how *pobladores* in neoliberal Chile have reshaped the agency embedded in the term *poblador* by both reclaiming the legacy of past urban mobilizations and constituting an effort-based narrative through which they signify ethically their experiences as working-class dwellers.

Ritualized Acts and the Production of Subjects

Performative theory is an epistemological perspective of social, philosophical, and linguistic analysis for which language, and particularly its discursive elaborations, forms what is said. John Austin (1962) points out that statements are performative when, instead of reporting or stating any given phenomena, the utterance itself is an action. In contrast to constative statements and their true-false criterion, performative utterances function under the principle of happiness-unhappiness. The definition of their felicity or infelicity is a matter not of empirical evidence, but of the enforcement and implementation of rules, procedures, and circumstances. For any performative utterance to be realized—and therefore to have perlocutionary effects—it must satisfy a certain number of social conventions. This is why performative speech assumes the character of a "ritual or ceremonial" act (Austin 1962, 19), which means that its force is materialized mainly through repetition.[5] Later work on the performative character of words concentrated on the performative power of rituals. While Derrida's (1977, 180) performativity is predicated on the capacity of the linguistic sign of being quoted—what he calls "iterability"—Pierre Bourdieu (1991) pays much more attention to the sociocultural backdrop in which performative statements are uttered. If Derrida practically rules out that the influence of social context on the production of performative linguistics marks, then Bourdieu sees in it the necessary condition for speech acts to exert a performative effect. For him, the force of the performative stems from what he calls "the performative magic of ritual" (Bourdieu 1991, 115). This refers to the institutional conditions that must be satisfied for a ritual discourse—for instance, that of a priest at mass—to be received and accepted as such.

Whether as "conventional acts" (Austin), "iterability" (Derrida), or "the performative magic of rituals" (Bourdieu), authors conceive of repetition as a fundamental aspect of the performative. What is, then, the role of the subject who is speaking in the performative? Is the subject able to deliver words with power? If so, can we speak of a sort of political agency—like that of the *pobladores*—in which individuals can have control over what they are saying and consciously articulate a speech as a form of progressive discourse? Or are they a mere effect of the constitutive capacity of language? The relationship between language and the subject's capacity to act in a sovereign manner is one of the main concerns of Butler (1997). For her, the process of subject formation derives not only from its implication in language but also from the corporeal encounters of the bodies that take part in ritual. The subject, therefore, can reframe the terms of his or her subjectivation by developing performative practices. This suggests that actions, like words, also have a formative character.[6]

Butler conceives of Austin's speech acts as an act of "interpellation" (Althusser 2001), a concept that refers to rituals of ideological recognition by means of which individuals acquire the status of subjects. One of these rituals, Althusser says, comes about when a policeman shouts on the street, "Hey, you there!" This compels the individual hailed to turn around and identify himself as a subject of law. The idea of interpellation leads Butler to raise a fundamental issue regarding the relation between subject and speech: the extent to which the subject constituted through being addressed by another becomes a subject capable of addressing others. This aspect, as we have seen, becomes crucial to understanding *pobladores* as, at some point in the political history of Chile, they became able to address the state through a language of rights.

In attempting to understand interpellation through a performative framework, Butler rethinks the role of the speaking subject—and his or her relation to language—in rituals of ideological recognition. While in Austin's model, Butler says, the subject who speaks precedes the speech in question, in Althusser's view the interpellating speech act that brings the subject into linguistic existence appears to be prior to the subject in question. To disentangle this theoretical disjunction, Butler borrows Shoshana Felman's idea that there is not a radical separation between the body and the speech act, since the former is constituted through the latter.[7] Hence, there is no transcendental subject capable of interpellating or, in other words, a subject whose existence is prior to language. "This means—adds Butler—that the subject has its own 'existence' implicated in language that precedes and exceeds the subject, a language whose historicity includes a past and future that exceeds that of the subject who speaks" (Butler 1997, 28).

For Butler, the speaking subject who interpellates has no control over that ritual, as he or she cannot estimate the perlocutionary effects of his or her speech. However, it is precisely the conventional character of the rituals of interpellation that allows Butler to recognize the possibility of a linguistic agency, different from that of relying on the sovereign subject. For her, the subordination involved in any process of interpellation—for instance, by being called a *poblador*—can be subverted on the basis of the defining condition of speech acts: their citational nature. Drawing on Derrida's iterability, Butler maintains that repetition always entails a form of alterity. If injurious speech acts need to be cited in order to have a perlocutionary effect, the repetition of such acts then opens up the possibility of linguistic insubordination, as their intended meanings can be recontextualized and resignified for subversive goals. In this sense, interpellation is not only a subordinating act (as conceived by Althusser) but also a condition for the agentival power of the "post-sovereign subject" (Butler 1997, 139), a subject whose discursive operations are open to an additional and unexpected delimitation. The very process of subject formation is, consequently, that which compels Butler to construe agency as the unanticipated, open-ended reformulation of the performative utterance, which can be resignified for different, or even radical, purposes.

In what follows, I describe the process of subject formation among low-income residents struggling for housing by examining how the category for the term *poblador* acquired a performative power through ritualized practices of city making. This task compels me to go back in time and examine the role of land occupations and autoconstruction processes—and the social discourses that began to speak about them—in the emergence of *pobladores* as a political subjectivity. I then discuss how housing protesters in neoliberal Chile, by invoking the performative power of the word *poblador*, constituted themselves as subjects endowed with agency in circumstances in which there is no actual performance of these ritualized acts.

Stories of *Callamperos*

As explained in chapter 2, in the first half of the twentieth century the implementation of urban renewal projects and Santiago's demographic changes contributed significantly to the housing crisis of the 1940s and, later on, to the development of the *pobladores* movement. The massive impact of the *lanzamientos* (evictions) of the poor from the city center not only redefined Santiago's geography of residential segregation but also gave rise to a phenomenon that would become a determining factor in formation of *pobladores*: the rise of illegal land seizures along the urban peripheries. Not able to afford a place to live in Santiago's central areas, *los sin casa* (those who do not have a home of their own) increasingly began to dwell as squatters in *poblaciones callampas* (shantytowns).[8] These *callampas* were located mostly on public-owned, vacant, peripheral area lots (e.g., riverbanks, channels, ditches), usually close to industrial areas. Who were these individuals who began to settle on empty lots on the outskirts of the city? What were the narratives through which social and cultural discourses produced them as an object of public inquiry, during a period in which *callampas* were deemed the most expressive icon of urban marginality?

Progressive Imaginaries and Views of the Catholic Church

The growing number of squatter settlements drew significant attention in the arena of public opinion in the early 1950s. As a large number of "modest citizens" were condemned to live in humble shantytowns, *callampas* appeared to reveal the unequal nature of Chilean modernization.[9] Squatters—then known as *callamperos*—became an object of media and cultural discourse, as they represented the materialization of the unexpected outcomes of an importsubstitution industrialization model, which could not absorb the migrant population from the countryside who had come to find work in the cities.

The first accounts of these new forms of urban inhabitance were characterized by a denunciatory language. This could be seen in leftist newspapers
such as *El Siglo, Democracia,* and *Vistazo,* as well as in the Jesuit-edited *Mensaje*
magazine. Although the political left and the Catholic Church conceived of *ca-*
llampas as an undignified type of residency that needed to be changed through
governmental policies, the ethical understanding of the phenomenon differed:
for the leftist papers, shantytowns were a vivid expression of the self-organizing
capacities of the urban poor, whereas for the latter these spaces served only to
demoralize, degrade, and corrupt working-class urban dwellers.[10] These opposing perspectives on shantytowns reveal themselves through two different cultural productions: *The Novel of "Poblaciones callampas"* and the documentary
Las callampas.

At the beginning of 1953, the progressive journal *Vistazo* began to publish
The Novel of "Poblaciones callampas," a tale divided into twelve, sequential,
short pieces that came out every Tuesday. Based on true events, the novel narrates the experiences of poor inhabitants who, once evicted from their urban
slum tenement (*conventillos*) in 1946, started living in different *callampas* until
they finally ended up taking over a vacant area. These actions would give rise
to the Toma Zañartu in 1947. Later on, the characters in the story were moved
to an urbanized area in which the Población Nueva La Legua would eventually be founded. In the first published episode of the novel, tellingly called "El
lanzamiento" (The eviction), *poblaciones callampas* are described as "a chapter
of misery and heroism, of embarrassment and struggle, of pain and effort that
arose in Chilean social life."[11] The author of the opening note, whose identity
is not revealed, argues that the story is the "most real, most human, and most
dramatic novel in Chile today." The message for the reader was clear: although
callampas maintained situations of never-before-seen forms of misery and social exclusion, they might also contribute to the rise of new kinds of solidarity-
based social relations, and even to the formation of political agencies. In fact,
most of the chapters follow more or less the same argumentative structure:
the squatters face a variety of threatening events—an eviction, a winter flood,
the spread of alcoholism among *callamperos*, one member's betrayal of the
group[12]—that they are able to overcome successfully through strong community ties and solidarity, decent moral values, and wise political consciousness.
For *The Novel of "Poblaciones callampas,"* the appearance of squatter settlements
created the conditions necessary for the formation of grassroots organizations

and, ultimately, class consciousness. *Callamperos*, although they received constant support from politicians and civil society, were able to overcome their dismal material conditions by themselves, through political struggle. The novel narrates the story of increasingly politicized subjects who, primarily by forming a strong community, were able to autoconstruct their homes while envisioning a future life full of promise and high expectations.

This optimistic account of the *poblaciones callampas* was absent in the narratives developed by the Catholic Church in the 1950s, which tended to emphasize the dehumanizing character of squatter settlements. During this period, the role Jesuits played was crucial, which was demonstrated through two major institutions that emerged under the auspices of this congregation: Hogar de Cristo (Christ's Home), a charity organization established in 1944 that provided *callamperos* with emergency housing, and *Revista Mensaje*, a magazine founded in 1951 that took on a leading role denouncing Chile's social inequality in the mid-twentieth century. The Catholic Church's view of squatter settlements is clearly expressed in *Las callampas*, a documentary directed by the Jesuit priest Rafael Sánchez (1958). The documentary describes the events that led up to the establishment of the Población La Victoria, the first working-class neighborhood that emerged from a large-scale land seizure (for more on this, see chapter 2). This film must be understood as an attempt to comprehend the experiences, motivations, and feelings of impoverished dwellers who, the documentary insinuates, were ultimately unable to integrate themselves into the modernizing process. In portraying the living conditions of *callamperos*, the film is thus framed by a language of despair, misery, and desolation.[13] The residents of Zanjón de la Aguada squatter settlements are depicted as hopeless *callamperos* who, after a fire consumed their shacks, were forced to occupy vacant lots in order to build their houses. It was during those fateful circumstances when, the documentary tells us, Catholic missionaries appeared to help out *callamperos*. The film's narrator says: "In those tough moments, when failure and grief threatened to break down the whole operation [the building of a new neighborhood], someone came dressed like a *callampero*. The [Hogar de Cristo's] Priest [Alejandro] del Corro showed up confident and enthusiastic. Here he built his tent and got mobilized from that moment on."

Later, the narrator continues to describe the process of moral transformation experienced by the former squatters. The *callampero*, "that man who seemed overwhelmed in a disorganized and unsanitary *población callampa*, jumps passionately at the chance to build his new home." The urban poor, unlike the story told by *The Novel of Poblaciones callampas*, are here seen as incapable of overcoming their condition as informal residents by themselves. It is only through the moral and technical guidance of the priest that former squatters were able to acquire capacities to make their new neighborhood. It is, in other words, through the Catholic Church's intervention that *callamperos* became city makers.

Unsanitary Housing, Subhuman Residents

The "unsanitary" nature of *poblaciones callampas*, such as that accounted for by Rafael Sánchez in *Las callampas*, was a widespread topic of debate in the 1950s. These sanitary approaches to *poblaciones callampas* can be found in different sources, such as the *pobladores*' own propaganda, national newspapers (both progressive and conservative), and the above-mentioned Jesuit magazine *Mensaje*. In all of them, the lack of basic sanitation in shantytowns, which resulted from the total absence of urbanization, was interpreted as a dehumanizing and undignified way of living. According to the Pobladores' Provincial Association, there were thousands of "citizens" who, by 1952, lived in "subhuman conditions" on the outskirts of the city, on account of the state's failure to halt land speculation in the city center.[14]

The eviction of the *callampas* and the emergence of new neighborhoods in areas with minimum standards of urbanization were therefore seen as necessary steps for creating more human and civilized forms of inhabitance. For instance, Miguel Lawner, a progressive architect who later would become the director of the Urban Improvement Corporation (CORMU) during Salvador Allende's government (1970–1973), was certain that the building of Población La Victoria in 1957 would enable *pobladores* to autoconstruct their homes in "human and hygienic conditions."[15] The conservative newspaper *El Mercurio* in a similar narrative described the massive displacement of other *callamperos* from Zanjón de la Aguada, which led to the rise of Población San Gregorio in 1959: "Thirty families, out of four thousand, were taken from the Zanjón de la Aguada *población callampa* to the San Gregorio ranch on army trucks. There, the residents themselves will build *viviendas definitivas e higiénicas* [permanent and hygienic houses]."[16]

Any notion of dirtiness, Mary Douglas (1966) argues, reveals symbolic systems of classification in which the elements of our social world are put into a hierarchical order. The presence of dirt always involves the existence of a systemic ordering through which elements deemed inappropriate are rejected. With respect to *callampas*, the appearance of cleanliness-based discourses can thus be examined as part of broader urban imaginaries inspired by particular ideas of urban modernity, ideas by which modern cities were thought of as able to provide industrialization not only with infrastructure and services but also with a more skilled—that is, educated—labor force. Industrializing agendas in Latin America construed the city fundamentally as both an economic and a cultural space in which modern life could be successfully achieved (Gorelik 2004). In congregating a large number of poor families residing in "pathetic living conditions," uncultured, dirty, and dehumanizing *callampas* were conceived of as a threat to such a premise.[17] Why? Because *callampas* would produce individuals unable to participate in modernization processes as human beings.

Although these sanitary approaches were also present in the *pobladores'* discourses, they understood early on the risks involved in reproducing the derogatory language commonly utilized by the mainstream media. In the Pobladores' Provincial Association's official propaganda paper, *El Poblador*, housing activists frequently said that working-class families lived "like animals" in *callampas*.[18] But they did so not to account for their socioeconomic backwardness; rather, they were putting forward a sort of human rights-based discourse that started out with recognition of *pobladores* as subjects who had been dehumanized by state policies. This housing organization complained about those who, by calling them *inadaptados social y culturalmente* (social and cultural misfits), denied them the right to live in dignified houses, a right, they said, that poor residents were entitled to simply because they were "human beings."[19] In this regard, for *pobladores* the spreading of social discourses that treated them as dirty, infected individuals—in opposition to those "sanitary citizens" who adopt hygienic practices for disciplining their bodies[20]—was a means of disenfranchising them. The negation of their human condition was conceived of as a denial of their rights as humans. However, they would "regain" the rights denied to them by derogatory discourses, by developing ritualized performances of city making, a set of practices for producing space through which *pobladores* constituted themselves as the main agents in the urbanization of the peripheries.

Ritualized Performances of City Making

The occurrence of land seizures since the late 1940s, graphically depicted in the feature production discussed in the previous section, had unexpected political outcomes in the years that followed. The foundation of the Población Zañartu

(1947) and the Población La Victoria (1957), two land occupations that resulted from the organized action of *pobladores* and militants of the Communist Party (PC), provided the poor with a model for political activism. During the 1960s and early 1970s, *tomas de terreno* (land occupations) would become one of the main strategies used by *pobladores* for claiming the right to housing.

It was actually through the propagation of land seizures—and the processes of autoconstruction that in some cases resulted from them—that *pobladores*, now more actively involved in housing struggles, began to be recognized by the state as individuals endowed with agency. In other words, it was through the making of the city that housing activists formed themselves as political subjectivities. This phenomenon occurred alongside the development of new discourses on the urban poor and the use of new signifiers to refer to them. Starting in the early 1960s, people living in squatter settlements were less often referred to as unsanitary *callamperos*. Instead, they were *pobladores*, a word that began to allude to active urban residents claiming the right to housing. This is the context in which, as discussed in chapter 2, social-science discourses elaborated theoretically on the *pobladores* movement. This new understanding of squatters as *pobladores* is closely related to a process of interpellation through which the state began to acknowledge poor individuals as city makers. This, of course, by no means suggests that *pobladores'* subjectivity stems exclusively from the action of the state. The terms employed in this ritual of ideological recognition, rather than being constrained by the state's interest, had always been open to further and unexpected resignification. Such a resignification materialized through the proliferation of highly politicized squatter settlements in the early 1970s and, consequently, the construction of *pobladores* as a revolutionary subjectivity.

Autoconstructing City Spaces and the Creation of Radical Subjectivities

The experience of autoconstruction engenders political actions regarding residency and aesthetic judgments of houses, through which working classes develop new kinds of social agencies (Holston 1991). In these processes of city making, autoconstructors turn "themselves into citizens and political agents, become fluent in rights talk, and claim the cities as their own" (Caldeira 2017, 3). Autoconstruction is a modality of producing the urban peripheries proper to cities of the Global South. In Santiago, the working classes began to self-build their houses and neighborhoods as early as the 1940s. Unlike other cases in Latin America, in which autoconstruction relied primarily on the actions of poor dwellers alone,[21] the state was significantly involved by both attempting to regulate the distribution of land and providing the poor with building materials. This modality of state-led autoconstruction would later give rise to housing policies in which *pobladores* themselves were expected to work on the construction of their residential spaces.

By the late 1940s, although large-scale land seizures were not yet a concern for the state, poor residents struggling for housing already understood autoconstruction as a right. In simple terms, this implied the request for technical assistance and loans to acquire building supplies from the state, with which *pobladores* sought to construct their residential spaces on their own. In 1947, the dwellers of the previously mentioned Población Zañartu, for example, asked the state to expropriate the plot they had seized and for construction materials to build their houses by themselves.[22] Thousands of poor families without a home of their own would make similar requests in the following years.[23] All of them considered autoconstruction the most effective way to gain possession of the land they were occupying, to then legitimate their residential property.

Squatters were not the only ones who demanded the right to autoconstruction. Since the late 1940s, *pobladores* living in state-planned neighborhoods with poor-quality housing or incomplete urbanization had demanded the right to autoconstruct in order to improve their *poblaciones*. That was the case of Nueva La Legua. The residents of this neighborhood, most of whom lived in overcrowded conditions, demanded the right to autoconstruction in order to avoid being provided with emergency housing made of asbestos cement sheets (*pizarreño*) since, in their view, these were toxic to their health.[24] Some years later, the residents of other renowned *poblaciones* like San Gregorio and José María Caro—both founded in 1959 as part of the Housing Plan of President Jorge Alessandri (1958–1964)—would also perform autoconstruction processes on a large scale.[25] The urban poor's growing experiences in autoconstruction would be crucial for the implementation of Eduardo Frei Montalva's (1964–1970) housing programs, particularly Operation Site. As I describe in chapter 2, this program was based on the allocation of title deeds and, ideally, urbanized plots in which *pobladores* would autoconstruct their houses under the supervision of state agencies.

Poor individuals' participation in these actions of city making led the state apparatuses (e.g., political parties, unions) to construe them as individuals with high-level organizing skills. As low-income residents were progressively incorporated into state policies, squatters were no longer referred to as marginalized *callamperos* but as responsibilized city makers. Autoconstruction, in this state-led modality, represented thus the spirit of progress and self-improvement of the poor. This idea is well articulated in an opinion column that appeared in 1966 in *La Nación*, the state-owned newspaper that, in practice, operated as the government's official propaganda. Entitled "Autoconstruction in Chile," the article starts by indicating that *el pueblo* (the people) might be used to receiving aid and assistance from paternalistic politicians. However, *el pueblo* "prefers to participate, through their own effort, in the solution to their problems."[26] The column goes on to say that both the formation of state-regulated housing cooperatives and autoconstruction "are the ideal form" through which "the State and the People associate with each other." It was precisely the establishment of such an association that initially led the state to acknowledge *pobladores* as agents that, under certain conditions, were capable of political intervention in the public sphere. Two events help to illustrate this *pobladores*-state relationship.

The first has President Frei Montalva as the main player. When inaugurating the Población Irene Frei in Conchalí—a working-class municipality on the north side of Santiago—in 1965, the head of the state said to the *pobladores*: "You made these houses by yourselves, so don't thank me for them."[27] In addition, Frei Montalva made another statement, one as provocative as it was unachievable: "I assure you that *poblaciones callampas* will be gone by the end of my government." Making such a promise, though far from fulfilled, reveals the nature of Frei Montalva's regime and the patronizing relationship it established with *el pueblo*—one in which, while *pobladores* were imagined as lacking the capacity to act politically in their own right, they were also often praised as active citizens who were virtuously engaged in urban politics through their involvement in state programs. Frei Montalva's speech act was directly addressed to lower-income inhabitants in a *población*, which suggests that, for the president, there was a direct link between himself and the urban poor or, in other words, between the state and those who, just a couple of years prior, public opinion had deemed to be living "like animals." His speech can thus be understood as a form of interpellation by means of which the state acknowledged individuals as responsibilized citizens by assigning them the capacity to act politically as members of a nation. In this case, such a ritual of ideological recognition—borrowing Althusser's words—had to do with the identification of the urban poor as a particular kind of subject: as city-making *pobladores*. But Frei Montalva's interpellation was framed by a broader ideological approach to urban poverty greatly influenced by the theory of marginality. As I discuss fully in chapter 2, DESAL's theory of marginality—the theoretical perspective that backed Frei Monatlava's Program of Popular Promotion—understood *pobladores* as a marginal population that, to become civilized citizens, had to be integrated into state programs. Frei Montalva's declaration, in that sense, was not only aimed at obtaining the *pobladores'* support and mobilizing them toward the government's own partisan objectives. It also sought to endow prospective homeowners with the capacity to look at themselves as subjects who had acquired a certain moral status through their participation in state-led autoconstruction processes.

The state's interpellation of the poor as *pobladores* is also revealed in another 1965 event, one in which the Christian Democratic congressman Sergio Fernández is the central figure. After holding a meeting with hundreds of housing activists and other prominent Christian Democratic politicians such as Patricio Aylwin, Fernández said to the press, "*Pobladores* are currently the most active element of the working classes in Chile."[28] Fernández's declaration is not surprising if we consider that, while the government he supported had established a patronizing relationship with the poor, the party he represented had the urban poor as its main political base (Garcés 2002). Nonetheless, it is indicative that he identified *pobladores* as *the* "most active" popular group, because such recognition accounts for the consolidation of new forms of working-class agencies developed fundamentally through urban struggles.

Both Frei Montalva's and Fernández's statements demonstrate that the *pobladores* of the mid-1960s, envisioned as autoconstructors, had become relevant political actors by engaging in ritualized performances of city making. It is in this context that the category *poblador* underwent significant transformations as its performative dimension began to prevail over the constative one. The result of this "performative shift"—adapting Yurchak's (2005, 24) terminology—was that, while the constative dimension of the word *poblador* changed from its original meaning, the performative dimension allowed for the formation of new political subjectivities. In being referred to as *pobladores*, housing activists developed unprecedented political capacities. But the emergence of this political subjectivity would not be completed through state-led autoconstruction alone. The state's interpellation of the urban poor as city-making *pobladores* would have unexpected performative effects regarding the constitution of a subjectivity whose political claims exceeded those anticipated by Frei Montalva's populist government. The formation of *pobladores* as political subjects would be fully achieved once they took on a decisive role in the implementation of radical agendas for social change.

The Rise of Campamentos

Between the mid-1960s and the early 1970s *pobladores* executed large-scale land occupations not only to demand urban land but also to develop innovative political tactics aimed at creating popular power. The spread of highly politicized *tomas de terreno* was accompanied by a change in the language utilized to account for them. Since then, the term *campamento* (encampment) has become increasingly used to refer to squatter settlements, coinciding with the progressive withdrawal of the word *callampas*. If the latter concept stood for the most severe expression of urban marginality, the former symbolized the *pobladores'* political radicalization and their committed participation in broader processes of social transformation. In chapter 2, I argued that the autoconstruction of the Población La Victoria in the 1950s was crucial for the development of the Chilean housing movement, as it played a key role in the consolidation of *pobladores* as relevant political actors. To achieve this, the residents of this neighborhood disputed common views of shantytowns by asserting that La Victoria was not a *población callampa* and that its residents, on account of their organizing capacities, deserved dignity and respect. In an editorial column in *La Voz de La Victoria*, the official propaganda paper for the *campamento*, the residents said: "Our *campamento* is an erupting volcano. The desire and enthusiasm of all of those who live in Chile's most combative *población* is huge. We want to demonstrate to the public across the American continent that we are not a *población 'callampa'* and that we neither tolerate nor will tolerate such a humiliating term. We deserve respect from every citizen without exception, because we have been an example for overcoming poverty that we wish other working-class *poblaciones* could imitate."[29]

Campamento La Victoria opened up an entire realm of action for *pobladores*. From that point, housing activists began to conceive of squatter settlement as a strategy for the configuration of a struggle "larger than a house" (Cortés 2013). Between 1964 and 1973—the period in which the *pobladores'* mobilizations became more politically significant—there appeared more than four hundred *campamentos* in Santiago (Cofré 2011). What were the distinctive elements of these squatter settlements? What kinds of performative actions did *pobladores* take when setting up a *campamento*? Generally, land seizures occurred overnight and followed a series of ritualized events. First and fore-most, organized housing assemblies—which could include as many as one thousand or two thousand families—searched in advance for empty public or private lots. Once the preferred lots had been identified, they usually got ac-cess to them swiftly, by breaking down the fences and setting up their provi-sional tents and *mediaguas* (shacks). The squatters, who often arrived by truck, cart, or wagon, carried their belongings and Chilean flags. Similar to an act of colonization, the flags were immediately planted on the territory in which they hoped to build their neighborhood. The events surrounding the building of the Campamento Herminda de La Victoria in 1967 followed this series of ritualized practices. Drawing on an epic narrative, the communist newspaper *El Siglo* described the appearance of the squatter settlement in this way: "A for-est of Chilean flags emerged in the dense fog that covered yesterday's dawn in the capital city. . . . We witnessed the rise of a four thousand-person *población* in just fifteen minutes."[30]

In addition to physically seizing a vacant lot, the *pobladores* would perform another crucial act: they would give the new *campamento* a name. The name assigned to the emerging squatter settlement was commonly based on the date of the occupation; political slogans; a living politician, generally leftist, who supported the *pobladores'* demands; a prominent Marxist figure (e.g., artists, intellectuals); historical events related to revolutionary struggles; or simply the imagination of the squatters who, through the name, sought to display their spirit of struggle.[31] What usually came next is no surprise: police repression seeking to evict the squatters, popular resistance to the evictions, and the ar-rival—sometimes immediately after the seizure—of mostly left-wing politi-cians, who helped the *pobladores* to negotiate with state authorities their per-manence on the occupied land. Once the *pobladores* were granted permission to remain, the building of the *campamento* began, a process in which it was common to see university students, Catholic priests, and a variety of volunteers from other civil-society organizations collaborating.

In a 1972 album titled *La población* (1972), the Chilean folk singer Víctor Jara brilliantly depicted the set of practices and imaginaries surrounding the rise of *campamentos*.[32] Among other elements, Jara sings about the rigorous organization of the *pobladores*; their sense of opportunity when seizing a plot of land; the risks that they faced as a result of the occupation; and, more impor-tantly, their views on a future full of promise for the squatters. This last point is well formulated in the last song on the album, "March of the *Pobladores*":

Poblador, comrade *poblador*, we'll keep on moving forward until the end
Poblador, comrade *poblador*, for the kids, the fatherland, and the home,
Poblador, comrade *poblador*, now history is for you. For a house, a shelter,
and bread, we'll march all together into the future.[33]

The formation of *campamentos* was thus predicated on the execution of a series of standardized practices that, in addition to the state's interpellation discussed above, helped configure the *pobladores* subjectivities. In view of the formative character of ritualized social practices, the very autoconstruction of *campamentos* can be conceived of as an essential element for *pobladores* to be able to transform themselves into political subjects. In this sense, the building of *campamentos* on the outskirts of the city led to the consolidation of political agencies that, as Víctor Jara sang, endowed the urban poor with a new status which allowed them to deal with their own future, the state, and history.

Fearing Campamentos

The growing political importance of *pobladores* expressed through the spread of highly ideological and organized *campamentos*—especially during Salvador Allende's government—led to novel narratives of squatter settlements. For right-wing groups, *campamentos* operated like "concentration camps" in which "extreme left-wing elements" indoctrinated *pobladores*.[34] The conservative press began to draw on fear-based discourses to conceptualize squatter settlements. In this view, *pobladores* were seen as hopeless masses whose despair, while "clouding their view of what is correct and legal," might lead to the implementation of Marxist political projects.[35]

The right wing's fear of *campamentos* was both material and symbolic. In the material dimension, this fear was fundamentally associated with the threat to the right of private property that the increase of squatter settlements entailed. This idea led to the appearance of several editorials in newspapers such as *El Ilustrado* and *El Mercurio* discussing the political risks involved in allowing squatters to remain on the occupied lands. *Campamentos*, some newspapers said, might even become the staging ground for the development of some forms of "urban guerrilla" warfare.[36] State repression was thus understood as inevitable, in order to avoid the spread of *campamentos*. However, repression had to be directed toward the "intellectual authors," namely, leftist parties, rather than the "material executors." For conservative groups, *pobladores* were merely victims of extremism, just like the landlords whose right to property had been violated.[37]

The fear of squatter settlements also involved a symbolic dimension related to the criticism of two founding practices through which, as I have shown, *pobladores* autoconstructed *campamentos*: the planting of Chilean flags on the seized land and the naming of the new neighborhood. Editorial opinions in conservative newspapers argued that these performative acts represented both the abuse of Chile's national emblems and the incorporation of foreign figures that did not stand for national values. Both actions were thus understood as a menace to national unity, as expressed in these two editorials:

> Why do we venerate our national flag? Because it symbolizes the unity of our nation. . . . These days we have seen how the Communist Party has distributed hundreds of Chilean flags among *pobladores* who were instigated to invade a private lot in the municipality of La Granja. . . . It is time to take measures aimed at preventing demagogy and divisive politicians from continuing to use a respectable emblem that belongs to and symbolizes our entire nationality.[38]

> We are going through a period of "Che Guevara," "Mao Tse-tung," "Fidel Castro," "Camilo Torres" [names of *campamentos*], which expresses an anti-Chilean deviationism that ignores our values. . . . [Some radical groups] encourage squatters to seize an empty lot, which starts by planting a Chilean flag as a sign of respectability with regards to their arbitrariness. There, the Chilean flag surely waves with less pride and historicity than at the Morro de Arica or La Concepción, as it later gets lost amid all the red flags.[39]

The latter editorial was accompanied by a drawing of a shack with a Chilean and a Soviet flag (fig. 3), a symbolic representation of what, for some groups, was happening in Santiago's working-class neighborhoods: the increasing penetration of external, Marxist agendas aimed at promoting class struggles and subverting Chile's constitutional order. For the right-wing media, the *pobladores'* performative acts, in being used as an "instrument" for the left, were becoming increasingly dangerous. Housing activists' actions were leading to the emergence of new, revolutionary forms of social life, materialized through the rise of "Marxist" *campamentos*. In these autoconstructed spaces, they would question both the political-juridical and ideological principles of the bourgeois society by fighting against the right to private property and the unity of the nation.

The heavy symbolism of the two recently described performative acts—the naming of *campamentos* and the "misuse" of the Chilean flag—became even more evident when the dictator Augusto Pinochet came to power in 1973.

FIGURE 3. The "misuse" of the Chilean flag in *campamentos*. Source: *Tribuna*, July 19, 1971, 4.

Understanding the importance of disputing the symbols displayed by radicalized *pobladores*, the military regime changed the names of the *campamentos* right after Pinochet took office. Nine days after the coup on September 11, 1973, the war admiral Jorge Paredes said in Concepción—the second-largest city in the country—that the renaming of the *campamentos* sought to "restore the patriotic values of our nation . . . [since] there are foreign-looking denominations related to names of individuals who have contributed nothing to our fatherland."[40] At the same time, the dictatorship stopped referring to squatter settlements as *campamentos* and began calling them *poblaciones*, a term that seemed to be less ideologically loaded.[41]

The names used to rechristen the *campamentos* were mostly based on well-known characters from Chile's history, names of battles, or made-up phrases that represented "truly patriotic" ideals that were less harmful to national unity.

For example, a Santiago *campamento* called Lenin was renamed Población Yungay to commemorate an 1836 battle in which Chile confronted the Perú-Bolivia Confederation. The Campamento Unidad Popular was denominated Población Los Copihues, in honor of the national flower of Chile. The Campamento Angela Davis was named Población Héroes de la Concepción, to memorialize the death of seventy-seven young soldiers who died during the War of the Pacific in 1882. Likewise, the Campamento Ho Chi Minh, "one of the most controversial of Santiago's *campamentos* during the past regime," was rechristened simply as Villa San Luis de Las Condes.[42] For the dictatorship, the erasure of Salvador Allende's legacy had to do not only with the physical decimation of its supporters but also with the destruction of the symbolism that his "Chilean road to socialism" had been built on. This led Pinochet's military regime to regard *pobladores*, at least in public, not as transformative subjectivities but as defenseless, poor residents who, in General Óscar Bonilla's words, had been deceived and politically exploited by previous "demagogic" governments.[43] The military regime's actions toward the urban poor were based thus on considering them as marginal dwellers incapable of deliberating on their own behalf. This, of course, entailed severe repression against them.

Pobladores as Allegados

As explained in chapter 2, three phenomena framed the *pobladores'* actions during Pinochet's dictatorship: dramatic repression of land occupations; the implementation of a new, subsidy-based housing policy; and the execution of large-scale slum eradication programs (*erradicaciones*), through which *campamentos* located in central areas were displaced to the urban peripheries. As people in need of housing were no longer able to access land through illegal occupations, they began to live predominantly as *allegados*. In simple terms, *allegados* were those working-class families without a home of their own, living in relatives' houses. *Allegados* were already the subject of public discourse in the mid-twentieth century. In the 1950s and 1960s, the media frequently talked about prospective homeowners who, incapable of accessing housing, were forced to live with their parents, mostly in overcrowded conditions.[44] However, it was during the 1980s that this residential situation drew the attention of scholars, as "a never-before-seen magnitude" (Chateau and Pozo 1987, 37) of over 152,000 families lived as *allegados*.

In sociological terms, Andrés Necochea (1987) defined *allegados* as young poor families residing in any of the following four conditions: as an economically dependent household sharing a house with another family; as an economically independent household living in another family's home; as a household that, being granted a portion of land, was dwelling in the backyard of a residential property; and as a family renting a room or a small housing unit within a residential property. In chapter 6, I discuss extensively how the domestic life of *allegados* is crucial to understanding the struggles for housing in neoliberal Chile. For now, I want to mention that it was precisely the reconfiguration of poor residents' subjectivity as *allegados* that led social scientists to conceive of the term *poblador* exclusively as a social identity category rather than a political one.[45] The almost total disappearance of ritualized, city-making practices that had enabled the formation of *pobladores* as autoconstructors resulted in a sustained lack of interest in examining the type of agency embedded in the signifier *poblador*. Starting in the 1980s, intellectuals increasingly began to refer to *pobladores* as any sort of disadvantaged residents rather than political agents. This was especially true when discussing the growing incapacity of the urban poor to carry out autoconstruction processes. *Pobladores*, accordingly, began to be thought of less as producers of space and more as marginalized inhabitants.

An early example of this approach can be found in the book *Espacio y poder: Los pobladores* ("Space and Power: The *Pobladores*"), a compilation of articles edited by Hernán Pozo (1987). In the preface, the author states that prior to the dictatorship, *pobladores* were defined by their work, their place of residence, their social relations, their expectations, and their ideas of progress. However, the military regime blocked *pobladores'* hopes, wishes, and projects, relegating them to a condition of being characterized as poor residents. "In this new scenario," Pozo (1987, 10) argued, "the *poblador* becomes a man who inhabits a specific place." The removal of the productive character of the *pobladores'* practices is also evident in the first part of the book, written by Jorge Chateau along with Hernán Pozo. In their attempt to sociologically identify the main features of *pobladores*, the authors offered an operational definition built upon the common understanding of the term. In particular, they conceptualized *pobladores* as all the poor residents who lived, either as homeowners or *allegados*, in any of the following places: squatter settlements, *poblaciones* resulting from Frei Montalva's Operation Site, or any other housing projects oriented toward solving the housing crisis (Chateau and Pozo 1987, 23).

The understanding of *pobladores* as poor dwellers rather than political agents appears to be dominant in most academic work during this period. Most social scientists analyzing the urban poor in neoliberal Chile systematically overlook the question of how *pobladores* can rearticulate their agency in a context in which land occupations are no longer utilized. This theoretical disregard can be seen, for instance, in the work examining the depoliticization of the urban poor after the return to democracy (Paley 2001) or the ways the urban poor make sense of and embody past state violence and current social welfare arrangements in neoliberal Chile (Han 2012). When ethnographically problematizing the notion of *poblador*, scholars look back to the past to find traces of a subject who had acquired a political character through land seizures, autoconstruction, and, more generally, large-scale housing movements. However, they say little about how such a political subjectivity could be reformulated once the mass housing rights movements had vanished. By assuming that being a *poblador* is simply a matter of residing in a *población*, they conceive of *pobladores* as a static social category resulting from the act of inhabiting rather than an agency that has yet to be reformulated. For these scholars, *pobladores* inhabit the city rather than make it. During the 1990s and early 2000s, this approach brought about the depoliticization of the term *poblador*, and the spread of a particular understanding of the term that took the concept for granted. Scholars barely accounted for the mechanisms through which *pobladores* develop their political agencies as *allegados* demanding urban rights. However, new generations of activists developed their own housing movements by participating in neoliberal housing programs, which has entailed the reconfiguration of their subjectivity as political agents.

New *Pobladores*, New Subjects

As demonstrated in chapter 2, housing protests forcefully reemerged in Santiago in the mid-2000s. Families in need of housing, by enrolling in state-regulated *allegados* committees, began to make new right-to-the-city demands, a process of remobilization that relied significantly on new generations of poor residents self-identifying as *pobladores*. This compels me to explore the practical and discursive mechanisms allowing for the formation of what, in a public statement released in 2011, the National Federation of Pobladores called "a new subject": "What do we seek? We seek to obtain dignified housing by struggling and organizing. We also seek to construct *un nuevo sujeto* [a new subject] who, through solidarity and dialogue, makes up a community capable of struggling for the right to the city and the building of a new neighborhood."

How can we understand the constitution of a working-class agency—one that public and academic discourses have referred to as *pobladores*—when its historical modes of subjectivation are absent? What are the main attributes of this agency, when it is no longer construed by autoconstructors, but by *allegados* enrolled in state programs? Through my ethnographic participation in housing assemblies, I witnessed a sort of linguistic rearticulation of the category *poblador*. It was striking to see that my interlocutors used the term *poblador* widely in their everyday lives as housing activists. They did so even though they had never autoconstructed their houses or participated in large-scale land occupations. However, they drew on the signifier *poblador* to reinterpret their role as *allegados* claiming housing rights in a neoliberal city. By recognizing and identifying themselves as *pobladores*, they made sense of their everyday experiences as a socially excluded population, endowed with the capacity to address the state using rights-based language. In the next chapter, I further examine the political implications involved in the rearticulation of the category *poblador*, which relates to a redefinition of the social understanding of rights and citizenship. For now, I focus on the discursive formulations through which the *allegados* I met considered themselves as *pobladores*. These narratives were built on two main elements. First was the consideration of *pobladores* as a unified form of subjectivity, which compelled my interlocutors to look to the past as both a source of symbolic power and a container of foundational events. In doing so, they were able to reclaim the legacy of the old *pobladores* movement while connecting present individual biographies to a history made collectively by past autoconstructors. Second was the development of effort-based discourses, through which they signified their condition as disadvantaged working-class inhabitants based on a moral framework. In doing so, they conceived of the category *poblador* as containing an ethical boundary that, while creating a cohesive type of identity, allowed them to distinguish between worthy and unworthy poor residents.

Looking to the Past through Land Seizures and Autoconstruction

The *pobladores* I encountered usually talked about the past. They did so to put their own struggle in a broader historical context and to make sense of their subjectivity as activists living and acting politically in neoliberal Chile. The militants of the Movimiento de Pobladores en Lucha, for instance, understood their protest movement as a contemporary expression of a long-term struggle for the right to live with dignity.[46] This organization construed the *pobladores* movement as composed of a number of historically situated mobilizations, such as the squatters' protests of the mid-twentieth century, or their own involvement in state-regulated housing assemblies. Affirming the historical continuity of the housing struggles enabled my interlocutors to recognize themselves as heirs of a social movement and, as such, reclaim the agency anchored in the category *poblador* under new historical circumstances. At stake for them was to bring the performative force of the term *poblador* into the present as a way to form themselves as political subjectivities. The question, in other words, was how to become *pobladores* in practice, when the urban poor no longer obtained housing through large-scale autoconstruction processes but through their involvement in subsidy-based housing programs.

Here is where the symbolic power of land seizures emerged as a central element to the political discourses and practices of the *allegados*. They often referred to land occupations as the most concrete realization of the transformative capacity of *pobladores*. This fact made itself clear when the people I met talked about the past in ways like "My parents participated in a land occupation and founded this *población*" or "My parents made this house on their own." For them, land seizures represented the materialization of a set of performative actions that provided low-income residents with a place to live, social recognition, and a sense of dignity.

These narratives related to *tomas de terrenos* were accompanied by the actual execution of symbolic, small-scale takeovers of state-owned buildings, public spaces, riverbanks, and even empty lots (fig. 4). In these actions, the *allegados*—just like the mid-twentieth century *pobladores*—carried Chilean flags, sang the national anthem, and gave the occupation a name. However, they did not consider these seizures as a means to demand the right to autoconstruction. They construed these performative acts as a way to make their demands more visible when they felt that the authorities were not paying enough attention to their requests. In this sense, my interlocutors saw mass land takeovers—such as those of the past—primarily as a linguistic resource to refer back to a heroic past rather than as an actual means to becoming homeowners.

This, however, does not mean that implementing an occupation was not crucial for their performances as urban activists. For them, participating in small-scale land seizures served as a form of political action enabling new generations of housing activists to imagine a symbolic link between past and present *pobladores*. In thinking of *tomas*—regardless of their scale—as one of the defining political strategies of *pobladores*, the urban activists conceived of themselves as performers of the "same" kind of practices that their parents and grandparents participated in several decades ago. The magnitude of the

FIGURE 4. Takeover of Río Mapocho's riverbank in downtown Santiago in 2014. The Campamento Mapocho, as the National Federation of Pobladores (FENAPO) called this occupation, lasted seventy-four days, from June 11 to August 23. Credit: Eugenia Paz.

occupation, the number of people involved in it, the historical circumstances in which it is realized, and even the environment and the specific places occupied might certainly vary. But the doers of these actions are, from my interlocutors' perspective, fundamentally "the same." Either during Salvador Allende's presidency in the early 1970s or during Sebastián Piñera's right-wing government in the early 2010s, the participant in a *toma* was a poor individual constituted as a *poblador*.

Sometimes, the widespread presence of romanticized discourses regarding past land seizures brought about a disjunction between the imagined capacities to perform an occupation successfully and the actual possibilities to carry it out effectively. I noticed this on November 30, 2013, when I attended an assembly of the Santiago branch of the National Federation of Pobladores (FENAPO). The meeting involved representatives of a dozen *comités de allegados* who discussed strategies to get the government to respond to the particular demands of each group. The main points of discussion were the creation of a public bank of urban land to facilitate the building of social housing projects in central areas, the allocation of subsidies for those families who had not yet received them, and the prompt construction of those housing projects already approved by the state. During the debate, Luciano, a construction worker in his fifties, argued passionately that the only way to be heard was to take over a vacant lot "like in the 1960s." The assembly rejected Luciano's proposal after one of the FENAPO spokespersons said, "*Tomas* are a means to an end, not an end in themselves," which was simply understood as "We don't have the capacity to lead any *tomas* like in the past." Some months later, when Luciano and I were having a more personal conversation, he would insist on this idea: "I'm sick of coming to meetings every week and marching to the Ministry of Housing and Urbanism once in a while. That is not working at all. Do you know what I would do? I would get all the FENAPO housing assemblies together and go take over the Sauzal [an empty lot located in Peñalolén]. If we do that, the government would surely pay attention to us."

Luciano was the leader of a housing organization that had never conducted a land occupation. Nonetheless, other *pobladores* successfully conducted small-scale *tomas de terrenos*. Months before I began to participate in July 2013 in the Comité de Allegados Don Bosco, the members of this housing assembly had illegally occupied a state-owned vacant lot in the municipality of La Florida, in particular on the corner of Departamental and Tobalaba Avenues. They did so to request that the government provide them with additional subsidies, needed to purchase the occupied land and have a social housing project built there. This *toma* was maintained on a daily basis by three families who began to live there as squatters. They did not expect to autoconstruct their houses. Rather, they wanted to put pressure on the government by, in their words, making visible the "undignified living conditions that President Piñera offers to the poor." The takeover lasted nine months, ending in December 2013. That month the government, in addition to promising to give the Don Bosco committee extra subsidies to pay for the land, hired a private construction company to implement the soil treatment required for the building of the social housing project.[47] The Don Bosco *allegados* saw this occupation as a triumph. It helped them get more resources while allowing them to show the public that—quoting Ernesto, a Don Bosco leader—"the *pobladores* are still a powerful social actor."

Both Luciano's opinions and Don Bosco's actions reveal the symbolic character of *tomas* among new generations of *pobladores*. Whether uttered in discourse or realized in practice, land occupations were imagined not only as a possible set of actions when it comes to formulating strategies for protests and mobilizations, but also as a means to bring the past into the present. This enabled contemporary housing activists to understand their political struggle as deeply attached to urban movements of the past and, in doing so, reclaim the legacy of the old *movimiento de pobladores*. It was only when my interlocutors identified themselves as heirs of such a legacy that they could be recognized as *pobladores* entitled to urban rights.

The people I met also looked to the past by configuring social imaginaries of autoconstruction. The reference to autoconstruction was associated particularly with an understanding of *pobladores* as a productive agency capable of engaging in processes of city making. The rise of these autoconstruction-based discourses surprised me, as none of my interlocutors had ever taken part in collective homebuilding processes. This modality of referring back to the past differed from that linked to land occupations discussed above, as the symbolic power of the latter relied on the realization of small-scale *tomas*. In contrast, the *allegados'* references to autoconstruction were essentially based on family and neighborhood memories, which they brought into the present in the form of idealized narratives of the old *pobladores* movement. Through these recollections, they reflected on past *pobladores* as city makers who were able to transform both the city's peripheries and their own lives.

I met María through Ernesto, her partner. María, a woman in her forties who was born and raised in the old Campamento Nueva La Habana, lived most of her life as an *allegada*. She was one of the 160 prospective homeowners who in 2009 obtained subsidized housing in the Villa Rodrigo Carranza through participation in the Don Bosco assembly. Until then, she and her three children had lived in her parents' home with her siblings, nephews, and nieces. More than twelve people lived together in one residential property. In 2014, I went to María's own home to discuss her longing to remain in her neighborhood, which had ultimately encouraged her and others to create a *comité de allegados* and struggle for the right to stay put. During our conversation, she, noticeably touched, said: "My dad had to look for rubble, sand, bricks. . . . [W]hen the *campamento* was formed everybody began to build their houses. . . . He made our house all by himself. One has to get a house where one was born; for our parents, because they struggled [for us]."

Others shared similar experiences with me. José, an *allegado* who lived with his partner at her mother's house, proudly told me that his father had worked on the construction of what would later become the Población Nueva La Habana in the early 1970s (see chapter 2). "My dad made our house," he said right after I asked him about the formation of the *población*. "These houses were way better than the ones the government gives to the poor now," added Ángela, José's partner. "How do you know that?" I replied. While turning to her partner, she said, "earthquakes have not done any damage to them." Earthquakes are a natural phenomenon that most Chileans use as an indicator to measure the quality of any construction. Then, José went on: "I think that the poor lived better in 1970s, because at least everybody worked together for the community."

These *pobladores* made sense of autoconstruction primarily as a recollection of family events in which their relatives worked privately on the construction of a house. But they also understood autoconstruction as attached to a larger, collective phenomenon: the making of a *población*. At the very outset of that process, quoting María, "everybody began to build their houses," which compels us to consider autoconstruction processes less as an individual fabrication of *a* house, and more as a social production of space materialized through the building of a neighborhood. For the people I met, autoconstruction, though not personally practiced, functioned as a sort of foundational act through which they connected their personal biographies to historically grounded neighborhood memories. In being evoked through family narratives, such performative actions serve as set of ideal, or even mythical events, enabling present *pobladores* to bring individual experiences into a collective history. Collective memories of autoconstruction have thus a "symbolic efficacy"—adapting Lévi-Strauss's (1963) classic work on the shamanistic cure—as they provide the activists with a set of symbols by means of which their everyday experiences can be expressed in terms of struggle, agency, and resistance. This makes it possible to understand the *pobladores'* political capacities as political identity linked to the processes of city making; an agency that could be reclaimed even by those who had not participated directly in autoconstructing the city.

Becoming Pobladores

A second mechanism the *allegados* I met used in order to conceptualize themselves as *pobladores* related to the creation of effort-based narratives through which they differentiated who is—and, accordingly, who is not—to be considered a *poblador*. If the previous discursive formulations were based on a retrospective look at the old housing mobilizations, the effort-based narratives entailed the generation of moral evaluations of present-day events. It is precisely through these moral appraisals that my interlocutors, while signifying their living condition as socially excluded inhabitants, developed everyday ethical procedures to constitute themselves as *pobladores*. They did so by articulating discourses through which they spoke about themselves, as a means to ethically construct the self (see Foucault 2005). As a result, they created distinctions based on moral frameworks, which helped them to consolidate an understanding of the category *poblador* as referring to a consistent type of political subjectivity.

At the beginning of this chapter, I explained that after interviewing a public servant, I became increasingly interested in asking housing activists about their understanding of the word *poblador*. One of the most common answers I got was this: "*Pobladores* are all of us." Initially, I construed such a rough definition as describing a form of universalizing, territory-based membership that would include everybody living in a *población*. Being a *poblador*, I thought, was like being a Chilean, a member of a political community framed by neighborhood or national borders to which one has emotional ties. But later I was forced to change my thinking dramatically. As my ethnographic work progressed, I realized that this "all of us" was restricted to the people who, whether involved in the struggle for housing or not, were socially recognized as hardworking individuals committed to their families and to the community.

On a warm day in late December 2013, Ernesto introduced me to Efraín—a member of the Don Bosco *allegados* committee—at a barbecue we had at his place. Around 4:00 p.m., after having eaten enough, the three of us went to walk around the empty lot that the housing assembly had taken over in March. The occupation had ended just three weeks earlier, in early December, right before a private construction company came in to treat the soil prior to the building of the public housing units. While wandering around the area, Efraín, who at that time was employed as a worker on the construction site, complained constantly about his employers: "This company sucks. It's getting really warm these days and they don't provide us with sunscreen. They don't even give us the right materials to do our job. The engineers have no idea what they're doing," he said. Perceiving his friend's mood, Ernesto laughed and, directing his gaze toward me, said: "This guy is a *poblador-poblador*," utilizing a modality of speaking frequently used by Chileans in which the same word is repeated to make a statement more categorical. He added, "He doesn't philosophize about anything; he just tries to make a living day to day here in the *población*." After hearing Ernesto's comment, I reformulated my initial premise. *Poblador*, I said to myself, seems to be less an essence, than a condition developed through practices valued by the community, be it a housing assembly or a *población*. Later findings seemed to suggest that I was right. "I started to call myself *pobladora* after entering into the committee," a female activist once told me, after I had asked her about what it meant for her to be a *pobladora*.

This small, apparently fragmented discourse helped to redefine my ideas. Although the material condition necessary for *pobladores* to emerge is poverty—I concluded—not all the working-class residents are *pobladores*. The urban poor *become*, rather than just *are*, *pobladores*. With this significant distinction in my mind, I asked several *allegados* if my thoughts made any sense to them. Here are some fragments of a conversation on this topic that I had with Ángela in 2014:

> For me, *pobladores* are those who struggle for what they want. . . . I'm poor, but I'm struggling to have something better to get out of poverty.
>
> *So, who would be the poorest?*
>
> The poorest? They are people who don't want to work and want to be poor. . . . Extreme poverty is laziness. *Los pobres-pobres* [the poorest people] are lazy people.
>
> *You are saying that not all the poor . . .*
>
> [She interrupts me] No, no. There are *gente pobre-pobre* [very poor people] that want to be poor. . . . There are people who could have their houses beautifully arranged, but they still have them like when we got there [in the early 1970s].
>
> *So, they wouldn't be* pobladores?
>
> Well, maybe. . . . But there are *pobladores* who are struggling to have a house, to have something better. For example, there are *pobladores* in the committee because they want to have something better for themselves and for their children. We're not going to get rich, but we'll have a something worth having.

Ángela, just like the rest of my interlocutors, conceived of being a *poblador* as a condition acquired mainly through effort, struggle, and sacrifice. Despite considering herself poor, she made a distinction between "the poorest people" and the *pobladores*. Such a difference was not only material—expressed, for instance, in the ways people take care of their houses—but also moral. For Ángela, there were a clear difference between morally mediocre residents who "want to be poor" and self-sacrificing individuals who, instead, struggle daily to "get out of poverty." To make this moral distinction, Ángela—similar to Ernesto—repeated twice the word *poor*, as though such a repetition would let me know clearly, without ambiguity, on which side of the equation she was.

Both Ernesto's and Ángela's affirmations reveal a conceptualization of *pobladores* that lays in the recognition of "effort" as the main attribute of their subjectivity. These effort-based narratives enabled them to identify two classes of urban poor: the *pobres-pobres* (extremely poor people) and the *pobres pobladores* (poor *pobladores*). In their view, *pobres-pobres* are those dependent, "lazy," lower-income residents who—as many people told me—"want everything for free." *Pobres pobladores*, in contrast, are those hardworking, responsibilized, and self-sufficient residents, who struggle to improve their living conditions. For my interlocutors, the differentiation between *pobre-pobre* and *pobre poblador* operated as a discursive formulation allowing them to signify their everyday experiences in ethical terms. *Pobre-pobres*, as roughly defined by my interlocutors, might not even exist. However, their representation as subjects whose moral values are opposed to those of the *pobladores*, allowed them to consider themselves as deserving dignity on the basis of the efforts they make to maintain and improve their everyday life.

How the very idea of dignity became a key element in the political discourse of *allegados* is the focus of chapter 6. For now, I want to highlight that, for the *allegados* I met, the set of moral values and attitudes attached to the category of *poblador* functioned as a matrix of morally acceptable practices, by means of which they constituted their subjectivity as political agents. This form of understanding *pobladores* has important ethical and political implications. By affirming their identity as ethico-political subjects endowed with dignity, housing activists construe themselves as capable of demanding rights from the state. This fosters what I call "politics of effort," an urban formulation of citizenship predicated on narratives of personal and collective effort, which new generations of *pobladores* draw on in order to become citizen city makers. I discuss this politics of effort in detail in the next chapter.

5 Politics of Effort

Urban Formulations of Citizenship

In the previous chapters, I showed that Chile's subsidy-based housing policies have been paradoxical for the poor. Although these policies helped reduce the housing shortage by allowing for the mass building of housing units—especially in the 1990s—they forced low-income families to move to the peripheries in order to become homeowners. The exclusionary nature of the subsidy-based policies led to the reconfiguration of the *pobladores'* protests. Joined together in state-regulated housing assemblies (*comités de allegados*), new generations of housing activists began to reframe their struggles on the basis of a new right-to-the-city language, manifested in what the National Federation of Pobladores (FENAPO) referred to as a territorial demand. As I explained in detail in chapter 3, my interlocutors conceptualized this demand as the right to become homeowners in their municipalities of origin or, in other words, as their "right to stay put."[1]

This chapter analyzes the *pobladores'* struggles for territorial rights by showing that these claims reveal not only a reframing of the right to housing but also a broader reformulation of their imaginaries of citizenship. This reconceptualization is directly related to the effort-based narratives through which, as argued in the previous chapter, members of housing organizations signified their social experiences as working-class residents. If in chapter 4 I accounted primarily for the moral narratives enabling urban activists to imagine themselves as *pobladores* deserving dignity and recognition, in this chapter I focus on how they consider themselves as *pobladores* deserving of rights by making use of effort-related discursive formulations. In that sense, I discuss how *pobla-dores'* right to stay put allows us to reflect on the rise of new forms of citizenship through which my interlocutors, by conceiving of themselves as responsibilized and committed residents of the city, constituted new criteria for the distribu-tion of rights and political membership.

The activists' self-understanding as subjects entitled to rights rested on what I call politics of effort. This concept refers to a system of rights distribution grounded on narratives of personal and collective effort through which the ur-ban poor legitimize their political membership and, as a result, their capacity to demand rights (e.g., to housing, to the city, to stay put). For my interlocutors, the politics of effort operated as an assemblage of political and moral obliga-tions by individuals to the community—materialized in specific technologies of control and accountability—by means of which they defined who has the right to have rights within the housing assembly. I argue that this politics of effort reveals an "urban" type of citizenship, one in which residency becomes a key criterion of political membership.[2] The concept of contribution is crucial to un-derstanding this residency-based form of citizenship. Poor residents, Holston (2008) argues, tend to legitimize their demands for rights on the basis of the contribution that they make to the city through autoconstruction, tax paying, and consumption (on the role of contributions, see Skrabut 2018). The *pobla-dores* I encountered articulated their demands for homeownership precisely by seeing themselves as hardworking city makers who contribute to the reproduc-tion of everyday life in the city. Similar to what Lazar (2013, 114) describes in the case of union activists in Argentina, the type of citizenship that my interlocu-tors developed relied on the creation of specific forms of self-making based on the "encompassment of the individual by the collectivity." Thus, the politics of effort helped them to configure an idea of citizenship in which the capacity to demand rights was seen as dependent on individual commitments to the col-lective *lucha* (struggle) for housing.

Understanding *pobladores'* politics of effort as a kind of urban citizenship allows us to examine the impact of urban movements on the redefinition of the ways social agents interpret the system for the distribution of rights that results from the national model of citizenship. In this chapter, I do not argue that the rise of forms of citizenship based on residency entails the undermin-ing of political allegiances based on nationality; nor do I imply that the urban poor in Chile disregard the nation as the primary political community. *Pobla-dores'* identification with the nation is, in fact, key to understanding how they have constituted their subjectivity as working-class political agents. As I argue in chapter 4, in the mid-twentieth century they used largely national symbols such as the Chilean flag when conducting mass land occupations, actions that I understand as performative practices of city making that transformed the poor into political subjectivities. During my fieldwork, I also observed urban activists flying Chilean flags, wearing the national soccer team jerseys, and proudly singing the national anthem at marches and street demonstrations, especially when protesting in front of state buildings. This suggests that the *pobladores* still construe the nation as a community to which they have political and emotional ties. However, their attachment to the nation has not prevented the development of other forms of political membership, which have even surpassed those defined by national citizenship. In this chapter, I show that, when it comes to justifying their rights claiming, my interlocutors conceive of the act of residing in the city—expressed through practices contributing to the reproduction of urban life—as the source of legitimacy for their demands. In doing so, they have configured particular criteria regarding the distribution of rights within their housing assemblies, based on a moral and political evaluation of the *esfuerzo* (effort) that prospective homeowners put into the struggle for housing. Their political practices were thus framed by both their understanding of the nation as an abstract, imagined political community—following Anderson's (1991) definition—and their view of housing assemblies as actual, concrete political communities to which they must contribute on a daily basis in order to be recognized as validated members.

In this chapter, I also discuss the extent to which housing struggles in neoliberal Chile have triggered the irruption of specific understandings of rights and citizenship, enabling the urban poor to rethink the terms of the relationship they establish with a neoliberal state. In this way, I disclose the transversal character of *pobladores'* mobilizations in Santiago: although these protests sought to question the material effects of subsidy-based housing policies, at the same time they enabled the formulation of ideas of citizenship and rights on the basis of a neoliberal ethics and rationality. Within this moral compass, my interlocutors construed themselves as individuals "who must actively construct a life through the practical choices they make about their conduct, and who must bear individual responsibility for the nature and consequences of their choices" (Rose 1999, 176). Thus, I attempt to shed light on the extent to which poor residents engaged in urban struggles have been able to advance agendas for social change while internalizing values and ideologies proper to the neoliberal project.

This chapter discusses primarily, though not exclusively, the Comité de Allegados Don Bosco's struggle for the right to stay put in the gentrifying municipality of La Florida. I particularly show how, in the context of increasing land prices, the Don Bosco members framed their territorial claims by recognizing themselves as "heirs" of the urban rights acquired by their parents and grandparents through autoconstruction. To delve into how contemporary *pobladores* articulate their right to stay put in different urban contexts, the chapter also presents the case of the Comité de Allegados Techo Ahora ("Roof Now"), a housing assembly formed in the municipality of La Pintana. Made up predominantly of working-class families, La Pintana has long been stigmatized as a dangerous municipality in the realm of public opinion.[3] Up until the 1980s, La Pintana was a semirural area, a fact that changed drastically with the arrival of a significant number of state-subsidized housing projects derived from the dictatorship's slum eradication policies.[4] Most of Techo Ahora's *allegados* were born and raised in state-subsidized neighborhoods built by real estate companies. However, La Pintana's *pobladores* also claimed territorial rights by considering themselves producers of their residential space. The inclusion of Techo Ahora sheds light on how *pobladores* have formulated right-to-stay-put narratives, even when they could not claim to be the "heirs" of autoconstructed city spaces. The case of Techo Ahora, in that sense, compels us to consider forms of city making in the absence of experiences with large-scale autoconstruction processes.

The ethnographic exploration of how Chilean *pobladores* struggled against displacement allows for reflections on the role of moral categories such as effort in the subjective understanding of citizenship and rights. In doing so, I problematize how these territorially situated resistances made the rise of a residency-based type of citizenship possible, through which my interlocutors have developed a particular conceptualization of themselves as rights bearers, one in which they legitimate themselves as citizen city makers on the basis of a neoliberal ethics.

Resisting Housing Affordability in La Florida

La Florida is a municipality located in southeastern Santiago that, according to the 2017 census, has a population of 366,916 people. Over the past five decades, the municipality has undergone significant transformations in terms of its social class composition, as a result of the changing role of the state in urban planning. In the 1960s and early 1970s, when La Florida was still part of Santiago's semirural periphery, *pobladores* carried out large-scale land takeovers. These actions were followed by autoconstruction processes in which poor families, under the technical supervision of the state, self-built neighborhoods such as Nuevo Amanecer, the site of my ethnographic fieldwork. In the 1980s, the implementation of neoliberal housing policies led to the construction of 23,906 subsidized housing units between 1983 and 1999, most of which are located in the western part of the municipality.[5] At almost the same time, real estate agents took advantage of the low price of urban land in the recently urbanized peripheral district to make private residential and commercial investments. In the following decades, La Florida's inhabitants witnessed the inauguration of two shopping malls—Plaza Vespucio Shopping Mall in 1990 and Florida Center in 2003—and the opening of a subway station—Bellavista de La Florida—in 1997. In addition, they observed the arrival of a middle- and upper-class population, which moved into the eastern area of the municipality, mainly in gated communities built into the gorgeous landscapes at the foothills of the Andes Mountains.[6]

Since then, La Florida—like other Santiago districts such as Peñalolén, Huechuraba, and Quilicura—has drawn the attention of scholars to the extent that it exposes the "colonization" of the poor periphery by the rich (Sabatini and Salcedo 2007). Following recent debates on social mixing and residential segregation, these studies have discussed to what degree the coexistence of lower- and upper-income families may bring about new forms of social integration or, to the contrary, processes of gentrification and displacement.[7] As a patent demonstration of this colonization, by the early 2000s, around 11 percent of La Florida's residents were characterized as "ABC1"—a concept used in Chilean public policy to refer to the richest 7 percent[8]—on the basis of data provided by the 2002 census (Asociación Chilena de Empresas de Investigación de Mercado 2008). Some estimates indicate that, in the following decade, the number of rich families residing in La Florida increased to such a degree that some planners argued that the area had consolidated its position as a municipality that upper-class households now perceive as attractive to live in (*La Tercera* 2015). This fact is depicted in map 4, which shows the dispersion of ABC1 households in Santiago between 2002 and 2013. La Florida appears, along with the municipalities in which the rich have traditionally resided,[9] as one of the municipalities in Santiago that congregates the highest number of bourgeois households.

These sociospatial changes have been accompanied by a sustained increase in land prices. Data provided by the urban economist Pablo Trivelli (*El Mercurio*

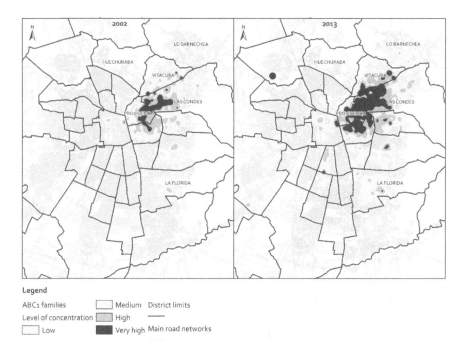

Legend

ABC1 families

Level of concentration

Low

Medium

High

Very high

District limits

Main road networks

MAP 4. Changes in the spatial distribution of ABC1 families in Santiago, 2002 and 2013. Source: Centro de Inteligencia Territorial-UAI, 2013. Credit: Juan Correa.

2012, B8–B9) shows that, between 1991 and 2011, the average land value in La Florida rose from 0.68 to 9.33 UF per square meter (US$24.60–$338 per square meter; table 4).[10] These numbers represent an increment of almost 1,400 percent, seven times higher than the increase observed in the Santiago metropolitan area during the same period (Trivelli 2011). By the early 2010s, subsidized housing projects for lower-income families were generally developed in areas where prices did not exceed 0.4 UF per square meter (Trivelli 2011). Thus, the notorious increase in land values in La Florida between 1991 and 2011 gave rise to a housing affordability problem for the 13 percent of the residents who, according to the National Survey of Socioeconomic Characterization, were poor in 2013. In fact, official data offered by La Florida City Hall indicates that, as of July 2015, 34,983 people were living as *allegados*, representing almost 10 percent of the total municipal population. It was precisely this phenomenon that triggered the Don Bosco assembly's struggle for the right to stay put.

TABLE 4. Increase in land
prices in La Florida.

Year	UF/m^2
1991	0.62
2001	5.43
2006	6.21
2011	9.33

Source: El Mercurio (2012).

"Because We Were Born and Raised Here, Here We're Going to Stay"

Why—I asked myself during the first stage of fieldwork—do the Don Bosco members want to keep living in La Florida so much, even willing to wait almost ten years for this possibility? Why don't they push for the development of housing projects elsewhere in Santiago? Their desire to continue to reside in La Florida, I soon realized, had a biographical explanation: most of them were children and grandchildren of those *pobladores* who, in the early 1970s, self-built the Población Nuevo Amanecer. Adriana, one of the social leaders of this organization, said:

> We noticed that our families, who had been displaced [*erradicadas*] to other municipalities, wanted to come back to La Florida . . . My sister received social housing in 1984 in [the southern district of] Puente Alto. . . . It was a two-floor, thirty-six square meters house that had a tiny patio, but they couldn't go out of the house because the neighborhood was really dangerous. . . . Those who were *más choros* (tougher) prevailed; it was like the law of the jungle. . . . We are struggling to stay here where everybody knows each other. . . . Elsewhere there is no sense of community that we have here in the Don Bosco, because those who formed this committee are all children of those who made this neighborhood.

The "sense of community" that Adriana talks about is rooted in the history of Nuevo Amanecer. On November 1, 1970, around two thousand families founded the Campamento Nueva La Habana under the leadership of the Movement of the Revolutionary Left (MIR).[11] After their arrival, Nueva La Habana's residents reached an agreement with the Ministry of Housing and Urbanism (MINVU) during Salvador Allende's government to allow the squatters

FIGURE 5. Autoconstruction in Campamento Nueva La Habana in the early 1970s. Source: Polumbaum and Polumbaum (1992, 30). Credit: Ted Polumbaum/ Newseum collection. Reprinted with permission.

themselves to work on the building of what would become the Población Nueva Habana. Thus, while the state provided construction materials, hundreds of *pobladores*—enrolled in a workers' front that united unemployed squatters—participated in the building of their houses (fig. 5).

The military coup of 1973 prevented the completion of the project. Augusto Pinochet's dictatorship assassinated several leaders of this *campamento*, changed its name to Nuevo Amanecer (New Dawn), and established a new and unfair system of housing distribution: those families who did not have the required amount of savings could not reside in the houses that they, as *pobladores*, had built themselves. Consequently, while some of them began to inhabit the *casas nuevas* (new houses) in 1975, many others continued to reside as squatters in what people started to call the *campamento viejo* (old squatter settlement). The "old squatter settlement," made up of almost four hundred residential properties, is now completely urbanized, and the former squatters have since acquired title deeds. By 2015, many of their children and grandchildren, however, still resided as *allegados* because of the lack of affordable housing available in La Florida. All of them claim their right to stay put as a way to

FIGURE 6. The Don Bosco *allegados* committee protesting in front of the Ministry of Housing and Urbanism. Credit: Photo by the author, October 2013.

preserve what Adriana calls "a sense of community." The slogan used in public protests by the Don Bosco assembly was telling in this regard: "Because we were born and raised here, here we're going to stay" (fig. 6).

Territorial Rights as a Legacy

For the *allegados* of the Don Bosco committee, their demand for the right to stay put in La Florida has a particular backdrop: the "invasion" of their municipality of origin by the rich. For the *pobladores*, this phenomenon, which occurred due to the growing interest of real estate companies to build housing developments for upper-class families, was central to understanding the housing affordability problem in La Florida. Clara, a member of the organization, conceptualized the arrival of wealthier neighbors in this way: "Here there are a lot of buildings for the rich, but there is no social housing. You know, *con plata baila el mono* [money talks]. [The rich] think that they are the owners of the municipality . . . the rich are invading this area. Private construction companies buy land to build houses that cost more than eighty million pesos [around US$100,820]. So, who is losing? We, the poor, are losing . . . Why don't I have the right to stay if I've lived all my life here? The rich weren't even born here!"

Many others expressed their frustrations regarding the "invasion" by the rich. They did so by arguing that upper-income families had no right to live in La Florida because they were outsiders. Such a complaint represented broader rights-based discourses developed by the new generations of housing activists who constituted their political language by taking the legacy of the old *pobladores* movement. They did this by recognizing themselves as endowed with rights to the city, earned by their ancestors through the autoconstruction process. This is well expressed in the case of María, who was born and raised in the Campamento Nueva La Habana. Back in the early 1970s, her parents participated actively in the construction of the Campamento Nueva La Habana, a fact that she considers the basis for her claim to rights. When I asked her to tell me her thoughts on Don Bosco's struggle, she responded: "I like it. We were born here so we have to stay here. . . . One has to get a house where one was born, for our parents, because they struggled [for us]. My mom tells me that people installed the poles for streetlights by themselves to have a better place to live. Back then people had neither running water nor electricity. . . . We have to stay here because Nueva La Habana is ours. This is what I think."

María's sense of belonging to Nueva La Habana/Nuevo Amanecer reveals something that can be theoretically understood using Lefebvre's (1996) concept of the right to the city: the idea that urban dwellers, as producers of space, are able to propose a political agenda reappropriating the city and its resources. Another ethnographic vignette illustrates how Don Bosco *pobladores* articulated their right to neighborhood spaces. In March 2013, the Metropolitan Service of Housing and Urbanism (SERVIU) told Don Bosco's members that the construction of Alto Tobalaba, a subsidized housing development that would be built in one of the vacant lots in Nuevo Amanecer, was not economically viable. To reverse this unfortunate decision, they took over the empty lot, located on the northeast part of the neighborhood, right on the corner of Departamental and Tobalaba Avenues. After months of intense negotiations, the SERVIU agreed to add more subsidies to the Alto Tobalaba housing project, which meant that 180 Don Bosco families could eventually have a house in that area.[12] The occupation ended in December 2013, when a construction company began to excavate the plot to initiate the process of soil treatment required for building the social housing units. This forced the three families that were living as squatters to search for a place to install their shacks. As part of that search, I accompanied them to talk to the neighborhood priest, to ask for space in a vacant area behind the chapel. He did not accept their request. "I'm not authorized to have people residing illegally on the property managed by the church," he said. In arguing with the priest, one of the women, Paula, said: "You can't do this to us, because you [the church] arrived [at the neighborhood] after the *pobladores*. The community gave you the chance to have a space here. It was not the other way around."

Both María and Paula legitimized this demand by considering themselves as producers of space, which results from the subjective acknowledgment of *pobladores* as residents who have played a crucial role in the urbanization of Santiago's peripheries. For them, the *pobladores'* performative actions have contributed to the improvement of the poor's living conditions, either by actually constructing the neighborhood or by demanding housing solutions within a municipality that has been "invaded" by the rich. The activists advocated for the right to exert full control over the fate of a part of the city that is deemed their own. This formulation of urban rights as detached from the actual making of homes and neighborhoods is analytically important, as academic work tends to relate the emergence of new social understandings of rights to the material action of homebuilding.[13] Housing movements in neoliberal Chile thus compel us to rethink the way this kind of legitimizing narrative comes into being. In the case examined here, autoconstruction functioned as an argument to demand rights, as it connected contemporary urban activists' personal biographies to historically grounded neighborhood memories. Home building, in being evoked through family narratives, served as a foundational discursive element that allowed Don Bosco members to bring individual experiences into a collective history, one built by their parents and relatives. As a result, Don Bosco *pobladores* thought of themselves as the legitimate heirs of the territorial rights acquired by their parents in 1970, which suggests that the subjective understanding of pobladores as city makers can actually emerge even when actual processes of home building are absent.

City Making without Autoconstruction

After spending six months in the Don Bosco *allegados* committee, I decided to examine another housing assembly to look into how housing activists who were not born in an autoconstructed neighborhood formulated their demands for the right to stay put. I wanted to explore how *pobladores* justified territorial claims over spaces that, in contrast to the Don Bosco members, neither their parents nor grandparents had helped build. In February 2014 I contacted the Agrupación Techo Ahora, a grassroots organization affiliated with FENAPO, situated in the municipality of La Pintana.

La Pintana is a peripheral municipality on the south side of Santiago, with a population of 177,335 residents, most of whom are working class. By the early 2010s, 55 percent were lower middle class, whereas 21 percent were poor (Cornejo 2012). The 2020 Social Priority Index—Índice de Prioridad Social, used by the Ministry of Social Development and Family to target social assistance to the poorest districts—categorized La Pintana as the most disadvantaged municipality in the Santiago metropolitan area.[14] The class composition of La Pintana is mainly explained by the large-scale evictions of squatter settlements that occurred during Pinochet's dictatorship, which resulted in the building of subsidized housing projects in the extreme periphery.[15] La Pintana received over fifteen thousand social housing units—mostly in the form of apartment blocks—in the 1980s (Tapia 2011). Since the early 1980s, the subsidy-based policies tended to locate social housing projects in southern areas of city, specifically in municipalities such as Puente Alto, San Bernardo, El Bosque, and La Granja. This trend continued throughout the following decades, especially in poor municipalities like La Pintana. In fact, more than 98 percent of the housing units in this municipality were publicly funded by the early 2010s (Cornejo 2012), making it one of the most homogeneous districts in socioeconomic terms. With respect to the housing shortage, official data provided by the Municipality of La Pintana reveal that 15,342 households were living as *allegados* in 2015, which represented 30 percent of all families residing in the municipality. This was the context in which the Techo Ahora housing assembly was formed.

The Techo Ahora Allegados Committee

Techo Ahora was created in 2010 in the Población San Ricardo to fight the lack of social housing in the municipality. According to Techo Ahora's activists, unlike the gentrifying district of La Florida, the housing affordability problem in La Pintana was not necessarily the result of an increase in land prices. Rather, quoting Laura—the president of the organization—it was the consequence of a "political decision" seeking to change the socioeconomic homogeneity that has characterized the area: "Local authorities don't want more poor people living here. They have told us that La Pintana is one of the most marginalized districts because it has too many poor families. There is land available for the construction of subsidized housing, but they [the municipality] want to develop middle-class-oriented housing projects."

Compared to the Don Bosco, Techo Ahora was a small housing assembly. By 2014, it had a total of forty-two families enrolled, most of whom lived in the Población San Ricardo. The rest resided in other neighborhoods of La Pintana, such as Santo Tomás and San Rafael. San Ricardo, Santo Tomás, and El Castillo, just to mention a few, were built in the 1980s as part of the new subsidy-based housing policies implemented during the dictatorship. Because of the peripheral condition of the areas in which these *poblaciones* are situated, they—and their residents—have long been subject to widespread stigmatizing discourses. In a case study of the Población El Castillo, the anthropologist Catalina Cornejo (2012) considers this territorial stigma as a form of symbolic violence, in which everyday suffering, in being misrepresented by stigmatizing social imaginaries, becomes invisible to the rest of society. In addition, the stigmatizing discourses are often internalized by La Pintana's residents, Cornejo argues. However, she notes that *pobladores* are able to develop positive feelings toward their *poblaciones*, resignifying the terms in which the territorial stigmatization occurs.

I observed such a resignification among Techo Ahora's members. Despite reproducing stigmatizing narratives by openly affirming that they lived in a "bad neighborhood," they demanded the right to stay put in La Pintana. Margarita, a woman in her thirties who lived in the Población Santo Tomás, admitted that, when applying for jobs, she avoided making it explicit that her house was located in La Pintana. "When I'm asked about where I live—she told me—I sometimes answer La Florida or La Granja." However, she wished to stay in La Pintana, a municipality that she and the rest of Techo Ahora's members were deeply attached to: "I'm used to living in La Pintana and I like it, although some people might not understand it. Some people say that La Pintana is a bad neighborhood. . . . Well, it may be true. There are actually bad people, but there are also good and hardworking people."

Memories of Exclusion and Displacement
How is it possible to account for the La Pintana *pobladores'* sense of belonging to severely stigmatized *poblaciones* that, in contrast to the case of La Florida, were not autoconstructed? For the people I met in La Pintana, family memories were framed not by events related to practices of home building but by

collective experiences of exclusion and displacement. Their recollections related fundamentally to the fact of being expelled to the periphery, as part of the dictatorship's squatter settlement eradication program known as *erradicaciones*. The *erradicaciones* implied that poor families, after applying individually for state subsidies, were assigned a housing unit without being able to decide either its location or the people they wanted to have as neighbors. Becoming homeowners on the outskirts of the city entailed a series of traumatic experiences, in which poor families had to both reaccommodate their life projects and remake their social networks.

"My neighbors came from different municipalities of Santiago, like Pudahuel, Peñalolén, Puente Alto, and Lo Espejo," explained Néstor, a Techo Ahora activist. "It was in the 1980s, in the midst of Pinochet's tyranny, when *pobladores* began to say '*me salió casa en . . .*' ['I received a house in . . .'] when they obtained housing," he added, when accounting for his family history. The phrase "I receive a house in . . ." speaks to the promising, though uncertain, process of becoming a homeowner in neoliberal Chile. This phrase is indicative of two main ideological principles of the market-oriented housing policies: the understanding of social housing as a commodity whose acquisition relies on the capacity of each family to both save money and apply for state subsidies privately, that is, on the urban poor's aptitude for behaving as rational economic agents, and the conceptualization of housing as a consumer good to be "received" by passive individuals through the market, rather than—paraphrasing Lefebvre (1996)—as an oeuvre collectively "made" by active city makers. The peripheral *poblaciones* that emerged from the subsidy-based policies were thus composed of families who, not knowing one another at the time of their arrival, had to deal with an unfriendly environment. Most of the time, their new neighborhoods lacked social services and appropriate public infrastructure. Néstor, raised in the Población Santo Tomás, described this process with an ironic, telling anecdote: "When we got here [in the late 1980s], there was a playground. It was really beautiful! Some military dictatorship authorities came to inaugurate it. But one week later, they packed all the equipment up and took it away. I swear! Then that place became a *peladero* [wasteland] and stayed that way for fifteen years."

Esteban, a founding member of Techo Ahora, went through similar life experiences when he moved in the Población San Ricardo in 1983. He was born in the well-known Población La Victoria in the late 1960s, and his grandparents participated eagerly in the autoconstruction of that neighborhood.[16] Tired of living as *allegados*, Esteban's parents decided to apply for subsidized housing and leave what had been their *población* for more than two decades. "In the early 1980s—he said—La Pintana was practically a *botadero* [garbage dump] for the poor. My family is part of those who got here in that period." As in the case of Néstor, Esteban's recollections of the process of arriving to his new *población* is full of descriptions accounting for the unfinished, incomplete, and deficient quality of his new neighborhood: "Logically, when we arrived at the Población San Ricardo, there was no grass, no pavement, and no trees. There was nothing. This was a damn wasteland. Gabriela Avenue [a major avenue in La Pintana] had only one lane . . . there was even a chicken coop nearby!"

It was precisely this lack of services and infrastructure that made displaced *pobladores* develop a sense of attachment to spaces initially seen as "wastelands." Because at the time of their arrival "there was nothing," drawing on Esteban's words, the new residents had to make everything. This making went certainly beyond the material building of a *población*, as performed in autoconstruction processes. In La Pintana, city making took the form of community practices through which *pobladores* sought to improve the conditions of habitability of their residential spaces. Their neighborhoods lacked green areas, playgrounds, soccer fields, and many other facilities, so they had to organize in order to get them. This type of city making led my interlocutors to produce a meaningful connection to their municipality. If, in their view, the state marginalized the poor by providing them with segregated and low-quality housing solutions, they had to make them livable by building up a strong community capable of struggling together for common issues. This required the constitution of an emotional bonding with the territory, which, once developed, served as an argument to demand urban rights, such as the right to stay put or the right to dignified housing. In Néstor's words: "Although we did not autoconstruct our houses, we do produce them on a daily basis. We give meaning [*le damos sentido*] to everything that surrounds our homes. That's why we have a sense of belonging, as rooted as that of those people who built their own homes. . . . We, like them, "constructed" [our homes] while living there."

Producers of Space

The very history of the Techo Ahora *allegados* committee can thus be understood as resulting from the symbolic attachment to a subsidized housing neighborhood. Its founders were mostly neighbors in San Ricardo who, before forming this housing assembly, had helped set up a cultural center, the Galpón

Cultural ("Cultural Warehouse"). This was a venue in which a variety of youth organizations—from soccer teams to rock and hip-hop musicians—met for gigs, workshops, film festivals, and the like. Esteban told me that they were not interested in participating in the cultural center run by the municipality, as it functioned under the logic of patronizing politics, in which local politicians allowed *pobladores* to take part in those activities as long as they supported them politically: "For that reason—he recalled—in 2006 we decided to create a self-managed cultural center to develop social activities by ourselves."

In this endeavor, they took over an abandoned lot within San Ricardo that, like other unoccupied areas in Santiago's peripheries, had become a small, illegal landfill as a result of municipal negligence. Using the renewed space as the organization's headquarters, the Galpón Cultural started to operate as a meeting point for activists, social leaders, and *vecinos comunes* (common neighbors). In addition to enjoying cultural events, they began to deliberate upon and demand what Castells (1983, xviii) calls "collective consumption," namely, "goods and services directly or indirectly provided by the state." Galpón Cultural's members engaged with a series of *cabildos* (popular assemblies) through which different grassroots organizations discussed the main problems affecting La Pintana's residents.[17] Such problems included the lack of public spaces, the need for adequate cultural resources, and the widespread presence of illegal landfills. At these gatherings, one of the topics that came up most often was the lack of affordable housing for *allegados*. Esteban and Laura, both of whom took part in these *cabildos*, agreed that this housing shortage was seen as an opportunity for creating Techo Ahora: "Back then we said: 'although we have no idea about housing policies, we have to channel this demand.' We did so because there were many people who were not receiving any support from the municipality in terms of how to apply for subsidies, how to deal with the SERVIU, etc."

Techo Ahora members' political involvement raises a crucial question: how should we reflect on these *pobladores*' sociospatial performances in terms of city making? I argue that this case illustrates what Lefebvre (1991) defines as the social production of space, that is, the process in which residents impugn hegemonic conceptualizations of space through the development of subversive spatial practices. By performing these practices, residents not only create new meanings to envision and signify space; space itself becomes an object over which they can claim rights to the city. In the Población San Ricardo, the municipality did not take care of the neighborhood soccer field for a long time, which eventually became an illegal landfill. However, by conducting cultural events for the community there, Esteban and his neighbors worked together to turn it into a productive space. They had to recondition a deserted lot and set it up for neighborhood activities. In doing so, they imbued the reconstituted space with new social dynamics, dynamics that established the possibility for *pobladores* to deliberate on public affairs and collectively demand the right to stay put. In other words, these residents were those who—borrowing Lefebvre's (1996) terminology—added "use value" to an area that had been left behind by the local administration. In Néstor's opinion: "We give use value to things. . . . It wouldn't make any sense to have schools, hospitals, etc. in this municipality if there are no people who use them. None of them would have any economic value if we don't give them use value."

Techo Ahora demanded that the state develop a housing project precisely on the former soccer field. "We know that this *población* needs public spaces, but the housing needs of the people are more important," Esteban told me. He also legitimized Techo Ahora's claim by arguing that this *allegados* committee had contributed to the *recuperación* (revitalization) of this piece of land through community-based actions. In a very Lefebvrian formulation, he was essentially advocating for rights over a space that is understood as an oeuvre belonging to those who produced it. In that sense, although Techo Ahora's members could not identify themselves as heirs of the rights acquired by autoconstructors, they conceived of the act of producing urban spaces as the source of legitimacy for their demand for rights to the city.

This case allows us to expand our understanding of the relationship between city-making processes and the emergence of a rights-based language among contemporary *pobladores*. When associating city-making performances with the formulation of urban rights, we must consider both the material and the symbolic production of space as two different, yet interwoven dimensions whose modalities of assemblage may vary historically. In both cases, however, the urban poor use the idea of contribution as the basis for their rights claiming, which speaks to the primacy of the notion of effort in the formation of *pobladores* as rights-bearing subjects.

Citizenship, Rights, and Effort

I have argued that both Don Bosco and Techo Ahora members' self-identification as city makers was predicated on the idea that *pobladores'* sociospatial practices have long contributed to improving the living conditions of the poor. By imagining autoconstruction as a source of symbolic and political power from the past, or by actually producing symbolic community spaces, all my interlocutors claimed their right to stay put in their neighborhoods of origin. What does this subjective understanding of the urban poor as city makers tell us about *pobladores'* views of citizenship? An answer to this question can be found by looking at the ways in which they thought of their housing assembly as a specific political community, formed by members with rights and obligations. Such an examination allows for a reflection on the extent to which the *pobladores'* political imagination makes the emergence of an urban type of citizenship possible.

"Only Those Who Struggle Win"

During my fieldwork, I often noticed that Don Bosco's social leaders uttered the phrase "sólo los que luchan ganan" (only those who struggle win) to emphasize that housing would be acquired only by the *allegados* who participated more actively in the committee. Likewise, many times I heard people say that those who did not struggle together with other pobladores did not deserve (*merecen*) housing. Both kinds of moralizing speech acts reveal a crucial characteristic of the *pobladores'* conceptualization of themselves as rights bearers: the consideration that such a condition is closely linked to the deployment of a sense of individual responsibility to their families and their organization.

To deal with the degrading effects of poverty and affirm their identity as responsible, decent, and self-sacrificing citizens, poor urban residents in Chile have long drawn on strict moral codes (Martínez and Palacios 1996). Housing programs have played a key role in the spread of this "culture of decency."[18] In the 1960s, these programs forced *pobladores* to save money systematically and pay monthly quotas. Policies like Frei Montalva's Operation Site did so not only to finance social housing projects but also to moralize the poor by inculcating values of responsibility, sacrifice, and effort.[19] Public opinion praised prospective homeowners for their "capacity for saving,"[20] as if such an action were a means for turning them into civilized citizens. But the state's imaginaries of responsibility took on a new face in neoliberal Chile, one related to the appearance of ideas of civility grounded in the consideration of the poor as individual rational economic actors. The widespread implementation of poverty alleviation programs in Chile beginning in 1990 led to the emergence of a "market citizenship" (Schild 2000). This type of citizenship involves modalities of subject formation through which working-class individuals are transformed into autonomous, independent, and disciplined citizens capable of actively partici-pating in the market.

In the case of the Don Bosco *pobladores*, the moral evaluation of each mem-ber's commitment to the housing assembly can be construed as an expression of this neoliberal ethics, one in which citizens, "once responsibilized and entre-preneurialized . . . govern themselves within a state-secured framework of law and order" (Rose 1999, 139). The capacity for demanding rights thus appears as intimately related to the very act of struggling for them and to the development of calculative actions through which pobladores actively seek to conduct their lives under a specific moral code. For them, rights are not "passively enjoyable" prerogatives—an aspect that Walzer (1989, 216) sees as characteristic of liberal regimes of citizenship—since the actual demand for rights appears as the con-dition for exercising them. To acquire the capacity to exert rights, they first had to constitute themselves as subjects endowed with a particular morality, based on a matrix of conduct that rests on ideas of calculation, individual responsibil-ity, and self-sufficiency.

The cultural dimension associated with the transformation of the poor into individualized, rational, and self-regulating citizens revealed itself when hous-ing activists verbalized discourses on personal and collective effort to establish ethical and political judgments about others and about themselves. These no-tions of effort allowed them to consider themselves as legitimate subjects en-titled with rights to the city. At the same time, their views of effort permitted them to create practical mechanisms to differentiate those who were worthy of rights from those who were not. This kind of urban politics relies on two in-terwoven understandings of effort. On the one hand, a political understanding conceptualized as willingness to struggle (*luchar*). This political meaning of ef-fort, as it related to the act of rights claiming, helped *pobladores* to produce dis-cursive definitions that establish the social and political conditions needed for individuals to exert their rights. On the other hand, effort was also construed ethically, expressed through the idea of sacrifice (*sacrificio*). By conceptualizing effort in terms of this ethical framework, my interlocutors managed internal conflicts within their housing committees on the basis of a moral definition of who "deserves" to have rights.

Effort as Struggle

To explore the political dimension of effort, I draw on a very tense, yet revealing event that I observed on a Saturday in March 2014. Don Bosco's leadership had scheduled a meeting with around sixty people who had gotten involved in the organization just three months prior. The *allegados* had agreed to get together at a five-a-side soccer pitch at 8:00 p.m. However, eight young men were using it when they arrived. Ernesto, a Don Bosco social leader, asked them to leave in order to start the meeting, but the players refused. Here is where the quarrel began. Some of the new members, assuming that the gathering would start at the established time, entered the playing field, provoking a violent reaction from the young men. In response, Ernesto himself vigorously confronted them, which made him the target of their threats. If Adriana and Rosa—two other members of the Don Bosco—hadn't had the courage to intervene, it certainly would have ended up in a fight, as Ernesto did not hesitate to defy the soccer-playing crew. Eventually, the players left and Ernesto started the meeting at around 8:20 p.m.

After Adriana and Rosa's pacifying intervention, I approached them to talk about the confrontation. Rosa said: "These *huevones* [idiots] don't do anything for the soccer field. It is in really bad condition. You can see how it is. It doesn't have lights to play at night and the goals are terrible. I have invited them to meetings to get it fixed but they don't show up, so they don't have any right to use it."

Rosa's understanding of rights, as a prerogative acquired through subjective involvement in public affairs, was widespread among the activists. This self-perception as rights bearers is grounded essentially on a self-identification as socially excluded residents that have to "struggle" on a daily basis to make a living. The signifier *struggle* is thus fundamental to capturing the full range of political practices realized by the *pobladores*, including the explicit claim for rights in the political arena and general demands for better living conditions. This explains why, along with advocating for the right to housing, urban activists' political discourses were also organized on the basis of critical judgments regarding Chile's high levels of social inequality, engendering a particular view of the poor as a dispossessed population whose rights have been denied by a neoliberal society. María's experiences are telling in this regard.

In the beginning of 2014, María was really concerned about her nineteen-year-old son, who had to make a decision regarding his academic future. He had graduated from high school in December 2013 and wanted to pursue undergraduate studies. He was immensely excited about the idea of becoming a college student, and he regularly asked me about university programs that might fit his interests. But María, working as a self-employed dressmaker with her mother, felt frustrated that she simply did not have the money to pay for her son's education, a disappointment that was broadly linked to her inability to access social rights that had been systematically privatized since the dictatorship. In discussing this subject with her, she said: "If you don't struggle, you get nothing. . . . This country never considers the poor [but] always the rich. For example, my son . . . even having a lot of interest in studying, he can't because we don't have money . . . that happens even in health care too: if you don't have money, you simply die."

In her view, similar to those of others, the *pobladores'* material precarity predisposes them to an everyday struggle to *parar la olla* (make ends meet). This predisposition is based on a social class–based understanding of effort. For my interlocutors, the poor, lacking the money to acquire commodities freely on the market, must necessarily exert themselves more than the rich in order to attain them. To feed their families and have a minimum standard of living, the poor must work extra hours, have two or three (precarious) jobs, and take out loans and credit with predatory interest rates from retail companies.[21] This perspective shaped their opinions of the rich, who were objectified as those who have no willingness to engage in a political struggle, as their economic power allows them to easily satisfy their material needs. "Why would they [the rich] struggle? They won't do that because they have money from inheritances they are getting [from their relatives]," a *pobladora* explained to me. She did so when describing why, in her view, bourgeois individuals do not "need" to struggle for rights since they have economic resources to take care of their own well-being. For the *pobladores* I met, the very act of mobilizing for rights was thus the precondition for their legitimate existence as political agents capable of addressing the state using a rights-based language. This idea was suggestively expressed by Rosa, who, with respect to the right to housing, said, "Maybe housing is a right for everyone because everyone should have a place to live . . . [but] you have to struggle for it because you can't have everything provided as a gift."

Effort as Sacrifice

The signifier effort was also conceptualized as a sacrifice, a connotation that derived from *pobladores'* understanding of their everyday practices as framed by a society that allocates opportunities differentially among its members. In this case, the concept of effort consisted of an ethical dimension that resulted in moral condemnations of those poor residents who, in the opinion of my interlocutors, have not sacrificed themselves enough to (broadly speaking) *salir adelante* (get ahead) in life. The idea of sacrifice was thus understood as a defining aspect of *pobladores'* subjectivity: they had to "sweat blood" to survive. In this context, those individuals who did not sacrifice themselves in the way that other *pobladores* did were subject to moral criticism, to the point of even denying their condition as rights-bearing subjects.

This approach to rights gave rise to the establishment of a set of norms through which Don Bosco members managed conflicts associated with how to distribute rights fairly among themselves. Every housing assembly faces a serious difficulty when it comes to deciding in which house or apartment their prospective homeowners will eventually reside. This is a sort of dilemma that can be expressed in the following question: which families have the right to choose first where they want to live if all of them are supposed to have equal rights? To solve this problem, the Comité de Allegados Don Bosco generated an evaluation system through which the leadership could "objectively" measure the performance of each applicant enrolled in the assembly in terms of the effort that he or she had demonstrated in the struggle for housing. The assessment scale used two criteria to evaluate people's behavior: commitment and participation, the former related to being up to date with monthly payments and the latter to being keenly engaged in the committee's activities. It functioned more or less like this: if a member acted properly (e.g., paying the committee fees on time), he or she received one point, which was written down in a notebook utilized exclusively for that purpose. To the contrary, if a person did not behave in accordance with the committee's internal rules (e.g., missing assemblies, marches, public demonstrations), he or she was not given any mark. This system was pretty straightforward: the more responsible one was, the more points one got.

The Don Bosco committee was split into smaller affinity groups—called *comunidades*—made up of groups of three to twenty people, generally friends and relatives, who planned to live next to each other when the housing projects were built.[22] To allow these *comunidades* to preserve the community-based relationships that their members had developed, the organization established that the decision regarding where each individual would eventually reside—either on which street or alley or in which apartment building—would be made collectively. This led to a critical point: although the assessment system operated on the basis of scrutiny of each person's behavior, the right to select where to live was not left to the individual him- or herself but, rather, to the affinity group (*comunidad*). Accordingly, the defining criteria for determining who "gained" this right was not each individual's score but the sum of the scores of those belonging to a *comunidad*, meaning that the affinity group with the highest score would be able to choose first. This had an important consequence in the way *pobladores* interacted with one another: everyone, in being a member of a *comunidad*, was supposed to act properly and self-govern their own conduct, so as not to lower the points of the group they took part in.

This mechanism for the distribution of rights gave rise to internal tensions between the "more" and "less" responsible affinity groups. These conflicts generally took the form of public condemnations of specific individuals who were considered "lazy," "selfish," or "opportunist." These moral appraisals were common in general assemblies, especially when the more energetic activists sought to legitimize themselves as deserving more rights (e.g., to housing, to speak in public, to be heard) than others. This particular conceptualization of rights even led to the expulsion of some members, given their "lack of commitment to the struggle for housing." Many of them showed up at Don Bosco general assemblies to vindicate themselves and avoid being expelled. Since the final decision was made by the general assembly, *pobladores* seeking exoneration often tried to convince the audience that they had good reasons for not attending the meetings or for being behind on their payments.

I witnessed such rites of exculpation twenty or more times over a period of twelve months, and only rarely did the assembly allow those expelled to continue participating in the organization. For instance, on October 5, 2013, a young woman notified of her expulsion came to ask for forgiveness. She had been absent for over six months, which would surely have a negative impact on the final score of her affinity group. For that reason, even some members of her *comunidad* wanted her out of the committee. One of them, after hearing her arguments, said: "If you can't come, you have to at least let us know." He continued: "All of us have problems to attend. We all work, study, and have children, but we come anyway." The verbal dispute escalated and, after realizing that she would not be reaccepted, the young girl shouted, "You're denying me the right to housing." By August 2015, more than forty members had been expelled, all of whom had been granted state subsidies. This implied that they were no longer able to become homeowners unless they enrolled in another *allegados* organization and applied again for subsidies elsewhere. Such an outcome, tragic for those who were disenfranchised, was conceived of by Don Bosco *pobladores* as an expected result of a morally unacceptable lack of personal sacrifice by those who simply "don't deserve rights."

Pobladores as Urban Citizens

Chile's Political Constitution of 1980 does not recognize housing as a constitutional right. Instead, it proclaims the right to reside without restrictions anywhere in the country as an expression of the rights to individual liberty. *Pobladores'* mobilizations in neoliberal Chile challenged such a conceptualization by conceiving of housing, and particularly housing within their home municipality, as a right that must be guaranteed by the state. They organized emergent right-to-the-city protests reframing the traditional right to housing on a territorial basis. In this chapter, however, I have shown that those who were involved in the struggle for the right to stay put made use of a neoliberal ethics when signifying their condition as poor residents struggling for urban rights. The *pobladores'* political imagination, in this way, reveals the transversal rationalities of housing movements in Chile: although their strategic orientation might be structured by demands challenging the logic of capital accumulation, they are not able to totally erode the moral grammar of the neoliberal project.

This paradox is particularly clear when reflecting on the extent to which housing activists' understanding of rights make the rise of new kinds of citizenship possible. I argue that contemporary housing protest movements have given rise to a residency-based formulation of citizenship that is grounded on the *pobladores'* subjective identification as citizen city makers endowed with rights to the city. In this sense, they see themselves as legitimate rights bearers not only through a formal membership in a national political community but also through active participation in urban politics. It is this "substantive" dimension of citizenship (Holston and Appadurai 1996, 190), as opposed to the formal one, which helped my interlocutors establish criteria for allocating rights: the capacity for rights, they said, is reserved for those who struggle (*luchan*). Nonetheless, they drew on these criteria—materialized through the use of evaluation systems through which housing assemblies assess the performance of their members—to morally condemn those who were seen as uncommitted or "lazy" and, through expulsion, denied them the right to have rights. When it comes to distributing rights among the members of housing committees, the *pobladores* thus considered the acquisition of rights as essentially a matter of effort, responsibility, and self-government.

Housing activists' conceptualization of effort is derived from the enactment of community-based social practices, organized around their participation in state-regulated *comités de allegados*. These housing assemblies, understood as political communities, became the entities through which they both mobilized for rights and developed ethical attitudes toward themselves and toward others. The primary role of the community in the structuring of *pobladores'* political and ethical practices reveals the rise of a form of governmentality that is specific to neoliberalism, one in which the subject constitutes him- or herself as a moral individual while becoming a member of a larger affinity group to which the individual has specific obligations and emotional ties (Rose 1999). As a "sector for government" (Rose 1999, 176), the community—and the social practices it entails—forms particular kinds of citizens who are responsible not only to themselves but also to others. It is, however, interesting to note that this modality of social action made the reemergence of urban protests possible. It is through these protests that *pobladores* have successfully struggled for the right to stay put. Indeed, by 2020 most of the families with which I had worked with between 2013 and 2015 were already homeowners. This is hardly a trivial point if, as I have shown in this book, we consider the difficulties involved with building social housing in well-located areas like La Florida, when housing policies are framed by market principles.

By using the right to stay put as a battle flag, *allegados* committees form a scenario for the rise of new forms of political mobilization capable of challenging the exclusionary character of housing policies. This complements most of the academic literature on housing protests and right-to-the-city movements in cities of the Global South. Research that focuses on autoconstruction processes has left the protests resulting from resident participation in subsidy-based housing programs unexamined. However, up to this point, I have shown that these programs have a dual role: on the one hand, they work as a strategic locus for implementing specific technologies of neoliberal governmentality; on the other hand, they make possible the appearance of urban protest movements that, although different from the old *pobladores* movement in terms of tactics and strategic orientation, challenge the dominance of the market in housing policies.

Can these struggles lead to the constitution of a truly transformative urban movement as, for example, conceived of by Lefebvre when discussing the right to the city? It depends on the capacity of housing activists to go beyond their well-articulated condemnation of the segregationist character of market-based urban policies. For this to occur, it seems crucial that their demands for territorial rights be linked to a deep criticism of the economic and ideological system of social inequality that structures Chilean (and, more generally, capitalist) society, which requires a radical questioning of the ethical foundations on which the *pobladores'* process of citizen formation is based. Advocacy for a more just city expressed through the right to stay put, in this sense, should be accompanied by the construction of subjectivities capable of defying the cultural values contained in what Schild (2000) has called "market citizenship." Not doing so entails accepting "social mixing" as the best way to promote spatial justice, without problematizing the effects of neoliberalism on the maintenance of social exclusion.[23]

In this chapter, I have illustrated the need to consider the political and the ethical as two interwoven dimensions of the citizen formation processes produced when housing movements demand rights to the city. I have done so by arguing that social change in neoliberal cities requires not only questioning the market rationality through which urban spaces are planned but also developing political subjectivities, the ethical orientations of which accommodate broader projects of social transformation. In the next chapter, I reflect on these political and the ethical dimensions by analyzing the role of moral concepts—particularly the idea of dignity—in the reformulation of the political horizons of the *pobladores* movement.

6 Toward a Life with Dignity

Ethical Practices, New Political Horizons

In 2011, the Movimiento de Pobladores en Lucha (MPL)—a housing organization created in 2007 that is one of the most active groups in Santiago—published a book that contains revealing reflections on the reemergence of housing
movements in neoliberal Chile. With the suggestive title *El retorno de los pobladores* (The return of the pobladores), the book was a sort of ideological mani-
festo in which new generations of poor urban dwellers stated that *la vida digna*
(a life with dignity) was the "political horizon" of their struggles; that is, the
long-term strategic demand that organizes their everyday political practices:[1]
"Housing is only the beginning of a long and ongoing struggle, the struggle
for *la Vida Digna* [life with dignity]. This is a choice of freedom that we do not
request, but rather struggle for on a daily basis. It represents a wide path including different dimensions of living and inhabiting in a territory, such as housing,
health care, education, work. . . . It is not an external ideal, but a horizon built
on people's dreams, wishes, and desires to have a good life" (Movimiento de
Pobladores en Lucha 2011, 31).

In the preceding chapters, I have largely shown that market-based housing
policies grounded in the allocation of subsidies have promoted the segregation
of the poor along the city's periphery. It is in this context that the *pobladores'*
right to *la vida digna* emerges. At first glance, this right stems from the idea that
living with dignity is not "external" to individuals' aspirations but is the result
of everyday practices. Dignity, in this sense, constitutes the *pobladores'* identity
as poor urban dwellers and can be claimed as a right when such an identity is

at risk. The right to live with dignity, as a right based on a moral category, allows the urban poor to articulate political claims that go beyond the demand for homeownership. By situating this right as the political horizon of housing struggles, they can thus demand better living conditions while reframing the terms of their participation in society as ethical-political subjects. The *pobladores'* right to *la vida digna* thus provides for an opportunity to reflect on the political role of moral concepts. In this chapter, I argue that moral categories such as dignity, while enabling vulnerable people to become ethical subjects, help them make sense of their everyday experiences in political terms. This has important consequences for anthropological research: moral categories, in addition to revealing how and under what circumstances human beings articulate their moral actions, also function as indicators that show how social movements seeking to transform people's precarious lives are formed.

Everyday moral concepts like dignity, as culturally situated categories that emerge in specific historical contexts, are critical for the study of ethics and moralities. For one of the dominant approaches in anthropology, that of so-called ordinary ethics, ethical practices are not grounded in a transcendental morality but are articulated through the words, categories, and actions of everyday life.[2] How human beings act morally, and the extent to which certain words enable individuals to signify their actions as moral subjects, are thus two key issues for the ordinary ethics approach. From this perspective, notions such as dignity can help people establish a moral criterion for practical judgment that, adapting Michael Lambek's (2010b, 40) work, makes them "routinely" do "what they think right or good." In addition, concepts like dignity can help us delve into how moral values circulate within the population, as well as the ethical procedures that enable moral subjects to form at a specific historical conjuncture (Fassin 2012).

But moral categories like dignity do more than allow for the construction of moral subjects or the establishment of criteria for practical judgment. Dignity has also been conceived of as a familiar moral concept, indicating certain ethical concerns that catalyze a political response through which people subjected to any form of vulnerability seek to change their living conditions (Zigon 2014). From this viewpoint, dignity is a "marker" (Zigon 2014, 752) that lets us know where to locate everyday ethical dilemmas and, accordingly, how individuals' moral experiences inform their political practices. Moral concepts can therefore reveal not only the moral procedures through which people become ethical subjects but also the practices and discourses that allow them to act politically.

FIGURE 7. "Struggle for Dignified Housing." Mural by the Don Bosco *allegados* committee. Credit: Photo by the author, October 2013.

The housing struggles of Chilean *pobladores* that I have accounted for in this book shed light on the ethical and political effects of using everyday moral categories in the development of rights-based mobilizations. The activists I met framed their collective actions as a struggle for dignified housing (fig. 7) and a life with dignity (fig. 8). In this chapter, I demonstrate that the right to *la vida digna*, a demand that became even more widespread after the 2019 social uprising, illustrates how poor inhabitants develop novel forms of political mobilization as they participate in neoliberal welfare programs. At the same time, this right reveals the ethical and political implications of using claims based on moral categories as the new strategic demand of a social movement.

Searching for Dignity through Market-Based Programs

In neoliberal Chile, *allegados* use subsidy-based housing programs to achieve their right to housing, which forces them to accommodate their everyday lives to these programs' requirements and demonstrate that they are responsible

FIGURE 8. "Our Struggle Is Larger than a House . . . Dignified Neighborhood and Life with Dignity." Banner made by the Don Bosco *allegados* committee. Credit: Photo by the author, June 2014.

economic actors. For them, becoming homeowners by participating in neoliberal housing programs involves an engagement with the state's apparatuses that can last for as long as ten years,[3] since it includes a number of mandatory steps. These steps include being recognized as eligible for subsidies by state instruments of socioeconomic assessment; forming state-regulated housing assemblies (*comités de allegados*) through which they apply for subsidies; saving money in a bank account that all applicants must open when they enroll in a *comité de allegados*; and, once prospective homeowners have received subsidies and raised the necessary money, purchasing housing built by real estate developers. As technologies of government, Chile's subsidy-based housing programs has aimed to turn the urban poor into citizens capable of governing themselves by inculcating values of responsibility, freedom, and individual autonomy.[4]

In Santiago, the persistence of urban inequalities and poor families' involvement in subsidy-based programs frame their claims for dignity. Their demands for a life with dignity emerge both as a struggle against segregation and as a criticism of how housing policies construe them as subject-citizens who can apply for welfare programs. But what kind of life do *pobladores* imagine when demanding dignity? Generally, the housing activists I encountered defined *la vida digna* using words related to ideas of security, justice, social recognition, comfort, and well-being. Their conceptualization of a life with dignity, in a broader sense, generally designated a "decent society," that is, a society "whose institutions do not humiliate people" (Margalit 1996, 1). In this sense, while achieving a home of their own is the *pobladores'* primary goal, what is ultimately at stake in their struggle is to be recognized as dignified, poor residents.

Hashemi (2020) argues that the search for dignity may entail actions oriented to either resist or adapt to dominant cultural values. Grounded in culturally instituted practices, people's quest for dignity assumes thus a variety of forms. In neoliberal societies, excluded populations' struggle for dignity, equal treatment, and social recognition materializes through everyday practices in which they deal with their experiences with vulnerability.[5] For some scholars, these practices, however, do not necessarily lead to political struggles for rights.[6] As a personal rather than a collective enterprise, the pursuit of a life with dignity would involve a set of actions and discourses that, developed fundamentally in the private and domestic spheres, allows the poor to respond critically to any form of economic, gender-based, or class-based exclusion. For example, in Chile the poor conceptualize dignity as a set of solidarity-based ideas and actions that, though emerging frequently in the everyday interactions among the residents of working-class neighborhoods, would not bring about public, collective mobilization for rights (Han 2012). In the United States, low-income women enrolled in welfare-to-work programs achieve dignity by engaging in "small acts of contestation," such as confronting their employers or quitting low-wage jobs (Cleaveland 2005, 55). Likewise, other authors point out that poor people's quest for dignity and social recognition through homeownership is framed by individual and private practices, which suggests that such a pursuit would not give rise to forms of collective action. The wives of migrating husbands in rural Mexico can individually renegotiate gender and kin relations—and thus attain dignity and agency—by building houses of their own using the remittances sent by their spouses (Pauli 2008). Brazilian dwellers participating in slum upgrading programs conceive of the search for dignified housing primarily as a personal undertaking that does not entail the use of a political language of citizenship; they do not construe themselves as rights bearers, nor do they see housing as a right that they can demand collectively (Nuijten 2013).

But is the pursuit of dignity in neoliberal contexts merely a private enterprise that neither results in the articulation of public demands (Han 2012) nor enables the urban poor to become rights-bearing citizens (Nuijten 2013)? The case discussed in this book, as well as the 2019 social uprising in Chile, shows the opposite. Working-class residents may privately want to live with dignity, but they also formulate public political demands in the form of a social movement. As both a moral category and a political signifier, the concept of dignity enables Chile's poor urban residents to constitute themselves as ethical subjects capable of addressing rights-based claims to the state. The discursive centrality of dignity among housing activists reveals itself, in particular, through the everyday experiences of female *allegadas*, as they tend to engage more actively in housing protests than men.[7] They are, in fact, the focus of this chapter.

The female *allegadas* I met through my ethnographic immersion in the Comité de Allegados Don Bosco were motivated in their struggle by two factors that they understood as expressions of a social system that humiliates and degrades the poor: first, the lack of affordable housing in La Florida, which forced them to reside in a relative's house;[8] and second, that the Survey of Social Protection—the instrument of socioeconomic assessment used by the state to allocate social welfare benefits—categorized them as a "vulnerable" population.[9] As *allegadas* constructed as "vulnerable" by the state, my interlocutors had everyday lives that were organized around a set of events in which, from their perspective, their dignity was compromised. It was only when they collectively dealt with the lack of affordable housing and the state's classification of them as eligible for subsidies that they could envision new political horizons on the basis of dignity.

Housing Movements as Struggles for Dignity

In Chile, dignity has long been a fundamental element of the political language used by *pobladores* in need of housing. In the preceding chapters, I showed that they often draw on this concept when demanding housing rights from the state. The notion of dignity has helped them to articulate political narratives in which they both envision themselves as subjects deserving of equal treatment and imagine the life for which they struggle. *Pobladores'* mobilizations for dignity have, nevertheless, changed over time. In the late 1960s, 16 percent of the population resided in shantytowns.[10] Under those circumstances, claims for dignity arose in response to the squatters' living conditions and homes, which, as the prototype of a life without dignity, were characterized by the state as "'irregular' and 'unhygienic'" (Murphy 2015, 83).

The Catholic Church played a key role in both denouncing the squatters' "subhuman" living standards and articulating a moral language through which *pobladores* could recognize themselves as dignified individuals. The *Revista*

Mensaje, a magazine founded by Jesuits in 1951, was one of the main platforms through which the Catholic Church spread its message of salvation and dignity based on the idea that human life, as a creation of God, is sacred and has intrinsic value. For the Catholic Church, dignity is the foundation of morality since it is an inherent attribute of human beings, one that allows everybody to be recognized as God's children. A society, thus, acts immorally when it jeopardizes human beings' dignity. This explains why the Jesuit priest Carlos Hurtado Echeverría (1957, 461) denounced Chile's social inequality, arguing that living in informal "undignified shantytowns" would lead to the *desquiciamiento moral y cívico* (moral and civic unhinging) of the urban poor. *Curas obreros* (worker priests) were, in this context, missionaries who, by constructing formal neighborhoods, could save the poor from becoming disturbed and immoral.

Housing activists soon questioned this view of dignity as dependent on the moralizing action of the Catholic Church. This questioning came about especially from the mid-1960s to 1973, when the growing politicization of *pobladores* and the emergence of mass social protest movements for housing transformed how they conceived of their existence as squatters. As observed elsewhere in Latin America, squatters no longer understood their informal settlements within the urban periphery as a subhuman, marginal type of inhabitance.[11] Rather, they saw them as an expression of their productive capacities as low-income residents. Having constituted themselves as transformative urban citizens through their involvement in city-making processes on the urban outskirts, housing activists began to be recognized as radicalized collective actors. In this context, the *pobladores'* sense of dignity was based on their ethical and political attributes as revolutionary subjects capable of taking part in projects for social transformation.[12]

Augusto Pinochet's military regime, which came to power after overthrowing Allende's government, had a profound impact on the *pobladores'* conceptualizations of dignity. On the one hand, Pinochet's dictatorship systematically repressed land occupations, carried out massive evictions of squatter settlements, and killed hundreds of poor residents. On the other hand, it implemented a new, neoliberal model of urban development that opened up the city to the market by removing land regulations. The poor could no longer squat, and the state persecuted those who engaged in housing struggles. Because people's lives were at risk, *pobladores* reframed their demands for dignity by articulating new claims for the right to live in freedom and safety. *Pobladores* thus focused their actions on the development, in most cases supported by the Catholic Church, of community-based survival strategies such as *ollas comunes* (cooking cooperatives) and *comprando juntos* (buying together).[13]

The neoliberal foundation of urban policies persisted when democracy was restored in 1990. As discussed earlier in this book, the governments that followed Pinochet's regime did little to change the market-based character of urban development. As of this writing, the Chilean state still understands homeownership as the result of an individual effort and housing as a commodity that the poorest families can attain through the private market. This model of housing provision, however, enabled an unprecedented number of social housing units to be built, especially during the 1990s. Thus, subsidized social housing expanded after the dictatorship as a result of relief programs that, by allocating subsidies on a large scale, sought to pacify the poor in contexts of social unrest, similar to the US welfare system (Piven and Cloward 1971). But this mass provision of housing has not necessarily resulted in better living conditions for the poor. Because subsidized housing units are often built along the segregated urban peripheries, *pobladores* have reformulated social movements for housing over the past decade, seeking to obtain housing in their own neighborhoods to avoid being relocated to the peripheries. In this context, the poor demand dignity no longer as a reaction to "subhuman" living conditions, as in the *pobladores* movement of the mid-twentieth century, or in response to living in a country where people's lives are at risk, as during the dictatorship. Rather, they demand dignity in order to respond to market-based policies that, along with segregating the poor, understand housing as a means-tested benefit distributed among those categorized as "vulnerable" by the Survey of Social Protection.

Living in the Backyard: The Life of *Allegadas*

The 2017 National Socioeconomic Characterization Survey (CASEN) showed that nearly 9 percent of Chileans lived below the poverty line. Compared to the 29 percent characterized as poor in 2006, this number represented a significant reduction in poverty levels over the intervening nine years.[14] Lower-income groups have had increasing access to credit since the 1990s, which has enabled them to purchase products that previously would have been regarded as expensive, sophisticated, and luxurious (Han 2012). Poverty is thus visible not so much through the lack of material goods but through the structural inability to find a stable job, live in proper housing, or receive suitable health care. One of these dimensions, the lack of housing, drives the poor to reside as *allegados*, which is a form of living that they consider undignified and degrading. Living as *allegados*, however, has allowed for the emergence of collective action by which prospective homeowners, especially women, seek to affirm their dignity as poor urban dwellers.

I met Ángela in August 2013 when I began to conduct ethnographic research in the Don Bosco *allegados* committee. A housewife in her fifties, she worked occasionally as a street vendor and for the Comité de Allegados Don Bosco doing administrative tasks, such as collecting fees, attending meetings at the Metropolitan Service of Housing and Urbanism (SERVIU), and taking notes during assemblies, for which she received a monthly salary of about US$500. At the age of six, Ángela came to live in the then newly built Campamento Nueva La Habana, and she continued to live in her parent's house until the late 1980s. She joined the housing protest movement in 2009, after living as an *allegada* in her mother-in-law's house for almost twenty years. "Before that," she told me, "I just was at home." I heard similar stories from other women, all of which caused me to wonder what had led a woman with little background in social organizing to stop "staying at home," join an *allegados* committee, and assume an active role in the political struggle for housing. When I visited her at home in January 2014, she explained, "*Mi vivienda* [my house] . . . I'm in the *comité* because I want my own house. It's really difficult to live as an *allegada* in another person's house."

Ángela and José, a construction worker and her common-law partner, had met in the late 1980s and, wanting to live as a family, decided to move in with José's mother in 1990. Like most of the houses in Población Nuevo Amanecer, the 150-square-meter residence (around 1,614 square feet), was a semidetached single-floor brick structure that was divided into three sections (living and dining room, kitchen, and bedrooms). Nevertheless, problems related to domestic violence soon arose, which led them to build a small wooden dwelling for themselves in the backyard. When daughters-in-law share space with their *suegras* (mothers-in-law), threats and violence are common (Pauli 2008). Virilocal residence, patrilineal descent, and patriarchy set the stage for those incidents since, as Julia Pauli suggests, wives are generally expected to behave as submissive daughters-in-law, which makes them a target for mistreatment by *suegras*. When daughters-in-law challenge such convention, violence tends to occur. Ángela told me what had happened: "At the beginning, living together with my mother-in-law was a disaster. Two women cannot live together, because they both want to be *dueñas de casa* [housewives]. *Las dos quieren mandar* [They both want to be in charge]. . . . We didn't get along at all, and even hit each other . . . so we decided to make this [our house] here out in the back."

Ángela and José's family were one of the 459,347 Chilean households that, by 2013, needed housing (Ministerio de Desarrollo Social 2014). Although they had been living in the backyard for over ten years, tension persisted between the women in 2014. The problem was that Ángela felt obligated to explicitly demonstrate that her family was economically independent and that, though residing on her mother-in-law's property, they could make a living on their own. In her view, being a woman in her fifties without a home of her own made her feel powerless. This forced her to legitimize her demands for housing by strongly asserting that her living situation did not signify that she lacked the means to provide for her family. She wanted to be recognized by her mother-in-law as self-sufficient. During the months I spent with her and José, I realized that paying the bills and cleaning the house were very significant to her, because they helped her to identify herself as a subject who was not exploiting José's mother. Ángela's persistent attempts to demonstrate economic independence and self-governing capacities sought to communicate that residing on another person's property as an *allegada* was dignified.

I observed many other cases in which the *pobladoras* I met endowed themselves with a sense of entitlement by asserting that they were economically self-sufficient. Nevertheless, all confronted the reality that they could not organize their everyday lives in the domestic sphere in accordance with their own norms. Their capacity for action was limited in ways that went beyond the mere fact that they had to share living quarters with others. In fact, one of the first responses that came up when I asked women about the downsides of living as *allegadas* was the lack of privacy, and the inability to autonomously decide what was and was not allowed in their houses. Many of the daily issues they faced were certainly uncomfortable and unpleasant, like sharing one bathroom with six or more people, or having to schedule laundry days when there was only one washing machine for two or three families. But much more frustrating was having no voice in deciding how domestic life was organized. This is why Ángela and other Don Bosco women described their lives as *allegadas* with expressions like "It's complicated," "It's terrible," or "I wouldn't wish this on anybody." Ángela's personal experience is telling in this regard: "I never invite people to my house simply because they have to go through the kitchen [of the main house], and my mother-in-law, who is very conservative, will begin to ask me a lot of questions. . . . You have to give explanations all the time, like 'He's a friend and wants to talk with me.'"

Allegadas' limited entitlement to their living quarters is manifested at specific moments, such as having to *pedir permiso* (ask for permission) or *dar explicaciones* (give explanations), in which they felt obliged to subordinate their subjectivity to the rules of the homeowner. They envisioned this mode of living as structured by everyday relations of subjugation, which compromised their individual dignity and agency. The idea of becoming homeowners thus emerged as the only possible way to subvert a private domain that restricts their capacity to act in a sovereign manner. Here is where the concept of dignified housing arises. Rosa, another Don Bosco *allegada*, understood dignified housing in these terms: "For me, dignified housing is a place where I can live comfortably, have *my* space, *my* living/dining room, *my* kitchen, *my* bathroom [and] rooms for my children." Dignified housing would therefore be a residence that allows each family to create a home according to a system of norms, rules, and expectations that its members freely define. As a precondition for achieving a life with dignity, dignified housing was imagined as the place where *allegadas'* understanding of what constitutes the private and the intimate would find a material and a social base—that is, a dwelling and specific family relations.

Predicaments of Poverty and Vulnerability

My interlocutors' concept of a *vida digna* was not only grounded in an evaluation of their residential circumstances as *pobladores* in need of housing but also informed by critical assessments of how the state characterized them as vulnerable in order to make them eligible for housing subsidies. In advanced liberal societies, welfare programs function as technologies of government that, through measurement and quantification, turn individuals into self-reliant, civilized, and autonomous citizen-subjects.[15] These programs seek to instill a specific form of political rationality in those who meet certain eligibility criteria so that they can "conduct their conduct."[16] If a poor family qualifies for welfare, it is not "on the basis of being citizens [in the liberal sense of that word] but on the basis of a means test, a calculation of their eligibility" (Cruikshank 1999, 108). In that sense, the *allegados* who qualified for housing subsidies confronted a distressing reality: to become beneficiaries, they had to subject their everyday lives to the scrutiny of state agencies and behave "properly," that is, according to the eligibility criteria (e.g., by methodically saving money exclusively for housing-related purposes, as promoted by subsidy-based housing policies). For the activists I spent time with, being held accountable for their actions was profoundly annoying. This was so because their own subjective class identification collided with the state's imaginaries of poverty, a phenomenon that reveals a tension between working-class individuals' views of what it means to be poor in a neoliberal society and the ideological principles that form the basis of state programs designed to alleviate poverty. How did *pobladores* envision and signify this collision between, so to speak, different concepts of poverty? To what extent did this collision give rise to specific modalities of political action? Furthermore, how did this tension make the appearance of political demands for dignity possible?

Condescension and Critical Acting

Housing activists' reaction against the state's imaginaries of poverty was based on a broader questioning of the ways they are seen and treated by other classes. The *pobladores* I met claimed to have gone through experiences of discrimination in their everyday interactions with middle- and upper-class people. This discrimination took the form of condescension, subtle disdain, and implicit arrogance. Either when applying for jobs or when dealing with state agents—to mention two events that my interlocutors usually referred to when accounting for experiences of discrimination—they felt as if they were being patronized. In Ángela's words, "Your prospective boss or the SERVIU people are not going to tell you to your face that you're a *choro* [thief] or a drug trafficker, but I'm sure that's what they think, by the way they look at you." Then, she added, "It's like those times where no words are needed because *tú cachai altiro lo que piensan* [you realize right away what they think]."

I observed firsthand such experiences regarding public officials' condescending attitude toward the activists, at several meetings that the Don Bosco members and I attended at SERVIU between 2013 and 2015. When interacting with the *pobladores*, the state agents—most of whom were upper-middle-class engineers and architects educated at the most prestigious universities in Chile—tried hard to show kindness. They greeted the activists with a kiss and a hug, as if they were close friends, but their greeting struck me as unnatural. During the meetings, they attempted to look empathic and were extremely polite when letting the *pobladores* know that, "once again, the housing projects have been delayed." But the housing activists' recognition of such symbolic violence did not seem to jeopardize their self-esteem or confidence. To the contrary, they fought patronizing attitudes by affirming their dignity as rights-bearing citizens, a kind of political resistance that revealed itself through humor and parody.

Rosa used to complain about how she and other Don Bosco activists were treated by the SERVIU professionals. However, in her complaints she rarely made herself out to be a victim of the system, meaning that she hardly ever uttered her complaints in a self-pitying way. Rosa's social criticism manifested itself when, hoping to amuse other *pobladores*, she made fun of her condition of poverty by unexpectedly playing the part of an upper-class woman having a condescending attitude toward the poor. Either at the committee's activities, in meetings with public officials, or in more personal conversations, she often acted as if she were a rich lady with little empathy for the *pobladores* who happened to be present. In these improvised stand-ups, Rosa performed the role of a gentry person who, in a ridiculous and exaggerated way, "spontaneously" verbalized common opinions that rich people have of the poor, statements that, if articulated by a middle- or upper-class individual, could have been regarded as inappropriate, harmful, or injurious. Unlike the "aesthetic of ambivalence" that Yurchak (2005, 251) discusses when describing the type of irony developed in the late period of the Soviet Union, Rosa's overidentification with an authoritative form—the gestures and manners of a rich woman—allowed her to develop an aesthetic of resistance. By sarcastically performing class-based discriminatory behaviors, she sought to expose the system of social inequality that stigmatizes the poor.

One of these performances took place in the context of a protest in downtown Santiago. In June 2014, the Don Bosco members, together with other *allegados* of the National Federation of Pobladores (FENAPO), decided to occupy the riverbank of the Río Mapocho under the Pío Nono Bridge, right in front the School of Law of the Universidad de Chile. To carry out this occupation, *pobladores* set up an encampment on the riverbank, which lasted for over seventy days. The goal of this action was to make the shortage of housing solutions for the poor visible, by "bringing the reality of peripheral *poblaciones* into the city center," according to Ernesto, the spokesperson of FENAPO. It was in these circumstances when Rosa began to perform her character. One time when we had stayed overnight at this riverbank seizure, looking around the encampment, she said: "For God's sake, look at how the poor people are protesting! They want a house for free . . . such vulgar people!" Then, directing her gaze toward a friend, she carried on with her performance: "I'm a professor of the

School of Law at the Universidad de Chile and am here accompanying the poor. What are you doing here, ma'am? Are you also protesting?" she said, pretending to display false interest in the other person's opinion.

Although Rosa's "routines" generally alluded to the *pobladores'* housing problematic, in many cases she addressed other concerns that were troubling for her and her family. The lack of economic resources to pay for her children's education was, for example, one of these disturbing issues. On another occasion, while waiting to enter a meeting at the Ministry of Housing and Urbanism (MINVU), she was telling other Don Bosco *pobladores* that her nineteen-year-old daughter, who had just graduated from high school, wished to pursue studies at a technical school (*centro de formación técnica*). This meant that Rosa's family needed at least US$2,500 per year to cover tuitions and fees, an amount that neither she nor her common-law partner actually had or could save. While narrating her situation, she asked one of her friends, "Do you have any idea how my daughter can apply for the scholarships offered by the state?" Before getting a response, Rosa ironically added: "I'm just curious. You know that two million pesos [around US$2,500] means nothing to me because I have tons of money [*a mí me sobra la plata*]."

Having these and other ethnographic anecdotes in mind, in July 2015 I visited Rosa to delve into how she made sense of her life experiences as a *pobladora* in terms of dignity. In particular, I wanted to explore how she problematized the issue of dignity by reflecting on her belonging to a group that, along with experiencing economic precariousness on a daily basis, is referred to as—using her words—"vulgar people" by others. The following is a transcription of part of the conversation we had:

> *Do you think that society, broadly speaking, treats* pobladores *in a dignified way?*
>
> Not at all; society excludes you from everything. Besides, people think that all of us who come from a *población* are criminals or thieves. This society marginalizes you.
>
> *When have you felt such discrimination?*
>
> Sometimes, when we have meetings at the SERVIU, I feel that the people who work there discriminate against you because they assume that, as we go to these meetings, we don't have an education or something like that. . . . I feel like if they kiss you on the cheek [to greet] it is because they feel the obligation to do so, but they don't really like it. . . . I think that we all have the same rights, regardless of our education. . . . For them we are all dirty and stinky . . . my

clothes may be very old, but I have to demonstrate that they are clean, that I smell good, that at least I take a shower before going to the meeting.

As discussed earlier in this book, *pobladores* have long made use of cleanliness-based narratives to construe the urban poor as marginalized subjects who, in spite of their social status, are endowed with dignity. This echoes what Martínez and Palacios (1996), in their cultural analysis of the urban poor, call a "culture of decency," conceptualized as a system of dispositions through which the poor are capable of overcoming the humiliating effects of poverty by embracing strict moral codes based on honesty, honor, temperance, and transcendence. *Pobladores'* self-recognition as being endowed with dignity is closely related to their subjective identification as nondirty individuals who, irrespective of their residential situation, deserve respect and equal treatment. In chapter 4, I showed that such an approach was tellingly revealed when, in the mid-twentieth century, housing activists conceived of the lack of hygiene of *poblaciones callampas* (shantytowns) as a degrading way of living that denied them their right to live in "humane" conditions. In doing so, they were able to formulate a language of rights as dignity-bearing people, which ultimately contributed to the emergence of the *pobladores* movement.

Currently, the *pobladores'* sanitary narratives are not reduced to critical appraisals of the structural forces preventing them from obtaining dignified housing. As demonstrated through Rosa's discourse and her performances, *pobladores'* expectations—such as her interest in finding economic support to fund her daughter's undergraduate studies—conflict with what they understand as social stigmas that categorize them as an unclean, uneducated, and an undesirable population. From the *pobladores'* perspective, this system of social categorization operates as a mechanism of symbolic domination that reinforces social hierarchies by assuming that poverty is, by definition, opposed to well-being. Under this dominant framework, *pobladores* can attain welfare, social respect, and dignity not only by getting out of poverty (see Han 2012) but also by denying their subjectivity as *pobladores*. This becomes even more problematic when Chile's neoliberal state draws on this ideology to allocate social spending.

Technologies of Objectification

Early in the morning on Tuesday, December 13, 2011, Santiago's residents awoke to the sound of housing activists blocking the city's main streets. As on many other occasions, hundreds of members of FENAPO had set up barricades at the intersections of major avenues in different sectors of the city, causing severe traffic congestion. On this occasion, however, the goal of the protests was not to demand more subsidies, but to criticize the changes to the system of socioeconomic classification, called the Survey of Social Protection (Ficha de Protección Social, popularly known as *la Ficha*). Proposed by Sebastián Piñera's first government (2010–2014), these changes sought to redefine the terms used to determine which families were eligible to receive benefits from social programs. This proposal, the activists said, would make thousands of families ineligible for housing subsidies. The changes initially suggested by this administration were never put into practice. In January 2016, however, Bachelet's second administration (2014–2018) replaced the Survey of Social Protection with a new instrument of socioeconomic stratification called the Social Household Registry (Registro Social de Hogares).

Both the Survey of Social Protection and the National Household Registry exemplify a paradigm of welfare distribution that, in Latin America, has been known as *focalización* (means testing for benefits). This methodology has resulted in policies that, in contrast to the principle of universality, are oriented exclusively toward the most vulnerable segments of the population.[17] To apply for housing subsidies, my interlocutors had to be categorized as vulnerable by the Survey of Social Protection. To do so, they had to attend an interview with a state agent, generally a city hall social worker. Some weeks later, they were given a score based on their responses, calculated by the Ministry of Social Development and Family. This score was used to assign them to a socioeconomic quintile and, accordingly, determined their eligibility for housing programs.[18] Most of the Don Bosco committee members were in the first quintile, meaning they obtained housing subsidies from the Solidarity Housing Fund, the program oriented to the lowest-income groups.

The Survey of Social Protection was developed by the first government of Michelle Bachelet (2006–2010) as part of a new System of Social Protection. As a policy characteristic of neoliberal welfare states,[19] Bachelet's social protection programs were intended to allocate social spending to poor and lower-middle-class families who have been unable to establish conditions for economic security. The Survey of Social Protection came to replace the Ficha CAS II—a new version of the Ficha CAS created in the late 1970s—which was a means-testing tool that classified families by measuring their household goods, type of housing, level of schooling, and access to basic services.[20] Unlike the previous CAS and CAS II, the Survey of Social Protection classification assumed that poverty is a dynamic condition, meaning that a family that was initially recognized as nonpoor could be reclassified as vulnerable later on, and vice versa. To improve the methodology used in CAS and CAS II, the Survey of Social Protection included other variables in its analysis of poverty, such as an individual's capacity for generating income, a measurement that is adjusted according to each household's particular needs.[21]

In 2011, Piñera's government tried to change the Survey of Social Protection to reveal the number of what former secretary of social development Joaquín Lavín called *falsos pobres*, literally translated as "fake poor people" (*El Mercurio* 2011). As a Chilean version of the North American "welfare queen," fake poor people were families who supposedly cheated on the survey.[22] Housing activists, however, saw Piñera's initiative as a way of making it more difficult for the poor to qualify for housing subsidies. In the December 2011 protest, FENAPO issued a public statement:

> We reject the Survey of Social Protection as a valid mechanism for measuring [poverty] because it is designed to falsify reality and hide poverty by classifying thousands of families . . . as nonpoor. We blame the Ministry of Social Development . . . for wanting to end poverty by decree. . . . With the excuse that poor people cheat, the government wants to meddle in our private information. We strongly reject this, as it constitutes not only a menace to our privacy, but is also an act of discrimination toward *pobladores* since, in this country, nobody surveys the rich nor enters their houses to measure them. (Federación Nacional de Pobladores 2011)

This statement not only questions how the state manipulates the production of scientific knowledge about poverty but also criticizes the objectifying nature of the Survey of Social Protection. This critique is reminiscent of Michel Foucault's (2010) conception of the subject in terms of determinant fields of knowable objects, meaning that subject formation is grounded in the construction of objects of knowledge. In this case, the protesters criticized the class-based character of the Survey of Social Protection: the state measures, evaluates, and classifies only the poor as objects of scientific knowledge, scrutinizing how they live or what they do in their private lives. The *allegados'* protest was framed not only by their aspiration to become homeowners but also by their desire to change the terms in which the state construes them as vulnerable.

Cheating as Resistance

For most of my interlocutors, there was nothing "objective" in the way the scores were calculated, an idea that was grounded in empirical knowledge. They all claimed to have relatives, friends, or neighbors who were assigned totally different scores despite having similar living standards. This opinion was bound to a sense of uncertainty: no matter how poor they were, they would never really know their score until they checked it online at the Ministry of Social Development and Family's web page. As a result, many *allegados* adopted strategies that would lower their scores, most commonly by cheating on the Ficha survey, to make sure that they qualified for housing subsidies. Cheating was not a practice that Don Bosco committee members necessarily condemned. For example, Carla, a single woman in her early thirties with a four-year-old son, who had studied at a university and worked as a preschool teacher, could not afford a house of her own on her salary of about US$615 a month. Applying for housing subsidies through an *allegados* committee was the only way she could become a homeowner. But she struggled to be recognized as eligible to join Don Bosco:

> It was really difficult for me to get into the *comité* because, at first, I was assigned 9,500 points just for having a college degree. . . . That's why many people cheat on the Ficha. You *have* to cheat. In my case, I went [to city hall] to talk with the social worker and had to bother her in order to get my points lowered. I told her, "Do you want me to not wash my face or not take a shower for a week? Do you want me to come in with my hair dirty? Do you want me to lie to you and tell you that I'm unemployed, that I haven't studied?" They [the city hall's representatives] lowered my points when I complained.

Housing activists cheated to deal with the anxiety caused by uncertainty. In the case of Carla, for instance, having a college degree turned out to be deeply problematic because it indicated her "nonvulnerable" condition. She viewed any improvement in her living standards as a risk, since it might result in her exclusion from welfare programs. This paradox compelled her to articulate her criticism of the Ficha as a matter of dignity. Carla's argument was that of a working-class woman for whom the "easiest" way to qualify for benefits was to renounce her dignity by presenting herself as a dirt-poor individual. She was unwilling to do that, however. She chose not to cheat, but she did not morally condemn those who did; moreover, she justified cheating. In that sense, Carla's assertion of her personal dignity did not entail following or obeying abstract, transcendental values like those of Christianity (e.g., honesty, integrity) but was expressed through her complaints about a welfare system that forced her to act in ways she considered unworthy and undignified of a *pobladora*.

"Now Everybody Can Have a Car"
Carla's story illustrates the disjunction framing *allegados*' participation in housing programs: their desire to move up (*surgir*) in life conflicts with how the state

and, ultimately, a class-based society measure poverty. This disjunction gives rise to a disturbing conundrum: the *allegados* construed their recognition as vulnerable not only as being based on banal misrepresentations of their living conditions but also as a threat to their subjectivity as dignified *pobladores*. This disjunction becomes even clearer when the *allegados* see themselves as rational economic actors who can acquire expensive material goods like cars.

On July 26, 2014, around 6:10 p.m., I was chatting with four *pobladores* at the entrance of the Villa Rodrigo Carranza's community center (*sede social*) while waiting for a Don Bosco housing committee meeting to start. We were talking about trivial matters, nothing related to housing struggles or urban politics. But everything changed when an applicant showed up around 6:15 p.m. A good friend of one of the guys I was talking with arrived in a car and parked it right in front of where we were hanging out. When he got out of the vehicle, his friend yelled at him "Buena po', vulnerable!" ("What's up, vulnerable man!"), which, of course, made everybody laugh. Unquestionably, the latter said this to his friend without the intention of being offensive. And his friend took it as what it was, as a harmless welcoming joke. The guy who had just showed up in his car did not join us in the conversation, but his arrival generated an illuminating discussion about the meanings of poverty in neoliberal Chile, articulated around a central question: can the poor buy a car? For one *poblador*, it was absolutely inconceivable that a member of an *allegados* committee had a car. He emphatically said: "If you can pay for a car, then you can also pay for rent, right? So, nobody who owns a car should be part of the *comité*. Furthermore, if the SERVIU finds out that many of the Don Bosco applicants have vehicles, they could be in real trouble because we're all supposed to be vulnerable. . . . Have you ever seen a *persona vulnerable* [vulnerable person] with a car?"

The three other people who were engaged in this spontaneous discussion group strongly disagreed. From their perspective, being vulnerable and possessing material goods—including a car—were not in contradiction. Thus, it was perfectly understandable that an *allegado* got to the meeting by car. One of the individuals supporting this point of view said: "In this country the poor are told that they can't get ahead, that they can't have a car. Let's make this clear. There are five social classes: extreme poverty, the poor, the workers, the middle class, and the upper class. A poor guy or a worker can have a car if they are capable of saving money and getting credit. Now everybody can get a car."

This debate, which lasted about ten minutes, ended when all the interlocutors agreed upon one point: common ideas of poverty are full of caricatures in which the poor are depicted as individuals who, using one the discussant's words, are "dirty, barefoot, and with muddy feet."

The ethnographic illustrations I have provided disclose a key aspect: the construction of the poor as vulnerable by state technologies of socioeconomic classification is built upon ideas, registers, and meanings of poverty that *pobladores* cannot decipher. Thus, the *allegados'* everyday experiences cannot be understood or read through the lens of social programs allegedly aimed at generating the conditions for overcoming poverty. Fearing not to meet the criteria to become eligible for subsidies, the urban poor seek to permanently accommodate their expectations to those of the state. This, however, turns out to be problematic, as it involves representing themselves as "dirt" poor residents, which my interlocutors conceived of as a menace to their dignity as *pobladores*. It is in this context that the right to a life with dignity emerged as the Chilean housing movement's new strategic orientation.

The Right to a Life with Dignity

In the quote with which I began this chapter, the Movimiento de Pobladores en Lucha stated that housing is the starting point in a long and permanent struggle for a *vida digna*, which they understood as a right that is "built on people's dreams, wishes, and desires to have a good life" (Movimiento de Pobladores en Lucha 2011, 31). How can we interpret the *pobladores'* right to a life with dignity, a right that is construed as the renewed political horizon of the movement and is based on a moral category such as "dignity"? As a process based on the use of moral categories, the search for dignity entails the realization of practices of self-fashioning and self-subjection that turn individuals into ethical subjects.[23] But the quest for dignity also involves a number of reflective practices through which individuals seek to overcome the ethical dilemmas they confront on a daily basis. Zigon's (2007) concept of moral breakdown alludes to a moment of ethical dilemma in which moral expectations and dispositions become insufficient for individuals to be-in-the-world, obligating them to perform reflective tactics in order to overcome these quandaries. In his words, moral breakdowns are "social and personal moments when persons or groups of persons are forced to step-away from their unreflective everydayness and think-through, figure out, work on themselves, and to respond to certain ethical dilemmas, troubles, or problems" (Zigon 2007, 140). Political claims for dignity thus respond to the "ethical imperatives" felt by those who realize that, at some point in their lives, they cannot live in everydayness that is "akin to being trapped in a world" (Zigon 2014, 756–57).

Allegados' everyday experiences were framed by events in which their dignity is called into question, revealing these ethical imperatives. I previously discussed two of these moments: first, the events surrounding their lives as *allegados* such as "asking for permission" or "giving explanations" about their private life; second, the moments when they are faced with the need to obtain a low enough score to qualify for welfare programs. While in the first case they feel obliged to subordinate their individual agency to, as in Ángela's experience, that of her mother-in-law to avoid domestic violence, in the second case *allegados* are forced to represent themselves as unworthy in order to qualify for housing subsidies. Confronted with these predicaments, my interlocutors performed reflective tactics to affirm their dignity, such as getting involved in housing assemblies, collectively applying for subsidies through *comités de allegados*, or cheating on the Survey of Social Protection. These tactics enabled a new dignity-based political language through which *pobladores* resisted the exclusionary character of neoliberal housing policies. The act of overcoming an everydayness that threatened the dignity of the urban poor thus established the conditions in which the right to a life with dignity arose as a new demand by housing movements.

Laura was a member of Techo Ahora, a housing assembly formed in the municipality of La Pintana, one of the poorest districts in Santiago (see chapter 5). Laura conceptualized *la vida digna* as "the life that one draws by oneself [no matter] if we want square, round, or small houses, if we build them as semidetached or detached houses [or] if we decide to have a park in the middle [of the neighborhood] or on a corner." A life with dignity, in her view, is a life that *pobladores* "build up on our own by exercising the rights that should be guaranteed by the state."

Laura's conceptualization of a life with dignity, which certainly echoes that of the Movimiento de Pobladores en Lucha, was framed by her hope to build a future life in her municipality of origin together with other *pobladores* with whom she worked in the struggle for urban rights. To arrive at such a definition, she identified two interrelated dimensions that, in different ways, speak to the conditions necessary for a *vida digna*. The first refers to the physical environment that she and her neighbors sought to develop as members of a grassroots organization. A life with dignity, in her view, was one in which the material aspects of urban space—houses, squares, public spaces—are constructed in accordance with the *pobladores'* expectations and wishes. This element takes us back to what I mentioned earlier when discussing how *allegados'* everyday experiences led them to imagine dignified housing as the condition for the possibility of making their own home. Both the demand for dignified housing and a life with dignity are, in that sense, determined primarily by specific material claims that neoliberal housing policies are not able to meet. Issues such as the location of housing projects, the inaccessibility of public services, or the quality of both housing units and their surrounding public spaces are thus understood as physical manifestations of an unequal society that segregates the poor. A life with dignity would start only when *pobladores* are able to subvert those material conditionings by collectively participating in social protest movements that fight for urban rights.

This perspective enables us to analyze the second element through which the housing activists I encountered made sense of the concept in question. When speaking about a life with dignity, Laura and the Movimiento de Pobladores en Lucha saw *pobladores* as agents that are able to both demand dignity as a right and achieve it by intervening politically in the social production of space. They alluded directly to community-based, everyday social practices as the source of the *pobladores'* transformative power: if they have been capable of demanding that the state build better quality housing for the poor, it is only because they have organized to transform their living conditions autonomously. For the activists I met, a life with dignity referred not only to a kind of life in which the material needs for inhabiting a territory are satisfied but also to one in which the community itself takes charge of its fate "on a daily basis." What is at stake for them is both the (material) construction of dignified city spaces and the constitution of an empowered community through which the urban poor can, using Laura's metaphor, "draw" their life projects on their own.

Recognizing the physical-material and the community-related dimensions as constitutive elements of a life with dignity is key to problematizing what it means to have such a demand as the political horizon for the contemporary *pobladores* movement. At first glance, a life with dignity appears to be an umbrella concept through which the urban poor can claim a number of social rights such as housing, employment, education, and health care. It is this attribute that has enabled *allegados* to maintain that their "struggle is larger than a house" (fig. 8), suggesting that they imagine their political mobilizations as broadly oriented toward improving their conditions as poor urban residents. Housing, in the context of such a mobilization process, represents the first and a necessary step toward achieving a life with dignity, but it is not the only step. The notion of dignity, in allowing the poor to imagine new possibilities for being-in-the-world (Zigon 2014), thus emerges as a right to be demanded only when it is situated in relation to other social rights.

The political value of the notion of dignity goes beyond its discursive utilization as an explicit right to be claimed by the poor. For housing activists, this idea also functioned as a signifier, allowing them to produce critical evaluations through which they politically analyze their experiences with social exclusion. In his theory of recognition, philosopher Axel Honneth (1992, 189) maintains that notions of integrity and disrespect make "implicit reference to a subject's claim to be granted recognition by others." The experience of disrespect, accordingly, is related to injuries that can even "cause the identity of the entire person to collapse." Honneth identifies three forms of disrespect—physical mistreatment, denial of rights, and degradation of the social value of individuals or groups—which are subjectively internalized as a dispossession of self-confidence, self-respect, and self-esteem.[24] The sentiment of misrecognition and social degradation can, however, transform into forms of political resistance, through which individuals and larger collectives can react to these forms of disrespect. Honneth (1995, 163) notes that "there must be a semantic bridge between the impersonal aspirations of a social movement and their participants' private experiences of injury." Dignity, in this case, is the "semantic bridge" enabling *pobladores* to deal collectively with different experiences of injustice, including the lack of affordable housing for the poor, or the very fact of being construed as vulnerable by discriminatory technologies of socioeconomic characterization. As a semantic bridge, the notion of dignity allows for the articulation of a political language in which the subjectivity of the urban poor establishes a relationship to the self on the basis of "positive modes of self-confidence, self-respect, and self-esteem" (Honneth 1992, 196).

Moral Categories and New Political Horizons

When discussing the relationship between neoliberal social programs and the everyday experiences of working-class urban residents in Chile, Clara Han (2012) contends that these programs are grounded in the idea that the poor achieve dignity only when they get out of poverty. However, people's quest for dignity, she continues, is made up of a different set of imaginaries and practices. Their living with dignity "is neither formalized nor publicly pronounced; it is neither isolatable nor pinned down as a moral code. Rather, its outlines emerge through sustained engagement with everyday life" (Han 2012, 69). In this chapter, I have shown that poor urban dwellers' desire for a life with dignity can also result in new forms of collective action in which, by conceptualizing dignity as a right, they reformulate the strategic orientations of housing movements. The case examined here contributes to problematizing the extent to which people living in poverty in neoliberal regimes, through the use of moral concepts like dignity, can develop emergent forms of politicization by participating in the very welfare programs they question, criticize, and mobilize against.

A significant part of the literature scrutinizing the relation between liberal welfare programs and excluded communities has underscored the disciplinary, even pacifying, effects of the former on the latter.[25] Unprivileged individuals, in most of these accounts, have been described as the result of specific subject-formation processes that constitute them as self-reliant, entrepreneurial citizens capable of governing themselves. In a similar fashion, anthropologists' reflections on ethics and morality have been concerned with the ethnographic analysis of the ways practices of self-fashioning and self-subjection make individuals into ethical subjects. The ordinary ethics approach, in particular, have concentrated on how groups and populations respond to structural conditioning through ordinary ethical actions and discourses occurring fundamentally in the private or domestic sphere. To expand on these perspectives, I have accounted for how the use of moral categories, while allowing vulnerable people to become ethical subjects, also permits them to signify their everyday experiences in political terms. Recognizing the political role of moral concepts has significant value for anthropological research: moral categories, in addition to helping verbalize criteria for practical judgment through which individuals act morally, also let us know how and under what circumstances social movements seeking to transform people's precarious lives arise. Moral categories, such as the one discussed here, are certainly utilized by individuals to act "in favor of the good and against the evil" (Fassin 2008, 334). But at the same time, they also operate as political signifiers by means of which people—especially those suffering any form of exclusion—articulate, configure, and assemble their claims to rights, equality, and social recognition.

As an emblematic example of the neoliberal shift, Chile is an important case study for examining how moral categories contribute to the emergence of social movements organized around a new rights-based language. As explained largely in this book, in neoliberal Chile social housing has become legally and formally sanctioned ever since it was converted into a commodity that low-income families can obtain by participating in subsidy-based programs. The commodification of housing has entailed segregation of the poor, forced to live in peripheral urban areas. This phenomenon has given rise to novel social protest movements fighting for the right to a *vida digna*. Dignity emerges here as a concept enabling poor residents to build critical judgments of their daily experiences—conceived of as degrading and humiliating—such as living as *allegados* and being objectified as a vulnerable population. This explains why *pobladores'* quest for dignity encompasses both political claims for homeownership and strong criticism of the state's instruments of socioeconomic characterization, which are understood as technologies of classification operating through class-based forms of degradation. This also helps us understand why, in the 2019 social uprising, civil-society activists drew widely on the idea of dignity to demand both the expansion of social rights and, more importantly, a new constitution.

Both residing in overcrowded conditions and being construed as welfare recipients are two structural determinants that housing activists experience and make sense of in their everyday life, through what Zigon (2007) conceptualizes as ethical imperatives. In these moments of ethical dilemma, they see their subjectivity as dignity-bearing dwellers endangered and feel compelled to deploy certain reflective tactics to affirm their dignity. It is only then that the moral categories used by people to deal with these ethical moments assume the form of a "semantic bridge" (Honneth 1995). This takes us to another important implication for anthropological research: the moments in which these ethical imperatives reveal themselves can inform us about how social movements establish the conditions for individuals to transform themselves into political subjectivities by performing ethical practices in everyday life.

Understanding dignity as a right and as a semantic bridge—two aspects that help us examine how the right to a life with dignity has become the new strategic demand of right-to-housing movements—thus invites us to reflect on the formulation of a politics of everyday life. In the case discussed here, *pobladores'* wishes and desires to move up (*surgir*) or get ahead (*salir adelante*) turn out to be profoundly political, since they are framed by their aspirations to achieve a *vida digna*. In organizing their ethical practices under this political horizon, they deal collectively with moments of ethical dilemmas while constituting themselves as ethical-political subjects. In doing so, they are able to consider themselves as endowed with a dignity that is not external to them, a dignity that, accordingly, can be claimed positively as a right when macro-structural forces jeopardize the *allegados'* existence as moral subjects. If they demand the right to a life with dignity, it is not because they lack or have lost dignity; rather, it is because they perceive that Chile's social inequality threatens their subjectivity as always-already dignified *pobladores*. It is thus the re-affirmation of their dignity as poor residents—a condition attained through a political mobilization for rights—that makes it possible for them to imagine a *vida digna*.

Conclusion

"Until Dignity Becomes Custom"

The first time I returned to the Comité de Allegados Don Bosco, after conducting the main field research for this study, it could not have been under more meaningful circumstances. In June 2015, upon arriving in Chile, I called some of the activists I had met in 2013 to inform them that I would be in Santiago for two months and that I wanted to continue to participate in the organization during that period of time. Ernesto told me: "Come over to the Altos de la Cordillera housing project, close to the corner of Mirador Azul Street and Froilán Roa Street. The SERVIU [Metropolitan Service of Housing and Urbanism] scheduled an inspection for us to see the structural work of it and make sure that everything is going well. It'd be great if you could check out by yourself how it looks! Let's meet there at 3:00 p.m."

Altos de la Cordillera (fig. 9) was one of the three subsidized housing developments for which Don Bosco *pobladores* had been struggling for over ten years. It consisted of 180 apartments distributed into fourteen, five-floor blocks in which more than one hundred families of the housing assembly would eventually become homeowners in 2016. In March 2014, the private construction company in charge of building Altos de la Cordillera had presented a project sketch to the Don Bosco members at a meeting held at La Florida City Hall. The *pobladores* were shown some PowerPoint slides with the housing plan and listened to an architect tell them what they already knew: that the locational attributes of this social housing project—which is surrounded by public hospitals, two shopping malls, supermarkets, and a metro station--"made it unique,"

FIGURE 9. Altos de la Cordillera Housing Project, La Florida. Credit: Photo by the author, June 2015.

quoting the architect. Fifteen months had passed since that occasion, and at this time the *pobladores* were able to see, in person, what their soon-to-be new neighborhood was like. The inspection I was invited to attend was therefore a milestone for them. And I could clearly notice this upon arriving at the site. Although it was a weekday, many of them had taken the afternoon off from work to not miss out on the opportunity to have a firsthand look at the project. They expressed genuine happiness about what they were seeing. When I entered the model apartment on display, I saw a man talking to his six-year-old son. "Get ready to have your own room," the father said proudly. Next to him, a woman jokingly said to a friend: "I won't ever let my *suegra* [mother-in-law] in!" Others simply took tons of pictures of the housing units with their cell phones.

While wandering around the apartment, I ran into José, a construction worker who had become my friend during the first stage of fieldwork. I saw him carefully measuring the length of a wall with his tape measure. "Hey! What's up? Long time no see!" he said, warmly. Then, showing me his measuring tape, he added: "I just want to make sure that I'm going to receive what I was promised: a fifty-eight-square meter [about 624-square-foot] apartment." "So, what do you think?" I asked. "This looks great," he stated. Then, while knocking on the wall, he added: "This is *hormigón* [concrete]. If we throw a party here, none of my neighbors will hear anything." Then we walked together around the apartment. During our tour, José gave me his views on the quality of the roof, the windows, and the doors. He also carefully examined the electrical system of the apartment. "You look very excited!" I told him. "This looks great," he replied. Then, he added: "I'm really happy. This housing project is going to be perfect for us. We are not going to leave La Florida and everything is nearby. But you know what is even better? That nobody gave this to us; we fought for this."

Urban Agencies

In this book I have reflected on how poor urban residents struggling for housing and dignity become ethical-political subjects through their engagement in neoliberal welfare programs. To do so, I have ethnographically analyzed the case of Chilean *pobladores* who, by participating in state-regulated *allegados* assemblies, have remobilized in a powerful way for·the right to stay put in their municipalities of origin since the mid-2000s. I also have shown that scholarly reflections on *pobladores* have, to a great extent, examined them as political agencies in contexts in which the popular sectors were able to politically engage in the public sphere. This explains why, specifically in the early 1970s and the mid-1980s, poor residents captured the attention of social scientists seeking to account for how urban protests could result in transformative social movements. This also elucidates why since 1990, once democracy was restored, *pobladores* were no longer conceived of as transformative subjects but as a vulnerable population falling into more general processes of demobilization. According to this line of reasoning, the very existence of *pobladores* as political subjectivities was thus subordinated to the level of their power to intervene in the political system as "insurgent" citizens—using Holston's (2008) terminology—capable of realizing political actions such as mass land occupations. To challenge these approaches, in this book I have demonstrated that new generations of poor residents have been able to reformulate their political agencies as *pobladores* by engaging in market-based housing programs.

Agency, Saba Mahmood (2012, 34) argues, "must be explored within the grammar of concepts in which it resides." I take such a proposal not only as an invitation to detach the idea of agency from the goals of progressive politics but also to account ethnographically for the terms, meanings, and senses in which it develops within historically situated processes of political mobilization. The type of working-class agency that is anchored in the signifier *poblador* results from both material and symbolic practices of city making, practices that enable housing activists to constitute themselves as subjects entitled to the right to have rights. The very concept of *poblador*, I contend, must be understood as a political category of subject formation endowed with a performative character, which makes the rearticulation of the agential condition of the urban poor in different historical circumstances possible. To reformulate their political powers and form themselves as subjects capable of demanding rights from the state, new generations of activists base their modalities of action on their self-identification as *pobladores*. In doing so, they establish a symbolic link to the *movimiento de pobladores* of the 1960s and early 1970s while producing a set of ethical narratives through which they make sense of their residential condition as people in need of housing.

Subsidy-based housing policies have been ineffective in tackling the shortage of social housing. This became more evident in the early 2020s, as the economic recession caused by the COVID-19 pandemic led to the deepening of the housing crisis. While housing deficit reached 600,000 units in 2021—100,000 more than in 2017—the number of families living in squatter settlements went up to 81,643 in 2021, around 34,500 more than in 2019.[1] The lack of affordable housing affected also Latin American and Caribbean immigrants, whose growing presence in the country helped transform the cultural landscapes of Chilean cities.[2] By 2021, 56 percent of the residents of *campamentos* in Santiago were foreigners, turning the settlements into new spaces of sociability, inclusion, and cultural diversification.[3]

The resurgence of *campamentos* in the early 2020s demonstrates that, when faced with economic precarity, vulnerable residents keep utilizing autoconstruction as a means to attain the right to housing. However, unlike the squatter movement of the mid-twentieth century, in neoliberal Chile housing struggles are not organized around this mode of city making. As the housing crisis intensifies, this may certainly change. Autoconstruction could become predominant again both as a practice developed by the poor and as a state-led means of housing production. But as of this writing, poor families do not expect to autoconstruct their houses and neighborhoods to become homeowners, and autoconstruction is not the primary force acting on the urbanization of peripheries. Likewise, the social movement they have engendered neither supports a socialist government like that of Salvador Allende nor seeks to challenge the right to property by massively occupying empty lots in the richest neighborhoods. "Housing or death" is no longer their battle flag, and politicians do not recognize them as the most active element of the working classes anymore. *Pobladores*, rather, enroll in state-regulated housing committees, participate actively in welfare programs, save money privately, and apply for housing subsidies to fulfill *el sueño de la casa propia* (the dream of one's own home). They look forward to becoming homeowners in order to make a home according their own criteria for privacy, based on ideas of autonomy and self-sufficiency. They also develop ethical practices—toward themselves and toward others—through which they legitimize themselves as worthy of rights, dignity, and social recognition. In this way, they see themselves as hardworking and honest, underprivileged individuals who make sacrifices for their families and neighborhoods. This leads them to configure moralizing appraisals, allowing them to differentiate between those who "deserve" housing rights and those who do not.

Even so, the people I encountered were still able to re-create their political agencies as *pobladores* and, furthermore, develop political performative acts that turned out to be profoundly transformative. By considering themselves as heirs of the territorial rights earned by their parents and grandparents, they took part in an emerging process of remobilization aimed at fighting a system of capital accumulation based on urban land speculation. They protested against exclusionary subsidy-based policies that forced them to live in the urban peripheries, and questioned the instruments of socioeconomic classification through which the state construes them as welfare recipients. In addition, by collectively engaging in grassroots organizations, they articulated rights-based narratives to resist the "accumulation by dispossession" (Harvey 2012) resulting from the commodification of the social right to housing. They were ultimately able to propose new strategic orientations for the *pobladores* movement, on the basis of their claims for the right to live with dignity in the neighborhoods in which they were born and raised.

Subjects of Rights

In a context of neoliberal urbanization, the constitution of *pobladores* as political subjects has had significant political outcomes. This process of subject formation has led contemporary poor residents to produce particular understandings of themselves as individuals endowed with rights to the city, enabling the development of residency-based formulations of citizenship. By conceiving of themselves as city makers, *pobladores* reclaim the legacy of past housing movements while articulating new political demands, giving rise to a renewed politics of urban life. What the National Federation of Pobladores (FENAPO) calls territorial demand—or the right to stay put in the *allegados'* municipalities of origin—is indicative in this regard. As I showed in chapter 5, this right has surfaced forcefully in working-class neighborhoods in which housing activists, despite the generalized increase in land prices, expect to become homeowners.

But the *pobladores'* view of themselves as subjects of rights is not only predicated on their self-identification as descendants of those who participated in the housing struggles of the mid-twentieth century. To form themselves as legitimate rights bearers, they also draw on a moral conceptualization of *pobladores* as responsibilized residents, strongly committed to their families, their neighborhoods, and their housing assemblies. The *pobladores'* self-understanding as moral subjects materializes through what I have called the politics of effort. As a system of rights allocation, the politics of effort results in technologies of evaluation through which, by "objectively" assessing the behavior of each individual, housing assemblies distribute rights among their members according to their own criteria of fairness and justice.

Pobladores become agents able to address the state using rights-based language through an urban formulation of citizenship. Their widespread use of national symbols like the Chilean flag or the national anthem indicates that they do continue to look at the nation as a community to which they have political and emotional ties. However, the rights-claiming practices that they develop in their everyday life go far beyond their self-recognition as formal members of a nation-state. If Chilean *pobladores* think of themselves as entitled to rights to the city, it is because they "struggle" for them on a daily basis. This implies that they consider residency a significant type of political membership in which their symbolic and material practices of city making transform them into legitimate rights-bearing citizens. This perspective on rights and citizenship reminds us of what Walzer (1989, 216) defines as a "republican" mode of citizenship: for *pobladores*, citizenship is understood less as a status that endows them with rights and more "as an office, a responsibility, a burden proudly assumed," which rests upon their active engagement in public affairs.

The housing activists' political imagination unveils a number of tensions and dilemmas in terms of the citizenship regime in Chile. First, it reveals their criticisms of the ideological rationale through which Chile's neoliberal state allocates social benefits among working-class families. For *pobladores*, these programs are the most visible expression of how a class-based society, rather than distributing welfare as universal social rights, selects "the poorest among the poor"—quoting one of my interlocutors—to determine who are eligible for these rights. The *allegados* I met strongly questioned the idea of housing as a commodity to be acquired in the private market. Instead, they openly proclaimed the social right to housing, which was at the heart of their movement. For them, welfare programs based on the principle of *focalización* (means testing of benefits) were illustrative of a social system that denies universal rights to its citizens. In their view, these programs, in considering them welfare "beneficiaries," also negate their very capacity to claim rights; that is, their very existence as *pobladores*.

This idea takes us to the second point of analysis related to the examination of the nature of social rights in a neoliberal regime, a subject that, in Chile, became popular among public intellectuals and social scientists after the 2011 student movement.[4] Like millions of Chileans who mobilized in October 2019, my interlocutors conceive of housing, education, and health care—to name a few—as universal social rights that, since the late 1970s, have been systematically commodified. They understood the capacity of individuals to exert these rights as grounded primarily on the possession of economic capital, a phenomenon that led them to maintain a clear political demand: that these rights be guaranteed by the state as a means to secure a truly democratic and universal access to them. Nonetheless, as I showed in chapter 4, housing activists' advocacy for social rights is framed by an ambivalent, even contradictory, understanding of these rights. All the people I encountered expressed a universal comprehension of social rights. In their opinion, all the members of a political community have the same right to have rights such as housing or education. But at the same time, their understanding of the universal nature of rights was not based on the consideration that these rights should *necessarily* be provided for free for everyone. In fact, for most of the *pobladores* I met, the very act of fighting for social rights seemed to be opposed to demanding that the state give them housing "as a gift," drawing on the words of one *pobladora*. Consistent with their politics of effort, they looked at the acquisition of rights as the result of their subjective involvement in urban struggles or, using their language, as the consequence of the *esfuerzo* (effort) they make on a daily basis to subvert their current conditions of exclusion. As citizen city makers, contemporary *pobladores* in need of housing see everyday life as the condition that establishes the possibility for transforming their own existence. Thus, they forcefully reject the idea that social rights are inherently free for everyone, even for those who "do not struggle" or those *cuicos* (rich people) who have enough money to provide for themselves. They do so because it is considered "unfair," and also because it would involve withdrawing the political praxis from their subjectivity as rights bearers. In the words of a *pobladora* of the Don Bosco committee: "The rich do have rights like everybody else. But they don't need them because they have money to pay for what they want. We, instead, have to struggle for what we want . . . so I don't think that it's fair that the rich don't pay for education or for a house, do you?"

Rights to the City, Rights to Dignity

As I largely discussed throughout this book, since their initial manifestations during the first decades of the twentieth century, the *pobladores'* claims for housing have been crucial for the expansion of citizenship rights among the poor. Housing struggles have served as one of the preferred forms of political activism for working-class residents. *Los sin casa* (those who do not have a home of their own) have been able to develop new political subjectivities by demanding the right to a physical presence in the city. Housing movements have developed through the actions of thousands of poor urban dwellers who, either as room renters, squatters, or *allegados*, understand the city as a space not only of injustice, oppression, and violence but also of insurgency, political contestation, and democratization.

It is precisely the pursuit of strategies for resistance that explains the Chilean *pobladores* mobilizations for the right to the city. Their quest for urban rights has resulted in historically contextualized repertoires of collective action through which they have reframed the character and orientation of the *pobladores* movement. Sidney Tarrow (2011, 6) argues that "contentious politics occurs when ordinary people—often in alliance with more influential citizens and with changes in public mood—join forces in confrontation with elites, authorities, and opponents." For him, ordinary people's forms of collective action are dynamic and open to innovation, which suggests that particular modalities of protest can either be reformulated, change their meaning over time, or eventually be left behind. In neoliberal Chile, housing movements no longer react to forcible evictions carried out by repressive state apparatuses but, rather, seek to resist market forces that silently obligate poor families to move out of their neighborhoods. Likewise, the *pobladores* no longer conceive of mass land takeovers as the first and foremost tactic for becoming homeowners. Housing activists still conduct land seizures to access housing, as well as to claim the symbolic possession of urban spaces and bring the agentival power of the old *movimiento de pobladores* into the present. Nonetheless, when it comes to achieving homeownership, they draw predominantly on state-regulated mechanisms of civic participation, technologies of government that postdictatorial governments used to pacify the poor in the early 1990s.

This book has thus showed the capacity of *pobladores* to adapt their struggles to shifting political contexts. In addition, it has also demonstrated that organizations like *comités de allegados* do not necessarily function as instruments for demobilizing the poor. I do not claim that subsidy-based programs have not been utilized for subordinating purposes. Rather, I argue that the forms of civic participation that result from the poor's involvement in technologies of governmentality are not constrained a priori to the type of politics these programs and policies allow for. The very history of the *pobladores* movement is telling in this regard. In chapter 2, I accounted for how populist governments like that of Eduardo Frei Montalva tried to pacify the urban poor by enrolling them in state-led grassroots associations. Nonetheless, the attempts of the state to channel the *pobladores'* demands gave rise to new forms of politicization, enabling them to develop social movements that, in the early 1970s, even acquired a revolutionary character. The participation of the urban poor in state-regulated *comités de allegados*, rather than being construed as a clear expression of their pacification, must be ethnographically scrutinized. It is only by doing so that we can fully understand the character of the present-day *pobladores* movement, its relations with the past, the political language that housing activists draw on to claim rights, their ideas of citizenship, and their new strategic demands.

In this book I have examined these mobilizations by questioning how market-based housing policies have contributed to the reemergence of urban social movements. My ethnographic approach to these protests aimed to illustrate how poor families exposed to being displaced from their neighborhoods have reframed the right to housing on a territorial basis. As a new stage in urban social movements, housing activists are fighting a neoliberal state whose polices segregate the poor, obligating them to live in peripheral areas of the city, and objectify them as a "vulnerable" population through discriminatory technologies of socioeconomic classification.

As Chile's neoliberal state has done little to stop the increasing privatization of social rights, the signifier *dignity* has assumed a renewed discursive centrality among poor residents. By claiming the right to have a life with dignity, *pobladores* imagine a future in which their aspirations, longings, and expectations find a material base for their manifestation. They struggle to be capable of attaining a new home as proprietors of subsidized housing and also to preserve the sense of community developed in their *población* through their inhabitance as *vecinos* (neighbors). It is in this aspect where *pobladores'* claims for dignity reveal a profoundly political character. Although neoliberal policies helped reduce the housing deficit in the previous decades, the large-scale construction of subsidized housing projects has entailed the displacement of hundreds of thousands of lower-income families from their neighborhoods. The *pobladores'* yearning to live with dignity in their municipalities of origin thus cannot be fulfilled without radically questioning the type of urban development that has come to organize urban spaces over the past four decades. This explains why their demand for dignity has arisen as the new political horizon of the housing movement. As a "semantic bridge" (Honneth 1995, 163), the signifier *dignity* makes possible the articulation of political demands built on daily experiences, which are envisioned as humiliating and degrading. The claim for the right to a *vida digna* can thus be interpreted as the result of a politicization of—following Das's (2012) conceptualization—the "ordinary," which means that this right emerges not from the embrace of transcendental ideals or values but from the *pobladores'* questioning of how their everydayness is structured.

"Until Dignity Becomes Custom"

October 2019 will be remembered as the month in which Chile's neoliberalism was politically defeated. While I was writing this book, wrapping up the ideas I developed through my ethnographic immersion in housing assemblies, Chile changed dramatically in a period of just over one week. After days of high school students' protests against an increase in Santiago's subway fare, on October 18 thousands of Chileans spontaneously took to the streets to protest against socioeconomic inequality. And they did so by claiming the end of neoliberalism. The next day, Santiago's streets were filled with barricades, and after protesters burned down some metro stations and looted several supermarkets, Sebastián Piñera's administration declared a state of emergency. For the first time since Pinochet's regime, a democratic government put Santiago under a curfew. But that didn't stop the demonstrators. One week later, on October 25, almost two million people joined street protests throughout Chile's major cities.

FIGURE 10. "Dignidad," a mural painted in downtown Santiago after the October social uprising. Credit: Photo by the author, January 2020.

Just as in the case of the *pobladores* I met between 2011 and 2015, the activists in 2019 articulated their anti-neoliberal agenda by demanding the right to live with dignity. Murals with the word *dignidad*, just like the ones that I had observed in working-class neighborhoods in the mid-2010s, began to pop up all over the city (fig. 10). Likewise, Santiago's most important public square, the Plaza Italia, was renamed Plaza de la Dignidad by the activists. Having coined a new motto, *hasta que la dignidad se haga costumbre* (until dignity becomes custom), the 2019 demonstrators demanded a new constitution, one that, by securing social rights, would put an end to Pinochet's neoliberal constitution.[5]

The *pobladores* assumed an active role in the 2019 *estallido social* (social uprising). My interlocutors participated keenly in the demonstrations—I ran into many of them at Plaza de la Dignidad on several occasions—while nightly clashes between poor residents and the police became commonplace in Santiago *poblaciones*. As for housing organizations, the FENAPO, Ukamau, and the Movimiento de Pobladores Vivienda Digna—to mention some of the most important *pobladores'* associations—were all part of Unidad Social (Social Unity). Founded in August 2019, Unidad Social was a broad coalition joining student unions, labor unions, housing assemblies, feminist movements, among other grassroots organizations. Given the delegitimization of political parties, Unidad Social was the only organization that seemed capable of channeling the protesters' demands during the 2019 uprising. Unidad Social, in fact, called for a national strike on November 12 that halted some of the most important economic activities, such as the mining and port industries. The strength of the daily protests that occurred between October 18 and November 12 forced Chile's congress to reach an agreement on November 15, allowing Chileans to have an unprecedented constitutional referendum.

The plebiscite took place on October 25, 2020. In this poll, the people could decide democratically if they "approve" or "reject" a new constitution and the mechanism to be used in order to draft it. This mechanism could be either through a "constitutional convention" (composed exclusively of citizens democratically elected to this convention) or a "mixed constitutional convention" (made up of both members of parliament and directly elected citizens). In the weeks prior to the referendum, the activists I met were enthusiastically engaged in the campaign for the *apruebo* (approval). Some leaders of the Don Bosco committee—particularly those who had political connections with the Socialist Party (PS) and the Party for Democracy (PPD)—appeared in the *franja electoral* (authorized political advertising on TV), calling on citizens to approve the new constitution and vote on the constitutional convention. In turn, many other housing activists who contributed to this book took part in grassroots campaigns in La Florida, Peñalolén, and La Pintana. The result of the plebiscite was overwhelming: 78 percent of voters approved of rewriting the constitution, and 79 percent voted in favor of the constitutional convention.[6]

The 2019 social movement has been largely interpreted as a mass reaction against social inequality grounded in a deep-rooted sense of *malestar social* (social malaise).[7] The 2012 Human Development Report published by the UN Development Program points out that the core of social discontent is to be found in the generalized perception that Chilean society does not respect its citizens' dignity and rights. Such a perception is, nonetheless, unequally distributed. Lower-income individuals feel themselves less capable of succeeding when dealing with such forms of injustice. According to the report, this demonstrates that social relations are structured by a "lack of recognition . . .

experienced in the micro-quotidian" (PNUD 2012, 210), affecting most especially the working classes. They were, in fact, those who were more actively involved in the 2019 movement.

The demand for rights to dignity thus emerges precisely when this sense of malaise is interpreted as a political problem, that is, when those who are more exposed to social injustice perceive it as something to be changed through social mobilizations for citizenship rights. This explains the centrality of the signifier dignity among the demonstrators of the 2019 social uprising, who conceived of their protests as largely oriented toward the attainment of decent standards of living. More research is certainly needed in this regard. In the meantime, we can approach this emergent phenomenon by exploring to what degree the urban poor's struggles for dignity enable them to go from particular, sectoral demands—for dignified housing, for dignified work, dignified health care—to more general claims for social transformation, such as the demand for a new constitution. The key issue is thus to examine how *la vida digna* becomes a renewed political horizon for social movements in Chile and elsewhere in the Global South.

When delving into the right to the city, Henri Lefebvre (1996, 179) argued that the working classes' claims are generalizable to the rest of society, as they represent "the general interests of civilization and the particular interests of all social groups of 'inhabitants,' for whom integration and participation become obsessional without making their obsession effective." It is significant to note how, in a context of planetary urbanization, urban social movements like the one I have analyzed in this book are increasingly organized through demands not restricted to, and even different from, the ones that characterize labor-based protests. Is the right to live with dignity advocated by *pobladores* struggling for the right to the city one of these generalizable claims that Lefebvre talked about? Maybe the remobilization processes that Chilean society is experiencing will give us the answer.

Notes

Chapter 1

1. For an historical analysis of Santiago's urban peripheries in the late nineteenth century, see De Ramón (1985).

2. For a detailed analysis of the *pobladores* movement, see Castells (1973, 1983); Pastrana and Threlfall (1974); V. Espinoza (1982, 1988); Garcés (2002); Murphy (2015). See more in chapter 2.

3. See, e.g., Chateau and Pozo's (1987) and Necochea's (1987) works on housing-related issues during the dictatorship.

4. See more in Schneider (1995).

5. See more in Oxhorn (1994); Paley (2001).

6. See more in Donoso and Bülow (2017).

7. See more in Sabatini (2000).

8. See also Caldeira (2017).

9. On the relationship between technologies of government and the process of subject-citizen formation, see Cruikshank (1999); Ong (2003).

10. For other perspectives on Foucault's concept of government, see Rose (1999); Cruikshank (1999); Ong (2003).

11. See, e.g., Bengoa (1996); Martínez and Palacios (1996); Han (2012).

12. On the demobilization of the urban poor in Chile, see Oxhorn (1994); Paley (2001). On the pacification of housing struggles in the 1990s, see Hipsher (1996); Özler (2012).

13. See, e.g., Márquez (2004); Salcedo (2010).

14. See also Koppelman (2018).

15. See, e.g., Ferguson (2010); Kingfisher and Maskovsky (2008).

16. See more in Mahmood (2012).

17. John Austin (1962) defined performative speech acts as those statements that, rather than reporting an action or phenomenon—what he called "constative utterances"—produce it. The verb *perform*, he said, "indicates that the issuing of the utterance is the performing of an action—it is not normally thought of as just saying something" (Austin 1962, 6–7). Thus, the main characteristic of performative utterances is that uttering them is by itself performing an action. "I do," as the accepted response in a marriage ceremony or "I name this ship *Queen Elizabeth*" as the act of naming a ship, Austin argued, are two examples revealing how speech acts perform an action at the time of their verbal expression.

18. To mention a few: Bourdieu (1991); Butler (1997); Yurchak (2005).

19. On the performative role of rituals, see Hollywood (2002); Yurchak (2005).

20. See, e.g., Vekemans (1969); Vekemans, Giusti, and Silva (1970).

21. See, e.g., Mangin (1967); Turner (1968); Perlman (1976); Adler Lomnitz (1977).

22. See also Holston's (2008) concept of insurgent citizenship.

23. In Caldeira's (2000, 221) words, "The urbanization of the periphery was left mostly to private initiative, with little control or assistance from government authorities until the 1970s . . . the process of opening and selling lots in the periphery . . . was chaotic." This meant that those workers who bought land on which to build their houses, "discovered eventually that their deeds were jeopardized by some form of illegality" (222).

24. It is interesting to note that almost 30 percent of those who, by 2021, lived in squatter settlements were international migrants. See more in Centro de Estudios Socioterritoriales (2021).

25. This definition of citizenship is based on the works of Kipnis (2004); Postero (2007); Holston (2008).

26. See more in Postero (2007); Lazar (2013).

27. For another perspective on *pobladores'* demands for dignity in relation to their housing claims, see Murphy's (2015, 24–39) concept of the urban politics of propriety.

28. For a detailed analysis of the emergence of the modern national state, see Skinner (1989); Spruyt (1994).

29. See, e.g., Marshall (1977); Walzer (1989).

30. Through the Declaration of the Rights of Man and of the Citizen of 1789, the French Revolution was key to the consolidation of the ideas and practices of the national citizenship. The declaration established that the universal rights of man—liberty, property, security, justice, and resistance to oppression—were natural and inalienable, and had to be guaranteed by the nation-state.

31. See, e.g., Young (1989); Pateman (1990); Taylor (1992); Kymlicka (1995); Benhabib (2002).

32. This form of criticism has been widely discussed among political theorists. For Fraser (1990), for example, the modern public sphere, as defined by Habermas (1991), constituted itself through the permanent subjection of other types of publics whose

demands were relegated to the private sphere. In a similar manner, Pateman (1990) argues that civil society emerged through the selective exclusion of women from the public sphere. This is why the private has been commonly deemed the realm of family ties, natural subjection, emotion, love, and sexual passion, whereas the public refers to a universal sphere of freedom, equality, individualism, reason, and impartial law. Thus, Pateman holds, civil society is by definition against women's interests, as it is based on a patriarchal definition of the public as well as the type of universality it entails.

33. Young's proposal echoes Taylor's (1992) "politics of recognition." Taylor, like Young, defends a politics of difference by arguing that the concept of equal dignity, in being blind to difference, has forced minorities to subordinate their cultural aspirations to a hegemonic culture.

34. Holston suggests that special treatment–oriented citizenships turn out to be conservative in the end, as such a model does not contest the very foundations of inequality; rather, it accepts it and reproduces it by organizing social difference according to a legalized hierarchy of privileged and disprivileged.

35. Postero's (2007) work on Bolivian citizenship sheds light on how a politics of recognition can bring about new types of exclusion. She shows that the implementation of neoliberalism in that country during the 1990s went hand in hand with the enactment of multicultural policies. But this form of neoliberal multiculturalism, rather than making the emergence of truly democratic forms of political participation for indigenous populations possible, reinforced the system of exclusion and racial domination that has long characterized Bolivian society.

36. Several scholars have analyzed the new political role of the city in urbanizing societies. See, e.g., Holston and Appadurai (1996); Appadurai (2002); Purcell (2003); Fawaz (2009); Blokland et al. (2015).

37. See, for example, Beauregard and Bounds's (2000, 243) definition of urban citizenship. On the basis of the idea that the urban public realm is "where people of diverse backgrounds engage each other," they propose a model of citizenship aimed at developing the "moral rights and responsibilities that people have as participants in the social activities of public and parochial spaces."

38. To mention some: Holston (2008); Fawaz (2009); Caldeira (2017).

39. See, e.g., Hipsher (1996); Özler (2012).

40. For an account of the role of the Movement of the Revolutionary Left (MIR) in the *pobladores* movement, see chapter 2. For a brief description of the story of the Campamento Nueva La Habana/Población Nuevo Amanecer, see chapters 2 and 5.

Chapter 2

1. After serving as a mayor of Peñalolén for two terms, from 2004 to 2012, Claudio Orrego ran in the 2013 presidential primary elections organized by the Nueva Mayoría (New Majority), a center-left coalition. Michelle Bachelet won the primaries and

became president of Chile, for second time, in 2014. In 2021, Claudio Orrego became the Santiago metropolitan area's first elected governor.

2. In episodes of contentious politics, Tilly and Tarrow (2015, 7) argue, "actors made claims on authorities, used public performances to do so, drew on inherited forms of collective action . . . and invented new ones, forged alliances with influential members of their respective polities, took advantage of existing political regime opportunities and made new ones, and used a combination of institutional and extra-institutional routines to advance their claims." Contentious politics, they add, "brings together three elements: contention, collective action, and politics."

3. See more in Gorelik (2004).

4. Developmentalist theory adopted a historical-structural method in order to propose measures aimed at facilitating the development of a capitalist economy in the region. It was proposed by economists belonging to the Economic Commission for Latin America and the Caribbean (CEPAL) in Santiago, Chile (e.g., Raúl Prebisch, Celso Furtado, Osvaldo Sunkel, among others). See also Bresser-Pereira (2011).

5. According to Claudio Lomnitz-Adler (1992), *mestizo* is a concept usually referring to a particular racial and ethnic group derived from the process of *mestizaje*, meaning from the racial mixture between Spaniards and Indians. This author highlights that *mestizaje* is the "process wherein communities are extracted from their cultures of origin without being assimilated into dominant culture" (Lomnitz-Adler 1992, 39). Thus, it not only entails fracturing the cultural coherence of a subordinate culture, but also limiting the conditions for the creation of a new, independent culture insofar as the *mestizo* groups, in being subordinated to local elites, acquire cultural status by adopting or reacting against the culture of the ruling groups.

6. See, e.g., Lewis (1961) and Adler Lomnitz (1977) in México City; Mangin (1967) in Lima; and Bonilla (1970) in Rio de Janeiro.

7. In Latin America, squatter settlements received different names depending on the country where they emerged. To mention some: *pueblos jóvenes* (Perú); *favelas* (Brazil); *poblaciones callampas* or *campamentos* (Chile); *villas miseria* (Argentina); *asentamientos* (Guatemala), and *colonias* (Mexico).

8. The country's population also increased in the same period, from 3,231,496 people in 1907 to 4,287,433 in 1930. See more in Almandoz (2008).

9. Once it joined the Third International, the POS turned into the Communist Party (PC) in 1922, which exists to this day.

10. Similar typologies of housing received other names elsewhere in Latin America: *tugurios* (Perú), *vecindades* (México), *cortiços* (Brazil). The term *conventillos* was, however, also used in Argentina and Uruguay.

11. Inspired by Pope Leo XIII's *Rerum novarum* encyclical of 1891, Catholic Church charity organizations had already been developing housing projects for the poor in the late nineteenth century. However, it is only since 1906 that the state assumed a more proactive role in this area. See more in Hidalgo, Errázuriz, and Booth (2005).

12. These local housing councils were called Consejos de Habitaciones Para Obreros. See more in Murphy (2015, 53–54).

13. Other countries that passed housing laws in this period were Argentina (1915) and Colombia (1918).

14. For a detailed account of these mobilizations, see V. Espinoza (1988, 79–117).

15. See more in Hidalgo (2002).

16. Other significant public interventions in housing policy during this period included the creation of the Caja de la Habitación Popular (Popular Housing Agency) in 1936, through which the state engaged directly in the building of social housing. For a detailed analysis of the Caja de la Habitación Popular, see Hidalgo (2000).

17. "30 Familias Afectadas por Acción del Especulador N° 1 de la Vivienda, Juan Elgueta Ruiz," *El Siglo*, January 7, 1947, 5.

18. "Lanzaron a cientos de personas ayer: En todos los barrios hubo desalojos inhumanos todo el día," *El Siglo*, January 15, 1947, 5.

19. To mention some: Castells (1973, 1983); V. Espinoza (1982, 1988); Garcés (2002); Murphy (2015).

20. Prior to the Pobladores' Provincial Association—Agrupación Provincial de Pobladores, in Spanish—during the 1940s the most important housing organization was the Housing National Front (Frente Nacional de la Vivienda). For an in-depth analysis of *pobladores'* grassroots organizations during this period, see Manuel Loyola's work (1989).

21. See, e.g., V. Espinoza (1988, 248–70); Garcés (2002, 120–50); Cortés (2014, 241–44).

22. In 1947, President Gabriel González Videla (1946–1952) passed the Ley de Defensa Permanente de la Democracia (Law of Permanent Defense of Democracy), also called Ley Maldita or, in English, "Damned Law." This legislation outlawed the PC and other leftist organizations on the basis of their role, according to the government, in inciting a climate of social instability associated with the emergence of increasing forms of mass mobilization. In addition to persecuting left-wing militants, González's regime also broke relations with the Soviet Union as a way to take a clear anticommunist position in the midst of the Cold War.

23. Some newspaper reports exemplifying this sort of idealization include "52 años de población La Victoria: 'Avanzar hasta la casa conquistar,'" *La Nación*, October 30, 2009; "Población La Victoria: A 57 años de la primera toma en Chile sigue congelada en el tiempo y vecinos acusan abandono," *Cambio 21*, October 29, 2014.

24. See, e.g., Paulo Álvarez's (2014) work on the Población Legua Emergencia. In it, he documents the existence of certain types of community-based autoconstruction in the emergence of Nueva La Legua in the late 1940s. As for land occupation carried out in the late 1970s, see chapter 4.

25. "Ocupación de predios," *El Ilustrado*, August 3, 1965, 3.

26. I briefly discuss the category of *los sin casa* (those who do not have a home of their own) in chapter 1.

27. "La lucha de los sin casa," *El Siglo*, July 31, 1965, 2.

28. These are the psychosociological, the architectural-ecological, the ethnographic, the traditional-modernizing, the culture of poverty, DESAL's approach, and radicalism theory. See more in Perlman (1976, 97–31).

29. In an attempt to reframe the Marxist theory of labor in the Latin American context, José Nun (2001, 87) argued that the *masa marginal* (marginal mass) was that "afunctional or dysfunctional part of the relative surplus population." The marginal mass differs from Marx's industrial reserve army in that, rather than alluding to a surplus labor force permitting capitalists to keep salaries low, it refers to those who can no longer be absorbed as labor force by the capitalist system. Aníbal Quijano (1972) arrives at similar conclusions through his idea of the *polo marginal* (marginal pole).

30. DESAL's perspective was, in this regard, very similar to some structural-functionalist approaches to urban marginality like that of Gino Germani (1973), who analyzed Latin American underdevelopment by making a distinction between traditional and modern societies.

31. "La 'Operación Sitio' es una solución Chilena," *La Nación*, August 13, 1966, 17.

32. "Viviendas que enseñan a vivir," *La Nación*, November 3, 1965, 9.

33. "Récord de construcciones," *La Nación*, November 2, 1965, 2.

34. See more in Gideon Long's (2016) article on Frei's Operation Site.

35. See more in V. Espinoza (1998).

36. According to Murphy (2015, 116), in some exceptional cases the right-wing National Party (PN) and the fascist organization Patria y Libertad began to sponsor land seizures as a way to reclaim already-occupied lands.

37. The occurrence of land occupations also exploded nationwide: 35 in 1969, 220 in 1970, and 560 in 1971 (Murphy 2015).

38. Cofré (2011) points out that the number of *tomas* cannot be confused with the actual amount of *campamentos*, because one squatter settlement might be the result of more than one land occupation.

39. "Prefieren el Barrio Alto: El MIR comenzó invasión de Las Condes," *La Prensa*, May 12, 1972, 16; "Vecinos logran desalojo de predio ocupado por miristas," *El Mercurio*, June 2, 1972, 24; "Vecinos de Las Condes desalojaron a pobladores," *El Mercurio*, August 15, 1972, 1.

40. "Atentado fascista en el Barrio Alto," *Puro Chile*, December 15, 1971, 12; "Cobarde agresión de nazis a pobladores," *La Nación*, August 15, 1972, 2.

41. To mention some: CIDU (1972); Duque and Pastrana (1972); Fiori (1973); Santa María (1973).

42. Nuevo Amanecer is the name that Pinochet's dictatorship gave to Nueva La Habana. The assignment of new names to left-wing *campamentos* was one of the first measures taken by the military regime after the coup. I discuss the dictatorship's politics of name changing in detail in chapter 4. With respect to the process of auto-construction in Nueva La Habana/Nuevo Amanecer, see chapter 5.

43. "Extremistas de 'Nueva La Habana' no permiten policías," *La Prensa*, April 30 1972, 5. See also Robert Moss's *Chile's Marxist Experiment*. As a special correspondent for *The Economist* who was in Chile during Salvador Allende's government, Moss (1973, 98) shows a map of Santiago in which Nueva La Habana is identified as one of the "key extremist encampments." In contrast, see, e.g., "Nueva La Habana: Una solución

comunitaria." *Ahora*, May 4, 1971, 30–32; "Nueva La Habana: Tradición de lucha, perspectiva de combate." *El Rebelde*, February 15, 1972, 8.

44. See, e.g., Fiori (1973); CIDU (1972); Castells (1973); Giusti (1973); Pastrana and Threlfall (1974).

45. In addition to Nueva La Habana, the Campamento 26 de Enero was another settlement led by the MIR that captured the attention of the public. See more in V. Espinoza (1988, 302–28).

46. Early criticisms came, paradoxically, from Jorge Giusti (1973), a former member of DESAL who pointed out that the rates of unemployment among *pobladores* were not considerably higher than the rest of the economically active population in Santiago. In a similar fashion, Manuel Castells (1973) argued that Santiago's *campamentos*, though congregating a heterogeneous segment of the urban poor, were importantly made up of blue-collar laborers who, working mostly in light industries and construction companies, had lower standards of living than other factions of the working class. For another criticism of DESAL's approach to urban marginality, see Sabatini (1981).

47. As Mario Garcés (2002, 149) suggestively maintains, there was an inconsistency among the Chilean communists when it came to characterizing their approach to housing struggles. Although they practically and materially endorsed housing mobilizations, the communist intelligentsia did little to reflect theoretically on *pobladores* as a new type of political subject.

48. The Ficha CAS—acronym for Social Assistance Committees—was replaced by the Ficha de Protección Social (Survey of Social Protection) in 2007 during Michelle Bachelet's government. In 2012, Sebastián Piñera's administration released a new version of it. In 2016, Michelle Bachelet's second administration created the Registro Social de Hogares (Social Household Registry), which replaced the Survey of Social Protection. See more in chapter 6.

49. At the same time, *pobladores* linked to the MIR organized the Coordinadora de Organizaciones Poblacionales (Neighborhood Organizations Coordinating Committee, COAPO). In 1984, METRO, COAPO, and Movimiento Poblacional Dignidad, pertaining to the Christian Left (IC), founded the Comando Unitario de Pobladores (Unitary Pobladores' Command, CUP). For a detailed description of the *pobladores'* organizations that emerged during the dictatorship, see Sergio Wilson's (1988) work.

50. See more in Hardy (1987); Campero (1987).

51. See, e.g., Tironi (1986); Touraine (1987); Dubet et al. (1989).

52. See, e.g., Tironi's (1986) pessimistic account of *pobladores'* mobilizations during the dictatorship.

53. The Concertación de Partidos por la Democracia (Coalition of Parties for Democracy) included the following parties, among others: the Christian Democratic Party (PDC), the Socialist Party (PS), the Party for Democracy (PPD), and the Social Democratic Radical Party (PRSD). As such, this coalition backed the governments of Patricio Aylwin (1990–1994), Eduardo Frei Ruiz-Tagle (1994–2000), Ricardo Lagos (2000–2006), and Michelle Bachelet (2006–2010).

54. See more in Schild (2000); Özler (2012).

Chapter 3

1. I describe the moral and political effects of *pobladores*' involvement in the system of socioeconomic characterization in detail in chapter 6.

2. Barry Schwartz (1974, 844), for example, interpreted the social distribution of waiting by understanding time as a scarce good allocated unequally among individuals in networks of power. Waiting, in that sense, is simultaneously a product and a mechanism for the reinforcement of social hierarchies, as "to be delayed is . . . to be dependent upon the disposition of the one whom one is waiting for." Bourdieu (2000, 228) conceived of waiting as "one of the privileged ways of experiencing the effect of power . . . [as it] always implies submission: the interested aiming at something greatly desired durably . . . modifies the behavior of the person who 'hangs' . . . on the awaited decision."

3. For another account of the generative role of waiting in Chile's housing struggles, see Koppelman (2018).

4. I describe Tarrow's (2011) definition of cycle of protests in chapter 2.

5. See more in Paley (2001).

6. As I show in the conclusion, the social movements that gave shape to the 2019 social uprising demanded the end of Pinochet's constitution. This led to a plebiscite in October 2020 in which the majority of Chileans approved of a new constitution through a democratically elected constitutional convention. This organ began to draft the new constitution in 2021.

7. See more in Winn (2004).

8. For an anthropological examination of Chile's "social debt," see Han (2012). For a complete description of the social programs developed during the Concertación government, see Arellano (2011).

9. See more in Hipsher (1996).

10. Between 1990 and 2000, the main subsidy-based housing programs implemented by the state were: (1) Programa de Vivienda Básica (Basic Housing Program, initially created by the dictatorship), which sought to fund the construction of housing projects for those who applied individually or collectively for subsidies; (2) Programa de Viviendas Progresivas (Progressive Housing Program), which differed from the former in that *pobladores* required less savings to get a smaller structure, equipped only with housing and a kitchen; (3) Programa Chile Barrio (Chile Neighborhood Program), a policy developed by Eduardo Frei's government (1994–2000) to specifically address the lack of housing of those living as squatters. For a complete description of the housing programs utilized by the Concertación governments, see Arriagada and Moreno (2006); Özler (2012).

11. With a population of around 130,000 people, Bajos de Mena is a large neighborhood composed of several subsidized housing projects developed in the 1990s.

12. See more in *La Tercera* (2018).

13. The housing deficit, however, increased again in the early 2020s because of the COVID-19 pandemic. See more in chapter 1 and in the conclusion.

14. The segregationist nature of the subsidy-based policies has been extensively documented. See, e.g., Ducci (1997); Rodríguez and Sugranyes (2005); Tapia (2011). For an account of the increase in land prices, see Trivelli (2011); Castillo and Forray (2014)

15. Unidad de Fomento (UF) is a Chilean unit of account adjusted to inflation. It is currently the preferred measure for estimating the value of real estate, housing, and bank loans.

16. While Catherine Valenzuela (2014) explains in detail the history of Esperanza Andina, Rodrigo Salcedo (2010) does so for the case of the Toma de Peñalolén.

17. See more in Trivelli (2011); Castillo and Forray (2014).

18. I discuss the struggle of the MPL fully in Pérez (2017).

19. See, e.g., Hartman (2002); Newman and Wyly (2006).

20. To examine the city from a Marxist viewpoint, Lefebvre (2003) adopted categories such as "ideology" or "value" to scrutinize a society structured by what he calls the urban problematic; that is, a society whose structuring force is no longer industrialization but urbanization. In Lefebvre's work, the right to the city must be understood as part of the emergence of an urban society, one in which "the urban" comes to replace industrialization as the content and meaning of social relations. The urban is "a mental and social form, that of simultaneity, of gathering, of convergence, of encounter (or rather, encounters)" (Lefebvre 1996, 131). Thus, the urbanization of society does not refer only to the geographic expansion of the city or to the demographic changes that industrialized societies underwent in the mid-twentieth century. Rather, it alludes to the spread of new social relations framed by "the urban," which Lefebvre (2003, 15) understands as a "productive force," given its capacity to constitute a novel politics of space articulated through the right to the city.

21. To mention some: Mitchell (2003); Purcell (2002, 2003); Holston (2008); Marcuse (2009); Harvey (2012); Blokland et al. (2015).

22. For the concept of interpellation, see Althusser (2001). See also the discussion in the next chapter.

23. The creation of these *listas* (groups) was due to a 2007 state regulation establishing that *comités de allegados* could not include more than 160 applicants for subsidies. This policy sought to avoid the building of overcrowded social housing projects, as was done in the 1990s. Nonetheless, the legal entity was the "Comité de Allegados Don Bosco," meaning that all the members were formally enrolled in it.

24. By 2015, La Herradura was still in process of formation. This means that it was not yet a legal entity (*personalidad jurídica*), nor could its members apply for state subsidies. The individuals enrolled in the Don Bosco as part of La Herradura, although they participated in the committee's activities, were not formally registered yet as prospective applicants in the Ministry of Housing's database.

25. *Curas obreros* was an appellative used in Spain and Latin America to designate those priests who, by working in low-income neighborhoods of Latin America as Christ's missionaries, engaged in political struggles for social transformation.

26. The Don Bosco's registry also showed that almost 60 percent of members were younger than thirty-five years old when they entered into the committee.

27. Several authors have analyzed women's engagement in urban struggles in Chile. To mention some: Murphy (2015); Paley (2001); Valdés and Weinstein (1993). For the examination of other cases in Latin America, see Caldeira (2015); Levy, Latendresse, and Carle-Marsan (2017).

28. See more in Levy, Latendresse, and Carle-Marsan (2017).

29. Focusing on the case of La Florida, I analyze in depth the housing affordability problem due to the increase in land prices in chapter 5.

30. The year of building of the housing project was: Altos de la Cordillera (2016), Portal La Florida (2018), and Alto Tobalaba (2020).

31. The Equality Party (Partido Igualdad) was created in 2009 by, among others, the same housing activists who had founded the National Federation of Pobladores in 2010. Lautaro Guanca, a member of the Movimiento de Pobladores en Lucha, was its first president.

32. I examine the role of political parties in the development of the old *movimiento de pobladores* in chapter 2.

Chapter 4

1. Authors have long characterized *pobladores* as a heterogeneous aggregation of poor individuals; see, e.g., Castells (1973); Salazar and Pinto (2002); Murphy (2015). In chapter 3, I present an ethnographic account of a *comité de allegados* (state-regulated housing committee), highlighting the occupational and ideological diversity of the people who participate in these organizations.

2. To mention some: Mangin (1967); Paley (2001); Holston (2008); Murphy (2015); Caldeira (2017).

3. See, e.g., Paley (2001); Han (2012).

4. See, e.g., Movimiento de Pobladores en Lucha (2011).

5. For a discussion on the role of repetition in performative theory, see Butler (1997); Yurchak (2005).

6. On the performative character of rituals, see Hollywood (2002); Yurchak (2005).

7. See more in Felman (2002).

8. The category of *los sin casa* is discussed in chapter 1.

9. "Hogar de Cristo en ayuda de damnificados," *El Mercurio*, October 31, 1957, 17.

10. For the former, "Solución al problema de vivienda," *El Siglo*, February 2, 1954, 4. For the latter, "Ante un hecho illegal," *Mensaje*, December 1957, 461.

11. "El lanzamiento," *Vistazo*, February 17, 1953, 19.

12. "La resistencia," *Vistazo*, March 10, 1953, 22; "La inundación," *Vistazo*, March 3, 1953, 19; "Nuevas amenazas," *Vistazo*, April 7, 1953, 24; "La traición," *Vistazo*, April 14, 1953, 24.

13. This approach to *callampas* certainly echoes Lewis's (1961) understanding of the "culture of poverty" as a system of values, beliefs, and behaviors that needed to be reformed for the sake of modernization.

14. "La 'solución' del régimen al problema de vivienda," *El Poblador*, May 31, 1952, 3.

15. "Terrenos conquistados defenderán pobladores: Cuentan con amplia solidaridad," *El Siglo*, November 1, 1957, 1.

16. "En el Zanjón de la Aguada," *El Mercurio*, May 7, 1959, 1.

17. "Ayuda a gente de poblaciones del Zanjón de la Aguada," *El Mercurio*, November 1, 1957, 16.

18. "Nuestro periódico," *El Poblador*, May 1, 1952, 2.

19. "La 'solución' del régimen al problema de vivienda," *El Poblador*, May 31, 1952, 3.

20. For a discussion on the concept of sanitary citizenship, see Briggs and Mantini-Briggs (2003, 10).

21. See, for instance, the case of São Paulo described in detail by Holston (1991, 2008) and Caldeira (2000, 2017).

22. "Expropiación de la población Zañartu piden sus habitantes," *El Siglo*, January 28, 1947, 13.

23. See, e.g., "Pobladores de Lo Encalada rechazan el alza eléctrica: Exigen estabilidad de los pobladores en los sitios que ocupan," *El Siglo*, November 25, 1952, 4; "Pobladores de Ñuñoa piden entrega de materiales para construir viviendas," *El Siglo*, February 17, 1953, 4.

24. "Agregados de Nueva La Legua tienen hoy una gran asamblea," *El Siglo*, January 19, 1953, 8.

25. See, e.g., "Se ha logrado instalar 76 familias en San Gregorio," *El Mercurio*, May 9, 1959, 15; "300 familias construyeron su propia población de emergencia," *La Nación*, June 11, 1965, 8.

26. "La Autoconstrucción en Chile," *La Nación*, October 16, 1966, 11.

27. Trained as a social worker and sister of Eduardo Frei Montalva, Irene Frei was a politician from the Christian Democratic Party. She died in 1964 in a car accident. On Frei Montalva's statement: "'Les aseguro que al termino de mi Gobierno habrán desaparecido las poblaciones callampas en el país'. Dijo el Jefe de Estado a los pobladores." *La Nación*, June 18, 1965, 3.

28. Some decades later, Patricio Aylwin would be the first president elected democratically after Augusto Pinochet's dictatorship. He served as president of Chile between 1990 and 1994. See also "Coordinación de labor de pobladores estudia congreso del Tercer Distrito," *La Nación*, October 17, 1965, 15.

29. "Nuestra posición," *La Voz de la Victoria*, May 1, 1959, 1.

30. "Defendieron con sus pechos el suelo conquistado," *El Siglo*, March 17, 1967, 7.

31. Examples of date: 26 de Enero (26 of January) and 22 de Julio (22 of July); of political slogans: Venceremos (We Will Overcome), Batalla de la Producción (Struggle for Production), Unidad Popular (Popular Unity), and Trabajadores al Poder (Workers, Take the Power Over); of politicians: Salvador Allende, Carlos Cortés, Tito Palestro, José Tohá, and Carlos Altamirano; of prominent Marxist figures: Carlos Marx, Vladimir Lenin, Fidel Castro, Che Guevara, Angela Davis, Fidel-Ernesto, Camilo Torres, Ho Chi Minh, Pablo Neruda, and Violeta Parra; of historical revolutionary events: Primero de Mayo (First of May), Vietnam Heroico (Heroic Vietnam), Asalto al

Cuartel Moncada (Attack on Moncada Barracks), and Nueva La Habana (New La Habana); and the spirit of struggle: El Esfuerzo (Effort), Los Luchadores (The Fighters), Paz y Progreso (Peace and Progress), and Fe y Esperanza (Faith and Hope).

32. This work was inspired by the Campamento Herminda de la Victoria—located in the district of Barrancas, currently the municipality of Cerro Navia—which was tragically well known for the death of Herminda, a baby girl who died of gunshot wounds from police bullets during the events that occurred after the land seizure.

33. "Poblador, compañero poblador, seguiremos avanzando hasta el final. Poblador, compañero poblador, por los hijos, por la patria y el hogar. Poblador, compañero poblador, ahora la historia es para ti. Con techo, abrigo y pan, marchemos juntos al porvenir."

34. See, e.g., "¿Campos de Concentración en Santiago?," *El Mercurio*, May 31, 1967, 3; "El caso de la 26 de Enero," *El Ilustrado*, 30 April 1970, 3.

35. "Ilegal ocupación de terrenos," *El Ilustrado*, May 5, 1969, 3.

36. "Ocupación ilegal de predios," *El Ilustrado*, February 24, 1969, 3.

37. "Ocupaciones ilegales de sitios," *El Mercurio*, May 3, 1969, 3

38. "Abuso del pabellón patrio," *El Mercurio*, May 13, 1967, 3

39. Morro de Arica and La Concepción refer to two battles during the War of the Pacific (1879–1883), in which Chile fought against Perú and Bolivia. Juan de la Cuesta, "Las ocupaciones y las fricciones," *Tribuna*, July 19, 1971, 4.

40. "Cambian denominación y nombres a las 'tomas' y 'campamentos,'" *El Mercurio*, September 20, 1973, 17.

41. "Cambiaron nombres a campamentos," *El Mercurio*, September 27, 1973, 23.

42. "El sectarismo fue reemplazado por trabajo," *La Tercera*, December 18, 1973, 4.

43. "'Los pobladores tienen que dejar de mirarse con odio,'" *La Tercera*, October 22, 1973, 22.

44. See, e.g., "Que el gobierno compre los terrenos de la caja de carabineros ubicados en La Legua," *El Siglo*, 27 January 1953, 4; "Allegados," *El Siglo*, August 2, 1965, 2.

45. See, e.g., Chateau and Pozo (1987); Paley (2001); Han (2012).

46. See more in chapter 6 and in Movimiento de Pobladores en Lucha (2011).

47. Alto Tobalaba, the name of the housing project, was inaugurated in 2020. See more in chapter 5.

Chapter 5

1. See also Hartman (2002); Newman and Wyly (2006).

2. I offer a brief definition of urban citizenship in chapter 1. For more on the concept of urban citizenship, see Holston and Appadurai (1996); Holston (2008); Blokland et al. (2015); Cohen and Margalit (2015).

3. See more in Cornejo (2012).

4. For a detailed analysis of the number of subsidized housing units built during the 1980s in Santiago's peripheries, see Tapia (2011).

5. See more in Tapia (2011).

6. See more in Hidalgo (2004b); Ruiz-Tagle (2016).

7. For a discussion on the relationship between social mixing and urban segregation, see Slater (2006, 2009). For debates on social mixing, gentrification, and displacement in Santiago, see Hidalgo (2004b); Sabatini and Salcedo (2007); Ruiz-Tagle and López (2014); Ruiz-Tagle (2016).

8. Chilean public policy generally uses a matrix of socioeconomic classification that is mainly based on the level of education of the head of household, and the possession of certain consumer goods. It divides the population into five socioeconomic strata (ABC1, C2, C3, D and E), with ABC1 being the upper strata and E the lower one.

9. Las Condes, Lo Barnechea, Providencia, Vitacura, Ñuñoa, and La Reina.

10. UF, acronym for *Unidad de Fomento*, is an inflation-indexed currency unit used for real estate transactions.

11. I describe in detail the events surrounding the emergence of the Campamento Nueva La Habana in chapter 2.

12. After years of delay, these *pobladores* became homeowners only recently in 2020. I discuss the mobilizing role of waiting in chapter 3.

13. See, e.g., Holston (1991, 2008); Fawaz (2009); Caldeira (2017).

14. The Social Priority Index was designed in 1995 by the Ministry of Social Development and Family to measure the socioeconomic level of districts and to allocate social welfare among the poorest *comunas* (districts). The index is based on the analysis of three elements: income and poverty; access and quality of education; and health-related issues such life expectancy and percentage of child malnutrition. See more in Gajardo (2021).

15. In the mid-1980s, Miguel Budnik, a journalist working for the progressive journal *Hoy*, developed a number of news reports describing the subjective experiences of *pobladores* who, after being eradicated, were moved to semirural, peripheral areas by the dictatorship. These news reports resulted in the publication of the book *Los marginados* (1986).

16. I describe the foundation of the Población La Victoria in chapter 2.

17. It is interesting to mention that more than four hundred *cabildos* emerged in Santiago right after the social uprising of October 2019. See more in Zambrano and Huaiqui (2020).

18. For the concept of culture of decency (Martínez and Palacios, 1996), see more in chapter 6.

19. See more in chapter 1 and in Murphy (2015).

20. See, e.g., "Pobladores demostraron su capacidad de ahorro," *La Nación*, November 2, 1965, 2.

21. See more in Han (2012).

22. In chapter 3, I provide a comprehensive description of the Don Bosco assembly's internal functioning.

23. See discussion in Slater (2006, 2009).

Chapter 6

1. See also Guzman et al. (2009).

2. On the ordinary-ethics approach, see Lambek (2010a, 2010b); Das (2012).

3. In chapter 3, I discuss how the state of waiting has become a modality of action that frames *pobladores'* engagement in urban politics.

4. For a discussion on the transformation of individuals into self-regulating citizens, see Cruikshank (1999); Ong (2003).

5. See, e.g., Cleaveland (2005); Pauli (2008); Han (2012).

6. The movements against structural adjustment in Santiago del Estero, Argentina (Auyero 2003) and the protests against fair trade in Ciudad Sandino, Nicaragua (Fisher 2018) are two exceptions in this regard. In both cases, working-class women developed forms of collective action through which, by demanding dignity, they either constituted themselves as transformative political agents (Auyero 2003) or created an alternative work ethic (Fisher 2018).

7. Other scholars have extensively accounted for women's role in housing struggles, either in Chile (Hardy 1987; Valdés and Weinstein 1993; Murphy 2015) or elsewhere in Latin America (Levy, Latendresse, and Carle-Marsan 2017). I describe the overwhelming presence of women in state-regulated housing assemblies in chapter 3.

8. In chapter 5, I explain in detail the lack of affordable housing in La Florida and the resulting appearance of the demand for the right to stay put.

9. For another anthropological approach to the idea of vulnerability in urban contexts, see Zeiderman's (2013) work on biopolitics and citizenship in Bogotá, Colombia.

10. See more in chapter 2.

11. See, for instance, the case of Lima (Mangin 1967), Rio de Janeiro (Perlman 1976), and Mexico City (Adler Lomnitz 1977).

12. As I explain in chapter 2, the *pobladores* movement never developed through a unified ideology. However, the recognition of the poor as revolutionary actors enabled them to become one of the more distinguishable social forces backing Salvador Allende's government.

13. To deal with the economic crisis caused by the COVID-19 pandemic, *ollas comunes* (cooking cooperatives) reemerged powerfully in 2020 as a collective strategy used by poor urban residents. For a detailed account of *pobladores'* survival strategies in previous decades, see Hardy (1987).

14. Based on the widely held assumption that measurements by income tended to underestimate the real number of poor families, in recent years the Ministry of Social Development and Family has added variables such as housing, work, education, social security, and health care to its measurements of poverty. The resulting multidimensional analysis of poverty has indicated that, in 2017, 21 percent of Chileans were poor. See more in Ministerio de Desarrollo Social (2018).

15. See more in Cruikshank (1999); Ong (2003); Schild (2000).

16. See more in Cruikshank (1999); Rose (1999); Ong (2003).

17. See more in Candia (1998).

18. The score scale for the Survey of Social Protection was divided into quintiles of vulnerability, starting with 2,072 points, which represents the most vulnerable condition. These quintiles were as follows: Quintile I: from 2,072 to 8,500 points; Quintile II: from 8,501 to 11,734; Quintile III: from 11,735 to 13,484; Quintile IV: from 13,485 to 14,557; and Quintile V: 14,558 and above. By late 2015, an overwhelming majority of families using the Survey of Social Protection belonged to Quintile I (54.1 percent).

19. See more in Ferguson (2015).

20. CAS is the acronym for Comités de Asistencia Social (Social Assistance Committees), which were created in 1979 during Pinochet's dictatorship. These Social Assistance Committees were municipal agencies in charge of implementing social programs at the local level. See more in Han (2012); Schild (2000).

21. See more in Larrañaga et al. (2014).

22. For a detailed account of the "welfare queen," see Cruikshank (1999, 104–21).

23. See, e.g., Lambek (2010b); Das (2012); Fassin (2012).

24. For each form of disrespect, Honneth (1992, 195) develops three different forms of mutual recognition, which are: love, rights, and solidarity. These, he argues, "set down the formal requirements for conditions of interaction within which human beings can feel assured of their 'dignity' or integrity."

25. To mention some: Piven and Cloward (1971); Cruikshank (1999); Schild (2000); Ong (2003); Han (2012); Nuijten (2013).

Conclusion

1. See more in *Diario Financiero* (2021); Centro de Estudios Socioterritoriales (2021).

2. According to statistics from the National Statistics Institute, around 1.5 million people of foreign origin lived in Chile in 2020. Whereas immigrants represented slightly less than 1 percent of the total population in 1992, they made up 8 percent in the early 2020s. See more in Instituto Nacional de Estadística (2020).

3. See more in Pérez and Palma (2021).

4. See, e.g., Mayol (2012); Atria et al. (2013); PNUD (2015).

5. As people's interest in constitutional issues started to grow, Chile's 1980 constitution became the most-selling book in November, 2019 (*La Tercera* 2019).

6. As of this writing, the constitutional convention has just started to draft the new constitution and is expected to finish in 2022 After that, Chileans will vote again in a plebiscite to determine if they approve or reject the new constitution.

7. The idea of social malaise has been central to the analysis of the process of politicization that Chilean society has experienced since the 2011 student movement. See, e.g., Mayol (2012); PNUD (2012, 2015); Vera (2017).

References

Adler Lomnitz, Larissa. 1977. *Networks and Marginality: Life in a Mexican Shantytown*. New York: Academic Press.

Almandoz, Arturo. 2008. "Despegues sin madurez: Urbanización, industrialización y desarrollo en la Latinoamérica del siglo XX." *EURE* 34 (102): 61–76.

Althusser, Louis. 2001. *Lenin and Philosophy and Other Essays*. New York: Monthly Review Press.

Álvarez, Pablo. 2014. *Legua emergencia: Una historia de dignidad y lucha*. Santiago de Chile: Ediciones Universidad Diego Portales.

Anderson, Benedict. 1991. *Imagined Communities: Reflections on the Origin and Spread of Nationalism*. New York: Verso.

Angelcos, Nicolás, and Miguel Pérez. 2017. "De la 'desaparición' a la reemergencia: Continuidades y rupturas del movimiento de pobladores en Chile." *Latin American Research Review* 52 (1): 94–109. https://doi.org/10.25222/larr.39.

Appadurai, Arjun. 2002. "Deep Democracy: Urban Governmentality and the Horizon of Politics." *Public Culture* 14 (1): 21–47.

Arellano, Juan Pablo. 2011. *Equity and Sustainable Growth: Twenty Years of Social Policies, Chile 1990–2009*. World Bank. http://www.cieplan.org/media/publicaciones/archivos/330/E_Book_Twenty_Years_of_Social_Policies_Chile_19902009_Equity_and_sustainable_growth.pdf.

Arriagada, Camilo, and Juan Cristóbal Moreno. 2006. "Atlas de la evolución del déficit habitacional en Chile, 1992–2002." Gobierno de Chile. http://observatoriodoc.colabora.minvu.cl/Documentos%20compartidos/ESTUDIOS%20OBSERVATORIO/AtlasEvoluci%C3%B3nD%C3%A9ficit1992-2002.pdf

Asociación Chilena de Empresas de Investigación de Mercado (AIM). 2008. *Grupos socioeconómicos 2008*. Santiago de Chile: AIM. http://www.aimchile.cl/wp-content/uploads/2011/12/Grupos_Socioeconomicos_AIM-2008.pdf.

Atria, Fernando, Guillermo Larraín, José Miguel Benavente, Javier Couso, and Alfredo Joignant. 2013. *El otro modelo: Del orden neoliberal al régimen de lo público.* Santiago de Chile: Debate.

Austin, John L. 1962. *How to Do Things with Words.* Oxford: Oxford University Press.

Auyero, Javier. 2003. *Contentious Lives: Two Argentine Women, Two Protests, and the Quest for Recognition.* Durham, NC: Duke University Press.

———. 2012. *Patients of the State: The Politics of Waiting in Argentina.* Durham, NC: Duke University Press.

Beauregard, Robert, and Anna Bounds. 2000. "Urban Citizenship." In *Democracy, Citizenship and the Global City*, edited by Engin F. Isin, 243–256. New York: Routledge.

Bengoa, José. 1996. *La comunidad perdida: Ensayos sobre identidad y cultura.* Santiago de Chile: Ediciones SUR.

Benhabib, Seyla. 2002. *The Claims of Culture: Equality and Diversity in the Global Era.* Princeton, NJ: Princeton University Press.

Blokland, Talja, Christine Hentschel, Andrej Holm, Henrik Lebuhn, and Talia Margalit. 2015. "Urban Citizenship and Right to the City: The Fragmentation of Claims." *International Journal of Urban and Regional Research* 39 (4): 655–65.

Bonilla, Frank. 1970. "Rio's Favelas: The Rural Slum within the City." In *Peasants in Cities: Reading in the Anthropology of Urbanization*, 72–84. Boston: Houghton Mifflin Co.

Bourdieu, Pierre. 1991. *Language and Symbolic Power.* Cambridge, MA: Harvard University Press.

———. 2000. *Pascalian Meditations.* Stanford, CA: Stanford University Press.

Bresser-Pereira, Luiz. 2011. "From Old to New Developmentalism in Latin America." In *The Oxford Handbook of Latin American Economics*, edited by José Antonio Ocampo and Jaime Ros, 108–29. Oxford: Oxford University Press.

Briggs, Charles L., and Clara Mantini-Briggs. 2003. *Stories in the Time of Cholera: Racial Profiling during a Medical Nightmare.* Berkeley: University of California Press.

Bruey, Alison J. 2012. "Limitless Land and the Redefinition of Rights: Popular Mobilisation and the Limits of Neoliberalism in Chile, 1973–1985." *Journal of Latin American Studies* 44 (3): 523–552. https://doi.org/10.1017/S0022216X12000399.

Budnik, Miguel. 1986. *Los marginados.* Santiago de Chile: Empresa Editora Araucaria.

Butler, Judith. 1997. *Excitable Speech: A Politics of the Performative.* New York: Routledge.

Cáceres, Gonzalo. 1995. "Modernización autoritaria y renovación del espacio urbano: Santiago de Chile, 1927–1931." *EURE* 21 (62): 99–108.

Caldeira, Teresa. 2000. *City of Walls: Crime, Segregation, and Citizenship in São Paulo.* Berkeley: University of California Press.

———. 2015. "Social Movements, Cultural Production, and Protests: São Paulo's Shifting Political Landscape." *Current Anthropology* 56 (S11): S126–36.

———. 2017. "Peripheral Urbanization: Autoconstruction, Transversal Logics, and Politics in Cities of the Global South." *Environment and Planning D: Society and Space* 35 (1): 3–20. https://doi.org/10.1177/0263775816658479.

Campero, Guillermo. 1987. *Entre la sobrevivencia y la acción política: Las organizaciones de pobladores en Santiago*. Santiago de Chile: Estudios ILET.

Candia, José Miguel. 1998. "Exclusión y pobreza: La focalización de las políticas sociales." *Nueva Sociedad* (156): 116–26.

Castells, Manuel. 1973. "Movimiento de pobladores y lucha de clases en Chile." *EURE* 3 (7): 9–36.

———. 1983. *The City and the Grassroots: A Cross-Cultural Theory of Urban Social Movements*. Berkeley: University of California Press.

Castillo, María José, and Rossana Forray. 2014. "La vivienda, un problema de acceso al suelo." *ARQ (Santiago)*, no. 86 (April): 48–57.

Centro de Estudios Socioterritoriales (CES-TECHO). 2021. "Catastro nacional de campamentos 2020–2021." Santiago de Chile: TECHO & Fundación Vivienda.

Chateau, Jorge, and Hernán Pozo. 1987. "Los pobladores en el área metropolitana: Situación y características." In *Espacio y poder: Los pobladores*, 13–74. Santiago de Chile: FLACSO.

Chatterjee, Partha. 2004. *The Politics of the Governed: Reflections on Popular Politics in Most of the World*. New York: Columbia University Press.

Chiara, María, and Claudio Pulgar. 2008. "Villa San Luis de Las Condes: Lugar de memoria y olvido." *Revista de Arquitectura* 18: 28–39.

CIDU, Equipo de Estudios Poblacionales. 1972. "Reivindicación urbana y lucha política: Los campamentos de pobladores en Santiago de Chile." *EURE* 2 (6): 55–82.

Cleaveland, Carol. 2005. "A Desperate Means to Dignity: Work Refusal amongst Philadelphia Welfare Recipients." *Ethnography* 6 (1): 35–60.

Cofré, Boris. 2011. "El movimiento de pobladores en el Gran Santiago: Las tomas de sitios y organizaciones en los campamentos, 1970–1973." *Tiempo Histórico* 2: 133–57.

Cohen, Nir, and Talia Margalit. 2015. "'There Are Really Two Cities Here': Fragmented Urban Citizenship in Tel Aviv." *International Journal of Urban and Regional Research* 39 (4): 666–86. https://doi.org/10.1111/1468-2427.12260.

Cornejo, Catalina. 2012. "Estigma territorial como forma de violencia barrial: El caso del sector El Castillo." *Revista INVI* 27 (76): 177–200.

Cortés, Alexis. 2013. "A Struggle Larger Than a House: Pobladores and Favelados in Latin American Social Theory." *Latin American Perspectives* 40 (2): 168–84.

———. 2014. "El movimiento de pobladores chilenos y la población La Victoria: Ejemplaridad, movimientos sociales y el derecho a la ciudad." *EURE* 40 (119): 239–60.

Cruikshank, Barbara. 1999. *The Will to Empower: Democratic Citizens and Other Subjects*. Ithaca, NY: Cornell University Press.

Das, Veena. 2011. "State, Citizenship, and the Urban Poor." *Citizenship Studies* 15 (3–4): 319–33.

———. 2012. "Ordinary Ethics." In *A Companion to Moral Anthropology*, edited by Didier Fassin, 133–49. Malden, MA: Wiley-Blackwell.

De Ramón, Armando. 1985. "Estudio de una periferia urbana: Santiago de Chile 1850–1900." *Historia* (20): 199–294.

———. 1990. "La población informal: Poblamiento de la periferia de Santiago de Chile, 1920–1970." *EURE* 16 (50): 5–17.

Derrida, Jacques. 1977. "Signature, Event, Context." *Glyph* (1): 172–97.

Diario Financiero. 2021. "Vivienda estima que déficit habitacional subió hasta 600 mil hogares en medio de la pandemia." March 4.

Donoso, Sofia, and Marisa von Bülow, eds. 2017. *Social Movements in Chile: Organization, Trajectories, and Political Consequences.* New York: Palgrave Macmillan.

Douglas, Mary. 1966. *Purity and Danger: An Analysis of Concepts of Pollution and Taboo.* London: Routledge & Kegan Paul.

Dubet, François, Eugenio Tironi, Vicente Espinoza, and Eduardo Valenzuela. 1989. *Pobladores: Luttes sociales et democratie au Chili.* Paris: L'Harmattan.

Ducci, María Elena. 1997. "Chile: El lado obscuro de una política de vivienda exitosa." *EURE* 23 (69): 99–115.

Duque, Joaquin, and Ernesto Pastrana. 1972. "La movilización reivindicativa urbana de los sectores populares en Chile: 1964–1972." *Revista Latinoamericana de Ciencias Sociales* (4): 259–94.

Espinoza, Marissa, and Pilar Colil. 2015. "Panorama CASEN 2015. Hogares y bienestar: Análisis de cambios en la estructura de los hogares (1990–2015)." Gobierno de Chile. http://observatorio.ministeriodesarrollosocial.gob.cl/documentos/Panorama _Casen_2015_Hogares_y_bienestar.pdf.

Espinoza, Vicente. 1982. "El movimiento de pobladores: Una evaluación crítica." *Proposiciones* 5: 41–52.

———. 1988. *Para una historia de los pobres de la ciudad.* Santiago de Chile: Ediciones SUR.

———. 1998. "Historia social de la acción colectiva urbana: Los pobladores de Santiago 1957–1987." *EURE* 24 (72): 71–84.

Fassin, Didier. 2008. "Beyond Good and Evil? Questioning the Anthropological Discomfort with Morals." *Anthropological Theory* 8 (4): 333–44.

———. 2012. "Introduction: Toward a Critical Moral Anthropology." In *A Companion to Moral Anthropology*, edited by Didier Fassin, 1–17. Malden, MA: Wiley-Blackwell.

Fawaz, Mona. 2009. "Neoliberal Urbanity and the Right to the City: A View from Beirut's Periphery." *Development and Change* 40 (5): 827–52.

Federación Nacional de Pobladores. 2011. "Declaración pública: La Federación Nacional de Pobladores se moviliza contra la ficha de protección social." December 13. http://metiendoruido.com/2011/12/declaracion-publica-federacion-nacional-de -pobladores-se-moviliza-contra-la-ficha-de-proteccion-social/.

Felman, Shoshana. 2002. *The Scandal of the Speaking Body: Don Juan with J. L. Austin, or Seduction in Two Languages.* Stanford, CA: Stanford University Press.

Ferguson, James. 2010. "The Uses of Neoliberalism." *Antipode* 41 (January): 166–84. https://doi.org/10.1111/j.1467-8330.2009.00721.x.

———. 2015. *Give a Man a Fish: Reflections on the New Politics of Distribution*. Durham, NC: Duke University Press.

Fiori, Jorge. 1973. "Campamento Nueva La Habana: Estudio de una experiencia de autoadministración de justicia." *EURE* 3 (7): 83–101.

Fisher, Josh. 2018. "In Search of Dignified Work: Gender and the Work Ethic in the Crucible of Fair Trade Production." *American Ethnologist* 45 (1): 74–86.

Flisfisch, Ángel. 1983. "El problema del poblador." *La Segunda*, September 8.

Foucault, Michel. 2003. *The Essential Foucault: Selections from the Essential Works of Foucault, 1954–1984*. Edited by Paul Rabinow and Nikolas Rose. New York: New Press.

———. 2005. *The Hermeneutics of the Subject: Lectures at the Collège de France 1981–1982*. Edited by Frédéric Gros. Translated by Graham Burchell. Reprint edition. New York: Picador.

———. 2010. *The Archaeology of Knowledge*. New York: Vintage.

Fraser, Nancy. 1990. "Rethinking the Public Sphere: A Contribution to the Critique of Actually Existing Democracy." *Social Text* 25–26 (January): 56–80.

Fundación Vivienda. 2019. "Allegados: Una olla a presión social en la ciudad." https://www.fundacionvivienda.cl/wp-content/uploads/2019/10/allegados.pdf.

Gajardo, Santiago. 2021. "Índice de prioridad social de comunas 2020." Secretaría Regional Ministerial de Desarrollo Social y Familia. http://www.desarrollo socialyfamilia.gob.cl/storage/docs/boletin_interno/INDICE_DE_PRIORIDAD _SOCIAL_2020.pdf.

Garcés, Mario. 2002. *Tomando su sitio: El movimiento de pobladores de Santiago, 1957–1970*. Santiago de Chile: Lom Ediciones.

Germani, Gino. 1973. *El concepto de marginalidad: Significado, raíces históricas y cuestiones teóricas, con particular referencia a la marginalidad urbana*. Buenos Aires: Ediciones Nueva Vision.

Gilbert, Alan. 2004a. "Helping the Poor through Housing Subsidies: Lessons from Chile, Colombia and South Africa." *Habitat International* 28 (1): 13–40.

———. 2004b. "Learning from Others: The Spread of Capital Housing Subsidies." *International Planning Studies* 9 (2–3): 197–216.

Giusti, Jorge. 1973. *Organización y participación popular en Chile: El mito del "hombre marginal."* Santiago de Chile: Ediciones FLACSO.

Goodale, Mark, and Nancy Postero, eds. 2013. "Revolution and Retrenchment: Illuminating the Present in Latin America." In *Neoliberalism, Interrupted: Social Change and Contested Governance in Contemporary Latin America*, 1–22. Stanford, CA: Stanford University Press.

Gorelik, Adrián. 2004. *Miradas sobre Buenos Aires: Historia cultural y crítica urbana*. Buenos Aires: Siglo Veintiuno Editores Argentina.

Grez, Sergio. 2007. *Los anarquistas y el movimiento obrero: La alborada de "la idea" en Chile, 1893–1915*. Santiago de Chile: LOM Ediciones.

Guzmán, Romina, Henri Renna, Alejandra Sandoval, and Camila Silva. 2009. *Movimiento de pobladores en lucha: A tomarse Peñalolén para conquistar la ciudad Santiago de Chile*. Santiago de Chile: Ediciones SUR.

Habermas, Jürgen. 1991. *The Structural Transformation of the Public Sphere: An Inquiry into a Category of Bourgeois Society*. Cambridge, MA: MIT Press.

Han, Clara. 2012. *Life in Debt: Times of Care and Violence in Neoliberal Chile*. Berkeley: University of California Press.

Hardy, Clarisa. 1987. *Organizarse para vivir: Pobreza urbana y organización popular*. Santiago de Chile: PET.

Hartman, Chester W. 2002. "The Right to Stay Put, Reprinted." In *Between Eminence and Notoriety: Four Decades of Radical Urban Planning*, 120–33. New Brunswick, NJ: Center for Urban Policy Research, Transaction.

Harvey, David. 2005. *A Brief History of Neoliberalism*. New York: Oxford University Press.

———. 2012. *Rebel Cities: From the Right to the City to the Urban Revolution*. New York: Verso.

Hashemi, Manata. 2020. *Coming of Age in Iran: Poverty and the Struggle for Dignity*. New York: New York University Press.

Hidalgo, Rodrigo. 2000. "El papel de las leyes de fomento de la edificación obrera y la caja de la habitación en la política de vivienda social en Chile, 1931–1952." *Revista INVI* 15 (39): 92–120.

———. 2002. "Vivienda Social y Espacio Urbano en Santiago de Chile: Una mirada retrospectiva a la acción del Estado en la primeras décadas del siglo XX." *EURE* 28 (83): 83–106.

———. 2004a. "De los pequeños condominios a la ciudad vallada: Las urbanizaciones cerradas y la nueva geografía social en Santiago de Chile (1990–2000)." *EURE* 30 (91): 29–52. http://dx.doi.org/10.4067/S0250-71612004009100003.

———. 2004b. "La vivienda social en Santiago de Chile en la segunda mitad del siglo XX: Actores relevantes y tendencias espaciales." In *Santiago en la globalización: ¿Una nueva ciudad?*, edited by Carlos A. De Mattos, María Elena Ducci, Alfredo Rodríguez, and Gloria Yáñez, 219–41. Santiago de Chile: Ediciones SUR.

Hidalgo, Rodrigo, Tomás Errázuriz, and Rodrigo Booth. 2005. "Las viviendas de la beneficencia católica en Santiago: Instituciones constructoras y efectos urbanos (1890–1920)." *Historia (Santiago)* 38 (2): 327–66.

Hipsher, Patricia L. 1996. "Democratization and the Decline of Urban Social Movements in Chile and Spain." *Comparative Politics* 28 (3): 273–97. https://doi.org/10.2307/422208.

Hollywood, Amy. 2002. "Performativity, Citationality, Ritualization." *History of Religions* 42 (2): 93–115.

Holston, James. 1989. *The Modernist City: An Anthropological Critique of Brasilia*. Chicago: University of Chicago Press.

———. 1991. "Autoconstruction in Working-Class Brazil." *Cultural Anthropology* 6 (4): 447–65.

———. 2008. *Insurgent Citizenship: Disjunctions of Democracy and Modernity in Brazil.* Princeton, NJ: Princeton University Press.

———. 2011. "Contesting Privilege with Right: The Transformation of Differentiated Citizenship in Brazil." *Citizenship Studies* 15 (3–4): 335–52.

Holston, James, and Arjun Appadurai. 1996. "Cities and Citizenship." *Public Culture* 8 (2): 187–204. https://doi.org/10.1215/08992363-8-2-187.

Honneth, Axel. 1992. "Integrity and Disrespect: Principles of a Conception of Morality Based on the Theory of Recognition." *Political Theory* 20 (2): 187–201.

———. 1995. *The Struggle for Recognition: The Moral Grammar of Social Conflicts.* Cambridge, MA: Polity.

Hurtado Echeverría, Carlos. 1957. "Ante un hecho ilegal." *Revista Mensaje* (December).

Iglesias, Mónica. 2011. *Rompiendo el cerco: El movimiento de pobladores contra la dictadura.* Santiago de Chile: Radio Universidad de Chile.

Instituto Nacional de Estadística. 2020. "Estimación de personas extranjeras residentes habituales en Chile al 31 de diciembre 2019." Gobierno de Chile. https://www .ine.cl/docs/default-source/demografia-y-migracion/publicaciones-y-anuarios/ migraci%C3%B3n-internacional/estimaci%C3%B3n-poblaci%C3%B3n-extranjera -en-chile-2018/estimaci%C3%B3n-poblaci%C3%B3n-extranjera-en-chile-2019 -metodolog%C3%ADa.pdf?sfvrsn=5b145256_6.

Jeffrey, Craig. 2008. "Waiting." *Environment and Planning D: Society and Space* 26 (6): 954–58. https://doi.org/10.1068/d2606ed.

Kingfisher, Catherine, and Jeff Maskovsky. 2008. "Introduction: The Limits of Neoliberalism." *Critique of Anthropology* 28 (2): 115–26. https://doi.org/10.1177/ 0308275X08090544.

Kipnis, Andrew. 2004. "Anthropology and the Theorisation of Citizenship." *Asia Pacific Journal of Anthropology* 5 (3): 257–78.

Koppelman, Carter M. 2018. "'For Now, We Are in Waiting': Negotiating Time in Chile's Social Housing System." *City & Community* 17 (2): 504–24. https://doi.org/ 10.1111/cico.12301.

Kymlicka, Will. 1995. *Multicultural Citizenship: A Liberal Theory of Minority Rights.* Oxford: Oxford University Press.

Lambek, Michael, ed. 2010a. *Ordinary Ethics: Anthropology, Language, and Action.* New York: Fordham University Press.

———, ed. 2010b. "Towards an Ethics of the Act." In *Ordinary Ethics: Anthropology, Language, and Action,* 39–63. New York: Fordham University Press.

Larrañaga, Osvaldo, Denise Falck, Rodrigo Herrera, and Amanda Telias. 2014. "De la Ficha de Protección Social a La Reforma de La Focalización." Programa de las Naciones Unidas para el Desarrollo—Chile. http://www.cl.undp.org/content/dam/ chile/docs/pobreza/undp_cl_pobreza_cap6_focalizacion.pdf.

Lazar, Sian. 2013. "Citizenship, Political Agency and Technologies of the Self in Argentinean Trade Unions." *Critique of Anthropology* 33 (1): 110–28. https://doi.org/ 10.1177/0308275X12466678.

Lazar, Sian, and Monique Nuijten. 2013. "Citizenship, the Self, and Political Agency." *Critique of Anthropology* 33 (1): 3–7. https://doi.org/10.1177/0308275X12466684.

Lefebvre, Henri. 1991. *The Production of Space.* Malden, MA: Wiley-Blackwell.

———. 1996. *Writings on Cities.* Cambridge, MA: Wiley-Blackwell.

———. 2003. *The Urban Revolution.* Minneapolis: University of Minnesota Press.

Lemebel, Pedro. 2003. *Zanjón de La Aguada.* Santiago de Chile: Editorial Planeta Chilena.

Lévi-Strauss, Claude. 1963. "The Effectiveness of Symbols." In *Structural Anthropology*, 186–205. New York: Basic Books.

Levy, Charmain, Anne Latendresse, and Marianne Carle-Marsan. 2017. "Gendering the Urban Social Movement and Public Housing Policy in São Paulo." *Latin American Perspectives* 44 (3): 9–27. https://doi.org/10.1177/0094582X16668317.

Lewis, Oscar. 1951. *Life in a Mexican Village: Tepoztlán Restudied.* Urbana: University of Illinois Press.

———. 1961. *The Children of Sanchez: Autobiography of a Mexican Family.* New York: Random House.

Lomnitz-Adler, Claudio. 1992. *Exits from the Labyrinth: Culture and Ideology in the Mexican National Space.* Berkeley: University of California Press.

Long, Gideon. 2016. "Story of Cities #33: How Santiago Tackled Its Housing Crisis with 'Operation Chalk.'" *The Guardian*, April 29. https://www.theguardian.com/cities/2016/apr/29/story-cities-33-santiago-chile-housing-crisis-operacion-sitio-operation-chalk.

Loyola, Manuel. 1989. "Los pobladores de Santiago, 1952–1964: Su fase de incorporación a la vida nacional." Santiago de Chile: Instituto de Historia, Pontificia Universidad Católica.

Lynch, Kevin. 1960. *The Image of the City.* Cambridge, MA: MIT Press.

Mahmood, Saba. 2012. *Politics of Piety: The Islamic Revival and the Feminist Subject.* Princeton, NJ: Princeton University Press.

Mangin, William. 1967. "Latin American Squatter Settlements: A Problem and a Solution." *Latin American Research Review* 2 (3): 65–98.

Marcuse, Peter. 2009. "From Critical Urban Theory to the Right to the City." *City* 13 (2–3): 185–97. https://doi.org/10.1080/13604810902982177.

Margalit, Avishai. 1996. *The Decent Society.* Cambridge, MA: Harvard University Press.

Márquez, Francisca. 2004. "Márgenes y ceremonial: Los pobladores y la política de vivienda social en Chile." *Política* 43: 185–203.

Marshall, T. H. 1977. *Class, Citizenship, and Social Development.* Chicago: University of Chicago Press.

Martínez, Javier, and Margarita Palacios. 1996. *Informe sobre la decencia: La diferenciación estamental de la pobreza y los subsidios públicos.* Santiago de Chile: Ediciones SUR.

Marx, Karl. 1978. "On the Jewish Question." In *The Marx-Engels Reader*, edited by Robert C. Tucker, Second Edition, 26–52. New York: W. W. Norton & Co.

Mayol, Alberto. 2012. *El derrumbe del modelo: La crisis de la economía de mercado en el Chile contemporáneo*. Santiago de Chile: LOM Ediciones.

El Mercurio. 2011. "Lavín denuncia 4 mil casos que mintieron en ficha de protección social." September 21. http://www.emol.com/noticias/nacional/2011/09/21/504346/falsos-pobres-lavin-denuncia-4-mil-casos-de-adulteracion-de-la-ficha-de-proteccion-social.html.

———. 2012. "En tres décadas, el precio del suelo en el gran Santiago subió casi 1.000%." June 24.

———. 2015. "Subsidios de vivienda: De 732 mil entregados en cinco años, cerca de la mitad se pierden." June 27.

Ministerio de Desarrollo Social. 2014. "CASEN 2013: Vivienda. Síntesis de resultados." Gobierno de Chile. http://observatorio.ministeriodesarrollosocial.gob.cl/documentos/Casen2013_Vivienda.pdf.

———. 2016. "CASEN 2015: Situación de La Pobreza En Chile." Gobierno de Chile. http://observatorio.ministeriodesarrollosocial.gob.cl/casen-multidimensional/casen/docs/CASEN_2015_Situacion_Pobreza.pdf.

———. 2018. "CASEN 2017: Situación de La Pobreza En Chile." Gobierno de Chile. http://observatorio.ministeriodesarrollosocial.gob.cl/storage/docs/casen/2017/Resultados_pobreza_Casen_2017.pdf.

Ministerio de Planificación. 2001. "Situación Habitacional 2000." Gobierno de Chile. http://www.ministeriodesarrollosocial.gob.cl/admin/docdescargas/centrodoc/centrodoc_20.pdf.

Ministerio de Vivienda y Urbanismo. 2004. *Chile, un siglo de políticas en vivienda y barrio*. Santiago de Chile: Pehuén Editores Ltda.

———. 2012. "Hacia una nueva política urbana: Antecedentes históricos." Gobierno de Chile. https://cndu.gob.cl/wp-content/uploads/2014/10/Antecedentes-Hist%C3%B3ricos1.pdf.

Mitchell, Don. 2003. *The Right to the City: Social Justice and the Fight for Public Space*. New York: Guilford Press.

Moss, Robert. 1973. *Chile's Marxist Experiment*. Newton Abbot, UK: David & Charles.

Movimiento de Pobladores en Lucha. 2011. *Siete y cuatro: El retorno de los pobladores*. Santiago de Chile: Quimantú.

Murphy, Edward. 2015. *For a Proper Home: Housing Rights in the Margins of Urban Chile, 1960–2010*. Pittsburgh: University of Pittsburgh Press.

Necochea, Andrés. 1987. "Los allegados: Una estrategia de supervivencia solidaria en vivienda." *EURE* 13 (39–40): 85–99.

Newman, Kathe, and Elvin K. Wyly. 2006. "The Right to Stay Put, Revisited: Gentrification and Resistance to Displacement in New York City." *Urban Studies* 43 (1): 23–57. https://doi.org/10.1080/00420980500388710.

Nuijten, Monique. 2013. "The Perversity of the 'Citizenship Game': Slum-Upgrading in the Urban Periphery of Recife, Brazil." *Critique of Anthropology* 33 (1): 8–25.

Nun, José. 2001. *Marginalidad y exclusión social*. Buenos Aires: Fondo de Cultura Económica.

Okin, Susan Moller. 1999. *Is Multiculturalism Bad for Women?* Edited by Joshua Cohen, Matthew Howard, and Martha C. Nussbaum. Princeton, NJ: Princeton University Press.

Ong, Aihwa. 2003. *Buddha Is Hiding: Refugees, Citizenship, the New America.* Berkeley: University of California Press.

———. 2006. *Neoliberalism as Exception: Mutations in Citizenship and Sovereignty.* Durham, NC: Duke University Press.

Oxhorn, Philip. 1994. "Where Did All the Protesters Go? Popular Mobilization and the Transition to Democracy in Chile." *Latin American Perspectives* 21 (3): 49–68.

Özler, Ş İlgü. 2012. "The Concertación and Homelessness in Chile Market-Based Housing Policies and Limited Popular Participation." *Latin American Perspectives* 39 (4): 53–70. https://doi.org/10.1177/0094582X10397917.

Paley, Julia. 2001. *Marketing Democracy: Power and Social Movements in Post-Dictatorship Chile.* Berkeley: University of California Press.

Pastrana, Ernesto, and Mónica Threlfall. 1974. *Pan, techo y poder: El movimiento de pobladores en Chile (1970–1973).* Buenos Aires: Ediciones Siap-Planteos.

Pateman, Carole. 1990. *The Disorder of Women: Democracy, Feminism, and Political Theory.* Stanford, CA: Stanford University Press.

Pauli, Julia. 2008. "A House of One's Own: Gender, Migration, and Residence in Rural Mexico." *American Ethnologist* 35 (1): 171–87.

Pavlic, Rodolfo Disi. 2018. "Sentenced to Debt: Explaining Student Mobilization in Chile." *Latin American Research Review* 53 (3): 448–65. https://doi.org/10.25222/larr.395.

Pérez, Miguel. 2017. "'A New Poblador Is Being Born': Housing Struggles in a Gentrified Area of Santiago." *Latin American Perspectives* 44 (3): 28–45. https://doi.org/10.1177/0094582X16668318.

———. 2017. "Reframing Housing Struggles: Right to the City and Urban Citizenship in Santiago, Chile." *City* 21 (5): 530–49. https://doi.org/10.1080/13604813.2017.1374783.

———. 2018. "Toward a Life with Dignity: Housing Struggles and New Political Horizons in Urban Chile." *American Ethnologist* 45 (4): 508–20. https://doi.org/10.1111/amet.12705.

Pérez, Miguel, and Cristóbal Palma. 2021. "De extranjeros a ciudadanos urbanos: Autoconstrucción y migración en el gran Santiago." *Estudios Atacameños* 67. https://doi.org/10.22199/issn.0718-1043-2021-0010.

Perlman, Janice E. 1976. *The Myth of Marginality: Urban Poverty and Politics in Rio de Janeiro.* Berkeley: University of California Press.

Piven, Frances Fox, and Richard Cloward. 1971. *Regulating the Poor: The Functions of Public Welfare.* New York: Pantheon Books.

PNUD. 2012. *Desarrollo humano en Chile: Bienestar subjetivo. El desafío de repensar el desarollo.* Santiago de Chile: Programa de las Naciones Unidas para el Desarrollo.

———. 2015. *Desarrollo humano en Chile: Los tiempos de la politización.* Santiago de Chile: Programa de las Naciones Unidas para el Desarrollo.

Polumbaum, Ted, and Nyna Brael Polumbaum. 1992. *Today Is Not like Yesterday: A Chilean Journey.* Cambridge, MA: Light & Shadow.

Postero, Nancy. 2007. *Now We Are Citizens: Indigenous Politics in Postmulticultural Bolivia.* Stanford, CA: Stanford University Press.

Pozo, Hernán, ed. 1987. *Espacio y poder: Los pobladores.* Santiago de Chile: FLACSO.

Purcell, Mark. 2002. "Excavating Lefebvre: The Right to the City and Its Urban Politics of the Inhabitant." *GeoJournal* 58 (2–3): 99–108. https://doi.org/10.1023/B:GEJO.0000010829.62237.8f.

———. 2003. "Citizenship and the Right to the Global City: Reimagining the Capitalist World Order." *International Journal of Urban and Regional Research* 27 (3): 564–90.

Quijano, Aníbal. 1972. "La constitución del 'mundo' de la marginalidad urbana." *EURE* 2 (5): 89–106.

Redfield, Robert. 1947. "The Folk Society." *American Journal of Sociology* 52 (4): 293–308.

Ribeiro, Darcy. 1971. *El dilema de América Latina: Estructuras de poder y fuerzas insurgentes.* México City: Siglo XXI.

Rodríguez, Alfredo, and Ana Sugranyes, eds. 2005. *Los con techo: Un desafío para la política de vivienda social.* Santiago de Chile: Ediciones SUR.

Rose, Nikolas. 1999. *Powers of Freedom: Reframing Political Thought.* Cambridge: Cambridge University Press.

Ruiz-Tagle, Javier. 2016. "La persistencia de la segregación y la desigualdad en barrios socialmente diversos: Un estudio de caso en La Florida, Santiago." *EURE* 42 (125): 81–108. http://dx.doi.org/10.4067/S0250-71612016000100004.

Ruiz-Tagle, Javier, and Ernesto López. 2014. "El estudio de la segregación residencial en Santiago de Chile: Revisión crítica de algunos problemas metodológicos y conceptuales." *EURE* 40 (119): 25–48. http://dx.doi.org/10.4067/S0250-716120140 0100002.

Sabatini, Francisco. 1981. "La dimensión ambiental de la pobreza urbana en las teorías latinoamericanas de marginalidad." *EURE* 8 (23): 53–67.

———. 2000. "Reforma de los mercados de suelo en Santiago, Chile: Efectos sobre los precios de la tierra y la segregación residencial." *EURE* 26 (77): 49–80.

Sabatini, Francisco, and Rodrigo Salcedo. 2007. "Gated Communities and the Poor in Santiago, Chile: Functional and Symbolic Integration in a Context of Aggressive Capitalist Colonization of Lower-class Areas." *Housing Policy Debate* 18 (3): 577–606. https://doi.org/10.1080/10511482.2007.9521612.

Salazar, Gabriel, and Julio Pinto. 2002. *Historia contemporánea de Chile IV: Hombría y feminidad.* Santiago de Chile: LOM Ediciones.

Salcedo, Rodrigo. 2010. "The Last Slum: Moving from Illegal Settlements to Subsidized Home Ownership in Chile." *Urban Affairs Review* 46 (1): 90–118.

Sánchez, Rafael. 1958. *Las Callampas.* Documentary.

Santa María, Ignacio. 1973. "El desarrollo urbano mediante los 'asentamientos espontáneos': El caso de los 'campamentos' chilenos." *EURE* 3 (7): 103–12.

Schild, Verónica. 2000. "Neo-Liberalism's New Gendered Market Citizens: The 'Civilizing' Dimension of Social Programmes in Chile." *Citizenship Studies* 4 (3): 275–305.

Schneider, Cathy. 1995. *Shantytown Protest in Pinochet's Chile*. Philadelphia: Temple University Press.

Schwartz, Barry. 1974. "Waiting, Exchange, and Power: The Distribution of Time in Social Systems." *American Journal of Sociology* 79 (4): 841–70.

Skrabut, Kristin. 2018. "Residency Counts and Housing Rights: Conflicting Enactments of Property in Lima's Central Margins." *Current Anthropology* 59 (6): 691–715. https://doi.org/10.1086/700758.

Skinner, Quentin. 1989. "The State." In *Political Innovation and Conceptual Change*, edited by Terence Ball, James Farr, and Russell L. Hanson, 90–131. New York: Cambridge University Press.

Slater, Tom. 2006. "The Eviction of Critical Perspectives from Gentrification Research." *International Journal of Urban and Regional Research* 30 (4): 737–57. https://doi.org/10.1111/j.1468-2427.2006.00689.x.

———. 2009. "Missing Marcuse: On Gentrification and Displacement." *City* 13 (2–3): 292–311.

Spruyt, Hendrik. 1994. *The Sovereign State and Its Competitors: An Analysis of Systems Change*. Princeton, NJ: Princeton University Press.

Tapia, Ricardo. 2011. "Vivienda social en Santiago de Chile: Análisis de su comportamiento locacional, período 1980–2002." *Revista INVI* 26 (73): 105–31.

Tarrow, Sidney. 2011. *Power in Movement: Social Movements and Contentious Politics*. 3rd ed. New York: Cambridge University Press.

Taylor, Charles. 1992. "Politics of Recognition." In *Multiculturalism and "The Politics of Recognition,"* edited by Amy Gutmann, 25–73. Princeton, NJ: Princeton University Press.

La Tercera. 2014. "Cerca de cuatro mil subsidios sin proyectos podrían caducar durante este 2014." September 8. https://www.latercera.com/noticia/cerca-de-cuatro-mil-subsidios-sin-proyectos-podrian-caducar-durante-este-2014/.

———. 2015. "Estudio muestra cómo ha cambiado el mapa social de Santiago." May 18. https://www.latercera.com/noticia/estudio-muestra-como-ha-cambiado-el-mapa-social-de-santiago/.

———. 2018. "El largo epílogo de las casas Copeva." December 15. https://www.latercera.com/reportajes/noticia/largo-epilogo-las-casas-copeva/446639/.

———. 2019. "Cómo la constitución política se transformó en el bestseller de la temporada." November 18. https://www.latercera.com/la-tercera-pm/noticia/como-la-constitucion-politica-se-transformo-en-el-bestseller-de-la-temporada/905673/.

Tilly, Charles, and Sidney Tarrow. 2015. *Contentious Politics*. 2nd ed. New York: Oxford University Press.

Tironi, Eugenio. 1986. "La revuelta de los pobladores: Integración social y democracia." *Nueva Sociedad* 83: 24–32.

Touraine, Alain. 1987. "La centralidad de los marginales." *Proposiciones* 14: 214–24.

Trivelli, Pablo. 2011. "La propuesta de modificación del Plan Regulador Metropolitano de Santiago PRMS 100 requiere una justificación más sólida." *EURE* 37 (111): 179–84. http://dx.doi.org/10.4067/S0250-71612011000200009.

Turner, John. 1968. "Housing Priorities, Settlement Patterns, and Urban Development in Modernizing Countries." *Journal of the American Institute of Planners* 34 (6): 354–63.

———. 1972. "Housing as a Verb." In *Freedom to Build: Dweller Control of the Housing Process*, edited by John Turner and Robert Fichter, 148–75. New York: Macmillan.

UN-Habitat. 2012. *State of Latin American and Caribbean Cities 2012. Toward a New Urban Transition*. Nairobi: UN-Habitat.

Valdés, Teresa, and Marisa Weinstein. 1993. *Mujeres que sueñan: Las organizaciones de pobladoras, 1973–1989*. Santiago de Chile: FLACSO.

Valenzuela, Catherine. 2014. "El movimiento de pobladores en Santiago: La memoria social del campamento Esperanza Andina de Santiago (1992–1998)." *Historia y Justicia*, no. 3: 109–35.

Vanderschueren, Franz. 1971. "Pobladores y conciencia social." *EURE* 1 (3): 91–123.

Vekemans, Roger. 1969. *Marginalidad en América Latina: Un ensayo de conceptualización*. Santiago de Chile: DESAL.

Vekemans, Roger, Jorge Giusti, and Ismael Silva. 1970. *Marginalidad, promoción popular e integración latinoamericana*. Santiago de Chile: DESAL.

Vera, Antonieta. 2017. *Malestar social y desigualdades en Chile*. Santiago de Chile: Universidad Alberto Hurtado.

Walzer, Michael. 1989. "Citizenship." In *Political Innovation and Conceptual Change*, edited by Terence Ball, James Farr, and Russell L. Hanson, 211–19. New York: Cambridge University Press.

Wilson, Sergio. 1988. *La otra ciudad: De la marginalidad a la participación social*. Santiago de Chile: Editorial Jurídica Ediar Conosur.

Winn, Peter. 2004. "The Pinochet Era." In *Victims of the Chilean Miracle: Workers and Neoliberalism in the Pinochet Era, 1973-2002*, edited by Peter Winn, 14–70. Durham, NC: Duke University Press.

Wirth, Louis. 1938. "Urbanism as a Way of Life." *American Journal of Sociology* 44 (1): 1–24.

Young, Iris Marion. 1989. "Polity and Group Difference: A Critique of the Ideal of Universal Citizenship." *Ethics* 99 (2): 250–274.

Yurchak, Alexei. 2005. *Everything Was Forever, Until It Was No More: The Last Soviet Generation*. Princeton: Princeton University Press.

Zambrano, Catalina, and Consuelo Huaiqui. 2020. "Geo constituyente: Cabildos y asambleas autoconvocadas. La recuperación de espacio público por parte de la organización popular." *Planeo* 40 (January). http://revistaplaneo.cl/2020/01/08/geo-constituyente-cabildos-y-asambleas-autoconvocadas-la-recuperacion-de-espacio-publico-por-parte-de-la-organizacion-popular/.

Zeiderman, Austin. 2013. "Living Dangerously: Biopolitics and Urban Citizenship in Bogotá, Colombia." *American Ethnologist* 40 (1): 71–87.

Zigon, Jarrett. 2007. "Moral Breakdown and the Ethical Demand: A Theoretical Framework for an Anthropology of Moralities." *Anthropological Theory* 7 (2): 131–50.

———. 2014. "An Ethics of Dwelling and a Politics of World-Building: A Critical Response to Ordinary Ethics." *Journal of the Royal Anthropological Institute* 20 (4): 746–64.

Index

poverty and, 39, 66, 163, 169; private, 69; resources and, 47; transportation, 4, 14, 78, 81

Servicio Metropolitano de Vivienda y Urbanismo (Metropolitan Service of Housing and Urbanism) [SERVIU], 29, 64, 72, 75, 83, 89–90, 131, 137, 156, 159–61, 166, 174

shacks, 54, 98, 106, 108, 132

Siglo, El (newspaper), 41, 46, 97

Skrabut, Kristin, 123

social identity, 6, 15–16, 18, 23, 56, 91–92, 111, 118, 139, 148

socialism: Allende and, 8, 12, 42, 55–56, 110, 177; *Comités de Allegados* and, 83–84; Montes and, 83; neoliberalism and, 8, 12–13; Partido Obrero Socialista (Workers' Socialist Party) [POS], 39, 190n9; Partido Socialista (Socialist Party) [PS], 46, 49, 84, 185, 193n53

social justice, 4, 7–8, 25, 78, 151, 186

social networks, 9, 135

Social Priority Index (Índice de Prioridad Social), 133, 199n14

social production of space, 20, 73, 118, 137, 169

social rights: citizenship and, 142; conclusions from, 178, 180–84; ethics and, 169–72; Marshall on, 23; neoliberalism and, 5, 8, 12, 17–18, 23–24, 28, 31, 33; *pobladores* movement and, 34, 56; poverty and, 169–72

Sociedad de Arrendatarios de la Defensa Mutua (Renters' Association for Mutual Defense), 40

South Africa, 14

Soviet Union, 108, 160, 191n22

squatters: *callamperos*, 45, 96–103; *campamentos* (squatter settlements) and, 8, 20, 26, 50, 52–53, 58–59, 105–9, 129, 177, 190n7, 192n38; Catholic Church and, 96–99; citizenship and, 128–29,

132–33, 135, 153–54; city making and, 45, 96–103, 105–13, 116; *Comités de Allegados* and, 69, 74, 194n10; displacement of, 13, 45, 57, 74, 110; fearing, 107–10; Mangin on, 20; MPL and, 34–35, 43, 71, 148, 195n18; neoliberalism and, 5, 7–9, 12–13, 16, 19–23, 26, 31, 177, 188n24; *pobladores* movement and, 38–59, 190n7, 192n38; reduction of, 177; right to dignity and, 177, 181; settlement names of, 190n7; shacks and, 54, 98, 106, 108, 132; subhuman living conditions of, 99–100, 153–55; unsanitary housing and, 98–101; Zanjón de la Aguada and, 41, 44, 98–99

status, 8, 24–25, 56, 84, 104, 107, 162, 179, 190n5

stigmatization, 125, 134, 160, 162

subhuman living standards, 99–100, 153–55

subject formation: citizenship and, 17, 28, 32, 139, 187n9; city making and, 31, 92–96, 110; democracy and, 176; historic modalities of, 22, 85; performative theory and, 6, 18, 31, 92–96, 177; political category for, 6, 16; poverty and, 164, 171, 178

subsidies: *allegados* (residents at relatives) and, 9–10, 63, 65, 71, 75–76, 85, 110, 116–17, 122, 125, 136–37, 144, 150–51, 158, 165–68, 182, 192n23; citizenship and, 122, 124–27, 131, 133–37, 144, 146, 198n4; city making and, 91, 110, 114, 116–17; *Comités de Allegados* and, 63–77, 82–83, 85, 194nn10–11, 195n14, 195nn23–24; conclusions from, 174, 177–78, 182–83; displacement and, 71, 74, 110, 183; ethics and, 148–53, 163–72; exclusion and, 122, 178; health issues and, 14; Location Subsidy, 69; market-based programs and, 5, 9, 14, 17, 56, 66–67, 148; neoliberalism and, 4–5, 8–17, 22–23,

CPSIA information can be obtained
at www.ICGtesting.com
Printed in the USA
JSHW040119020322
23465JS00005B/5